1
LEADER'S
GUIDE

JUNIOR CHILDREN'S CHURCH

1
LEADER'S GUIDE

JUNIOR CHILDREN'S CHURCH

David C. Cook Publishing Co., Elgin, Illinois/Weston, Ontario

JUNIOR CHILDREN'S CHURCH 1 LEADER'S GUIDE

DAVID C. COOK PUBLISHING CO.
Elgin, Illinois/Weston, Ontario
JUNIOR CHILDREN'S CHURCH
©1987 David C. Cook
Publishing Co.

Published by David C. Cook
Publishing Co.
850 North Grove Avenue
Elgin, IL 60120
Cable address: DCCOOK
First printing, 1987
Printed in the United States
of America

TABLE OF CONTENTS

Unit 7 Prayer

Unit 8 Sermon

Unit 9 Worship Leaders

Unit 10 Our Role

Unit 11 The Sanctuary

Unit 12 Benediction

Creative Team
Editors:
Kathryn Lewis
Scottie May
Eric Potter
Lucy Townsend
Designer:
Catherine Colten
Illustrators:
Andre LeBlanc
Johann Schumacher
Chris Sharp

Contributing Writers:
Karen Dockerey
Neta Jackson
Kathy Johnson
Sandra Karls
Robert Klausmeier
Kathryn Lewis
Scottie May
Eric Potter
Robert Spanton
Lucy Townsend

Management Team
David C. Cook III, Editor in Chief
Ralph Gates, Director of Church
Resources
Marlene D. LeFever, Executive
Editor of Church Resources
Jim Townsend, Bible Editor
Randy Maid, Director of Design
Services

We would like to thank Robert Spanton for sparking the idea for this product by sharing the creative ways he has been using the Picture Bible in children's worship in his church in Plainfield, Illinois.

A YEARLONG WORSHIP ADVENTURE

You are about to embark on a adventure not unlike the one made by the Hebrew people in the Old Testament. God led the Hebrews on a journey through the wilderness for 40 years, and though the Hebrews had a destination in mind, God was more concerned with the process than the product. He wanted them to learn to trust Him and obey Him until He was the only focus of their worship.

In *Junior Children's Church 1*, we want to assist students with this process in two ways—

• By helping them understand how God works with and cares for His people—to help in this understanding, students will go through the Old Testament chronologically.

• By helping them worship God better—students will learn the significance of the parts of the worship service from invocation to benediction.

The curriculum will aid in this process, but our concern, and we believe God's, is not so much with reaching the destination, as with the process—students struggling with ideas, comparing their lives with the principles of Scripture, discovering creative ways to live out the Word, and worshiping the Lord in response to the unfolding of His story and His guidance on the journey.

As you guide this adventure, *Junior Children's Church 1* offers you the "equipment" you will need—

• The *Leader's Guide* will give you ideas for facilitating the process of spiritual growth in your students on their adventure. But just as no two people are alike, no two classes are alike either. We urge you to adapt this guide to your students and your situation.

• The *Picture Bible* has the great stories of the Bible, presented chronologically, in full-color action pictures designed for children.
• *Worship Time Music Book*
• *THE Idea Book*
• Maps
• Activity pieces (in the back of this book)

We pray that this adventure into God's Word and worship will be a growing time for you as well as your students. For on this adventure, none of us has "arrived." We can only guide students as we walk beside them. As Thomas Groome, author of *Christian Religious Education*, has said, "We are fellow and sister pilgrims alongside them, of whom they ask the way. As we point ahead of them, we also point ahead of ourselves."

> **W**e can only guide students as we walk beside them.

THROUGH THE OLD TESTAMENT

WHAT SHOULD HAPPEN IN EACH LESSON?

Ideally, each session of children's church should help the student move from an examination of his or her life as it is, to the Bible, and then to a life response.

LIFE ➥ BIBLE ➥ TRANSFORMED LIFE (LIFE RESPONSE)

The life response in these lessons has two parts. First, the students respond in corporate worship. Then, the students respond individually in the "Responding Personally" time. Thus, the parts of the lesson can be outlined as follows:

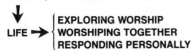

LIFE ➥ GETTING STARTED

BIBLE ➥ EXPLORING THE BIBLE

LIFE ➥ { **EXPLORING WORSHIP** **WORSHIPING TOGETHER** **RESPONDING PERSONALLY** }

Let's explore the purpose of each of these sections more closely.

GETTING STARTED

It is easy to think of the "Getting Started" activities as ways to keep the children busy until all of them have arrived or as ways to help children settle down for the lesson. While we may need to do both of these things, the wise teacher will see that the "Getting Started" time has a much more important purpose. The ideal use of this section is to help the student examine his or her own life in the area that will be addressed in the lesson.

In the lessons you will find two kinds of "Getting Started" activities. These differ in the kind of motivation they give the student.

● Interest—Some lessons will begin with activities designed to arouse curiosity about the day's theme or story. For example, during Session 3, the children go outside to measure off an area to show them how large Noah's ark was. This gets the children into the Bible story.

● Felt need—Some lessons will begin with the students discovering a need they have. This is the preferred way of beginning a lesson because it takes the student beyond surface interest to a real need he or she has in the present. Motivation to learn is stronger in a lesson that begins with this kind of activity. For example, in a "Getting Started" game in Session 43, students discover how easily they are distracted by peers. This activity is preparation for a Bible lesson on how Hezekiah resisted peer pressure and was able to keep worshiping God.

As you get to know your students and their needs, every week you should feel free to adapt these opening activities to address a felt need of your students. A high priority of these first moments of each lesson should be to listen and get to know your students. The more you know their felt needs, the more you can personalize the Bible application later in the lesson.

EXPLORING THE BIBLE

Once you have helped the students discover their needs, the transition to the Bible lesson should be easy. The students need to see that the Scripture is relevant to their needs today. While God's Word is authoritative, it can make no difference in the child's life unless he or she interacts with it. The purpose of this section of the lesson is, first, to help the students experience the dynamics and truth of the Bible story and, second, to help them critically reflect on its meaning in their own situations, to try to figure out what it says to them today. Learning in "Exploring the Bible" should be active and interactive.

The *Picture Bible* is a wonderful tool for active learning because it lends itself so well to drama. Roleplay is used often in these lessons to get the students involved in the story. Other active methods for Bible learning are creative storytelling, skits, and the use of puppets.

However, action without interaction is not enough. Try to help your students reflect on the Bible lesson and on its application. It is important in discussion times to emphasize exploration and creative thought. How did the character feel? How might he or she have acted differently? How can we apply the truth today?

Many teachers forget to ask the how and why questions because they are caught up with "right answer" questions—who? what? when? and where? Children should be able to answer these factual questions, but it is more important that they think and *interact* with God's Word.

An attempt has been made whenever possible to highlight aspects of the Bible story which teach principles of worship found in the same lesson. Study the lessons carefully to see connections which you can help students make between these two sections.

EXPLORING WORSHIP

This part of the lesson is designed to teach the students about the parts of the worship service so that the service takes on new meaning for them. Each unit highlights a different aspect of worship. This is also a time to help your students begin to prepare for and plan their corporate worship response to the day's Bible lesson.

WORSHIPING TOGETHER

This section of the lesson indicates the time for your group's corporate worship service. At this time you may distribute copies of "In Worship" and lead your students in a worship service. The key word for this section is participation. Involve as many students as possible. Make sure that different students get to participate each week. Remember that this is the student's life response to God's Word. You cannot respond for them.

RESPONDING PERSONALLY

At this point your students will already have begun their life response to the lesson by worshiping God together. This section of the lesson, following the worship time, provides a chance to personalize the life response. If students discovered and expressed felt needs in the "Getting Started" time, this is the time to finish the circle by tying the lesson truth back to their individual needs.

Often these activities take one of two forms.

● Formulating a plan—students may devise a plan for what they will do differently to respond to God in problem areas that have been discussed.

● Creating reminders—students may do some craft or create some other kind of tangible reminder to help them recall the truth of the lesson throughout the week.

You can see how this final section closes the circle begun in "Getting Started."

Keep this cycle in mind as you prepare lessons each week. You may wish to review this section frequently to help you remember the bigger picture behind the lesson activities.

WHAT SHOULD I KNOW ABOUT LEADING CHILDREN'S CHURCH?

This is the first time I've worked with Junior Children's Church. Since I have no experience, how do I go about leading the In Worship time?

● For every session we have provided a worship outline to guide you and your students. Adapt or modify it anyway you'd like so that it resembles the order of your adult worship service.

● Be familiar with the order of the worship time so you can help students who are participating to be ready at the proper time. You want to help worship flow smoothly, without interruption.

● Use the "Worship Questionnaire," activity piece 1A in the back of this book, to determine how your students would like to participate.

● Since participating as worship leaders may be new for your students, you might want to assume the major responsibilities for the first few sessions. We want students to feel good about helping in worship, not that its a chore. Let them volunteer for various parts rather than be assigned them.

● You will want to copy the In Worship page each week so students can follow along. It can be the "bulletin" for children's church.

● For each session we've suggested at least three songs that fit in with the theme. One is from your hymnal and two are from *Worship Time Music Book.* Feel free to make your own selection—songs that are special or familiar to your students and congregation. Select a hymn of praise

to God to be sung after the Call to
Worship.

- Be flexible. Do what works most
effectively with your students.

**How can I help prepare a child to
give the Student Worship Talk?**

- First of all, read the Bible story
and think through the worship talk as
if you were going to give it. This will
help you to be able to guide the
student.

- If possible, give him or her a copy
of In Worship a week in advance.

- The lesson in each session is
taught from the *Picture Bible*, but
references during the worship time
are from related passages in Scripture.
Sometimes the student will not be
able to complete the talk without
knowing the whole Bible story so
advance preparation would require
the *Picture Bible*.

- Call the student during the week
to encourage him or her and answer
any questions.

HELP! HOW DO I LEAD A CHILD TO CHRIST?

- Help the child know the basics
about salvation. The child needs to
know that God loves him or her, but
each of us has done things that
displease God. Jesus, God's Son who
never sinned is the only One who
could take away the wrong things we
have done. He did it by dying on the
Cross. We must believe that Jesus
died to forgive us for these wrong
things so we can become a part of
God's family—become a Christian—
by asking Him into our lives. We
know we are Christians when we
have done this. The child needs to
know that we are to live in a way
that pleases God when we are part of
His family.

**How can I know a child is sincere in
wanting to accept Christ?**

- Avoid using emotional or dramatic
stories to get children to respond.
Often many will respond, but it may
be out of fear or a feeling prompted
by the story.

- Let the Word of God be the
stimulus for prompting a child to
come to Christ.

- Some kids this age will want to
know Christ personally; others will
not. But the influence of peers in
making a decision can be great.

- A child is usually sincere in his or
her desire if he or she must take the
initiative to talk to you. If a lesson
offers an appropriate place to present
the plan of salvation, you might close
by saying, "If any of you would like
to accept Christ into your life today,
I will wait in the back of the room to
talk with you."

- Meet with students individually if
possible. This allows you to help with
specific needs and questions.

- Remember that many children at
this age still think concretely—they
don't understand abstract symbolism.
You might have the child explain
back to you what has just happened
so you can clarify any misconceptions
that can result from spiritual
terminology.

- Encourage the child to tell his or
her parents about what has taken
place. You may want to follow up
with the parents. Continue to
encourage the child in the coming
weeks.

What Scriptures do I use?

- Here is a list of familiar verses that
are important for salvation.

    John 3:16
    I John 5:11, 12
    John 1:12
    Romans 3:23
    Romans 5:8
    Romans 6:23
    Romans 10:9, 10

**How can I provide opportunities for
students to accept Christ?**

- First of all, pray for opportunities.
- Look ahead in the lessons to note
those that naturally allow for a
salvation emphasis. Be well prepared
when you get to them.

- Be available after sessions if a child
wants to speak with you.

- Share your own story of how you
came to Christ.

*. . . listen and get to
know your students. The
more you know their felt
needs, the more you can
personalize the Bible
application . . .*

TELL ME ABOUT THE *PICTURE BIBLE.*

I've never seen a Bible like this before. How in the world do I use it?

● The *Picture Bible* is an illustrated version of the Bible for children. The cartoon-like format makes it very readable and exciting.

● It is divided into short stories, taking events chronologically through from Genesis to Revelation. Each story is titled; under the title is the Scripture reference where that story can be found. (Our editors enjoyed working with the *Picture Bible* very much because it simply, logically puts the events of the Old Testament in sequence.)

● Use the coupons for the *Picture Bible* provided in the product box. Parents may be given one so a copy of the book may be ordered for their child. The *Picture Bible* also provides an excellent resource for the home.

HOW CAN I ADJUST THE LENGTH OF THE SESSIONS?

What do I do if one Sunday I have 90 minutes for children's church and the next Sunday I only have 45 minutes?

● Read through the lessons carefully so you can spot activities or sections that can be flexible in length.

● The easiest solution is to use only one of the options in the various sections if you have little time, or use all of the options if you have a lot of time.

● Try not to eliminate activities that help students realize their own felt needs and those that help them personally respond to the truth of the lesson.

I NEVER KNOW HOW MANY KIDS WILL SHOW UP?

What if one Sunday I have six kids and the next Sunday I have sixty? Wow! Does that call for flexibility! For six kids—

● Keep students in a close circle or group.

● Each of them will get to participate in all activities.

● Be sure to let them volunteer for responsibilities. It's easy to put someone on the spot when numbers are few.

For sixty kids—

● Be sure you have enough helpers.

● Divide into groups or double up for drama parts.

● Be sure to have plenty of general supplies on hand.

WHAT SUPPLIES WILL I NEED?

☐ *Picture Bible*—ideally, one for each student; you may make photocopies of the lesson so each student has access to a copy.

☐ Bibles (NIV has been used in lesson preparations.)

☐ Hymnals

☐ Chalkboard

☐ Newsprint

☐ Marking pens

☐ Crayons or felt-tipped markers for pupil use

☐ Pencils

☐ Scissors

☐ Scotch tape

☐ Masking tape

☐ Glue (Glue sticks are less messy, but you may want bottled glue for some crafts.)

☐ Magazines, catalogs, newspapers, or a file of pictures

☐ Colored construction paper

☐ Paper for writing and drawing

☐ Hole puncher

☐ Yarn, string, ribbon

☐ Stapler and staples

☐ Shelf paper or butcher paper

Many teachers forget to ask the how and why questions because they are caught up with "right answer" questions—who? what? when? and where?

WHAT ARE KIDS THIS AGE LIKE?

I have only worked with younger children. How are junior children different from preschoolers and primaries?

● The junior child is less self-centered and more concerned about what others think of him. The student compares himself or herself to peers and is sensitive to criticism.

● The junior child enjoys activity but may be less active than younger children because some of his or her energy is directed toward mental activity. The energy of a younger child is almost totally directed toward developing physical skills.

● The junior child is interested in developing and using skills which will help him or her adapt to problems and threats in his or her world.

Sometimes these students seem deep in thought and preoccupied. What are the major questions on their minds?

● Children of this age may seem withdrawn at times. They need time to process all the new information that they are collecting from their world and at school. They are developing an increased ability to think, so they need time to reflect on how all this new knowledge fits together.

● Junior children tend to be preoccupied with their own ability. They are developing a self-concept based on how they perceive others think about them. They ask themselves, "Can I succeed in my world?"

How can I help to build self-esteem and promote healthy development in my students?

● Give students opportunities to be creative.

● Praise them for their efforts.

● Don't compare or criticize their work.

● Encourage students to participate actively.

● Allow students to use their developing abilities—writing, reading, and critical thinking.

Since this age is sensitive and easily made to feel inferior, what things might I be doing unintentionally which may contribute to feelings of inferiority in my students?

● Because of their sensitivity to comparison with others, individual competition in any form may contribute to students forming a wrong self-concept.

● Asking "right answer" questions can make the student who doesn't know feel inferior. It can be painful for a student to hear that his or her response is wrong or even to hear "Yes, but . . . ."

● Remember that students are constantly evaluated at school. Many of them have already learned to fail and label themselves as failures. Children's Church and Sunday school should be places where they don't have to fail.

DO KIDS THIS AGE NEED MUCH DISCIPLINE?

What do I do if my students get out of hand? What kind of rules are best for this age child?

● Include the junior child in the process of forming rules for children's church and in setting the consequences for rule breaking.

● They still need some structure so they feel comfortable and safe to be themselves. You won't need a lot of rules, but the rules that are made must be enforced.

● Remember discipline means training and helping children to achieve self-control, not simply punishment.

● Correct a child's behavior, not personhood. Avoid statements like "You never listen."

Sometimes I feel that the misbehavior of students has underlying causes. What are some reasons children disobey?

● Children may not know the rules. Remind all students occasionally.

● Children will misbehave if rules conflict. Be careful not to state a rule that cannot be enforced. Children know which rules are real.

● Children may misbehave to vent frustration with some aspect of the learning experience or classroom activity. Search for the cause of the frustration rather than disciplining the misbehavior.

● Children may misbehave because of boredom. Keep learning active and relevant. Be prepared and excited about what you are teaching.

● Children may misbehave because of poor home situations. Be sensitive to the effect that family life can have on behavior in the classroom. ■

UNIT 1 WORSHIP SERVICE FOCUS: INVOCATION, CALL TO WORSHIP

Welcome to this exciting year-long journey that will explore worship for the junior church student and look at God's wonderful involvement in the lives of Old Testament characters. During each session you will help children to understand and then participate in worship. Every unit of this journey focuses on a different aspect of worship. This first unit reminds us that a worship service begins by telling people that it is time to come together to praise God. It also presents the importance of inviting Christ to be part of our worship. Sometimes we need to be reminded of His presence.

Children will work their way through the Old Testament chronologically. This may be the first time many of them have followed the Bible's story from beginning to end.

In this unit we will look at God's Creation, Adam and Eve, Noah and Abraham. From each story, children will learn important truths for their own lives. Please feel free to adapt these lessons to fit the needs and personalities of your students. Class time will be fun-filled with drama, choral reading, puppet plays, art projects, and more.

You may want to get your students involved in a project that can last the whole unit. The choral reading, "In the Beginning," will help the children see Creation in a new way. Another project could take the full year to complete—like having the class make an Old Testament picture time line.

Have a great time as you start this adventure. ■

SESSION 1 WORSHIP AIM:

PRAISING OUR CREATOR

Journey into Genesis 1—2: God creates our world (pp. 3-6).

Special Things You'll Need:
☐ Copies of "In the Beginning," pages 14-17 of THE Idea Book
☐ "Worship Journey Notebook," page 6 of THE Idea Book (Optional)
☐ Copies of "God's Favorite Creation," page 98 in THE Idea Book
☐ "Worship Questionnaire," activity piece 1A in the back of this book (optional)
☐ "Old Testament Picture Time Line," page 7 in THE Idea Book; roll of paper 24" wide (Optional)

GETTING STARTED

We have such a creative God. This lesson will help students realize and celebrate just how great His Creation is.

While the children are assembling, the Getting Started time provides activity ideas which will prepare the students for exploring the Bible lesson and exploring worship. This time also gives you and your helpers a chance to get to know each student. You can talk with the children about their favorite created thing, ask them about their week at school, see if baby brother is walking yet, etc.

Select one or more of the following ideas.
☐ Divide the room into seven areas or learning centers labeled according to the seven days of Creation: Day 1, Day 2, Day 3 . . . Each area needs enough space for several children to be able to draw. At each center place large sheets of drawing paper, colored markers or crayons, and two copies of the Picture Bible or photocopies of pages 3-6 from the Picture Bible.

Students may select one or more

centers at which to work. They should look up the corresponding day in the Picture Bible and draw a picture of what they consider to be their favorite thing that was created on that day.

Help students start to think about certain areas of God's Creation. Ask about a favorite form of light (light on a Christmas tree, campfires, stars, etc.) or favorite bodies of water (lakes, the ocean, a trickling stream in the forest). Day 7 will be more difficult for the children to relate to. That learning center may need a helper to guide their thinking to include many aspects of Sunday activities. Help them to see that holidays/vacation times may also provide rest.

Have the children put their artwork on the bulletin board. They may want to refer to it during the worship time.
☐ Have helpers take small groups of students on brief nature walks around the church property. Have the children collect a variety of things God created. Upon returning to the classroom, each group can arrange its findings on a table for the other groups to enjoy.
☐ Distribute the "Worship Questionnaire" to each child. Explain that those who want to will be able to help lead worship time each week. The questionnaire is to let you know what they would enjoy doing. (Optional)
☐ Consider starting the Old Testament picture time line. This could be used as a teaching aid throughout the whole year.
☐ Since much of today's lesson revolves around the children presenting a Creation play, you might want to use this time to assign special parts.

EXPLORING THE BIBLE

Our Getting Started time has focused on the greatness of God's Creation. Now we want to see what Scripture says about how all things began. For some children this is a very familiar story—one that they may have heard over and over. To bring a freshness to the story and to gain new appreciation for what God has created, we want the students to present a choral reading during the lesson time.

Before beginning to work on the reading, use the following question to help the children to think about the significance of God's Creation.

● **What would it be like if God had not created?**

List all the students' observations on a chalkboard or newsprint. A student might answer, "Nothing would be here." If this response is given, help the class explore the meaning of that response.

Students will learn today's lesson through the choral reading "In the Beginning." We've included information on how to present a choral reading along with the script.

Distribute copies of "In the Beginning" to each student. Read through the piece with them. Assign volunteers for the various roles. This morning it will be helpful to go through the reading two times. Between readings, help the children experience what is happening during the choral reading.

Be aware of how you feel about God and His Creation while you are acting out this reading. Encourage the students to imagine that they are performing before an audience that doesn't know about God, and they want to convince the

people of the greatness of our Creator.

After going through the reading the second time, use the following questions to discuss the lesson and what the children have just experienced.

● **What were you feeling while you were acting out the reading?** You might help them by suggesting feelings. **Maybe some of you felt nervous or embarrassed. Maybe someone felt full of joy or excitement. Share with us what you felt.**

● **How did you feel about God during the reading?**

● **Did you learn anything about Him?**

● **Do you view God's Creation any differently now?**

● **Why is it important to know what God has created?**

● **You and I are people. Why is this Bible lesson important to us?** (It helps us know that God specially created us, that we did not just happen or evolve.)

● **What do you think is important about Day 7?** (It is the day God rested.) **Why?** (Maybe He wanted to enjoy what He had created.)

● **How do God's people observe the Day of Rest?**

● **What kind of things does your family do to remember this special day?**

● **What would happen without the specialness of Day 7?**

EXPLORING WORSHIP

The five lessons in this unit help the student understand the meaning and purpose of the Call to Worship, a song or reading which tells the people of God that now is the time to

worship, and the Invocation, invoking or asking God to join the people in their worship. These questions will help you be sure each child understands.

● **What does Call to Worship sound like it would mean?**

● **Who would it be calling to worship?**

● **Does anyone know how people were called to worship in Old Testament days?** If no one is able to answer this question, explain that this custom actually began many thousands of years ago in Israel. Friday evening at dusk, the Hebrews began their day of rest, the Sabbath. People knew when it was time to begin worship because someone would blow a ram's horn. Since the people might be scattered over a large area, something that would make a loud noise had to be used.

Let the children make their own ram's horn by forming their hands over their mouths like a megaphone. Let them pretend they are calling people to worship from far away. Make this fun by controlling the volume of their horns by raising and lowering your arms.

● **What kind of things are used to call people to worship today?** One response might be a church bell, but also help the children to think

So God created man in his own image,
  in the image of God he created him;
  male and female he created them.
—Genesis 1:27

13

about things in our worship services that might be considered a Call to Worship like Scripture, a hymn or song, or a reading.

Distribute copies of today's In Worship. Have the students find the Call to Worship and share what they feel its purpose is in the worship service.

Next, use the same type of questions directed at the Invocation.

- **What is the Invocation?**
- **Why do we have an Invocation in our worship service?** Explain that many churches follow the Call to Worship with an Invocation. It's as if we were saying that we don't want to have this worship service without our guest of honor, so let's invite God to join us.
- **Do you think that it really is an Invocation? Why?**
- **What if we didn't have an Invocation? Does that mean God isn't present?** No, of course not. But it does help to remind us that God is present when we worship Him.

WORSHIPING TOGETHER

It is now time for the children to worship God because of His great Creation. We want the children to see God as Creator, and He has

> **G**od creates out of nothing. Wonderful, you say, yes, to be sure, but He does what is still more wonderful: He makes saints out of sinners.
> —Soren Kierkegaard

created all things good. The worship time will also allow the children the opportunity to participate meaningfully in two elements of worship about which they have just learned—the Call to Worship and Invocation.

Follow the outline for In Worship. The students have already been given a photocopy and will follow it throughout the worship time. Find a student who would like to lead the prayer, another to read the Scripture and another to do the Student Worship Talk. You might want to lead the other sections of worship at first (Sections 1, 2, 3, 6, and 8). Help make the transitions to other sections so that participating students will know what to do. The students will enjoy gradually taking complete charge of the worship time.

Help the student who does the worship talk. He or she might need to get ideas from you on how to complete the open-ended sentences in Section 7. (For additional information on leading the worship time, see the introduction to this book.)

As you select hymns for In Worship, let the message of the words also have an emphasis on God's Creation, such as "This Is My Father's World" from your hymnal. *Worship Time Music Book* contains several Creation songs, like "A Wonderful World," page 7, and "Mighty Fine," page 6, which you might teach your students.

It is now time for the children to worship God because of His great Creation. We want the children to see God as Creator, and that He has created all things good.

RESPONDING PERSONALLY

Now that students have worshiped together, we want them to respond individually to our creative God. Begin the worship journey notebook activity. Give the children an opportunity to personalize what they have gained from today's worship experience by writing an entry in it as if it were a worship diary.

During Getting Started students drew their favorite thing that God has created. Now they should realize that they are the favorite thing that God has created. Have each student complete "God's Favorite Creation" and share it with someone. ■

IN WORSHIP
WE PRAISE GOD FOR HIS CREATION

1. Call to Worship—*Read responsively.*
Leader: Come and worship God!
Children: Everyone come to church and praise Him!
Leader: God is our Creator.
Children: Come and worship Him!
Leader: God has made all people and the world we live in.
Children: He is a great God!

2. Invocation—Dear Lord, we have come here to worship You. But it wouldn't mean very much if You weren't here with us. We want You to share in our joy. Please join us in our celebration for Your Creation. In Jesus' name we pray. Amen.

3. Hymn - Song

4. Scripture Reading—Genesis 1:26, 27, 31; 2:1, 2.

5. Prayer—*Remember the pictures you drew when you first came today? Why not thank God right now for what you drew? Finish this sentence prayer,* "God, my Heavenly Father, I thank You for making _____, because _____."

6. Hymn

7. Student Worship Talk—*Complete the following sentences with your own words.*
 I. Read Genesis 1:1.
   A. This verse is important because it tells us that _____.
   B. I am glad to know that God was "in the beginning" because _____.
 II. Review God's activity on Days 2-6.
   A. The things God did on those days shows us that _____.
   B. Three things that God's great Creation helps me realize about Him are _____.
 III. Read Genesis 1:27a, 31a.
   A. Two important things these verses say about people are _____.
   B. Even though sometimes I don't feel good about myself, I know that God _____.

8. Benediction—May the Lord help you to enjoy His Creation, and may you learn to love Him more each day. ■

UNIT 1
WORSHIP
SERVICE
FOCUS:
INVOCATION,
CALL TO WORSHIP

SESSION 2
WORSHIP AIM:

P LEASING GOD

Journey into Genesis 3—4: God is displeased with Adam, Eve, and Cain because they disobeyed Him (pp. 7-14).

Special Things You'll Need:
☐ "Puppet Patterns," page 18 in *THE Idea Book*
☐ "Puppet Stage," page 19 in *THE Idea Book*
☐ Small paper sacks
☐ Large jelly candies (enough for seven per student)
☐ Toothpicks
☐ Small strips of paper 1/2″ x 3″
☐ A variety of small wrapping paper scraps and ribbon
☐ Plastic food saver bags
☐ "Worship Journey Notebook," page 6 in *THE Idea Book* (Optional)
☐ Small leaves; fake fur (Optional)

GETTING STARTED

Today's story reviews how Adam, Eve, and Cain displeased God by disobeying Him. You will help your students to see that their goal is to do the opposite: to please God by obeying Him. Here are some activities the children can get involved in as they arrive.

☐ To get ready for today's Exploring the Bible, have the children form groups of five. Allow each one in the group to select a character from today's lesson: Adam, Eve, Cain, Abel, or Narrator. Have each child make a hand puppet depicting that character to use as his or her group reads through the story and during Exploring the Bible.

Because Abel has a small part, you might have that student also read the parts where God is speaking. (God should not be represented by a puppet.) Have students find their

parts on pages 7-14 of the *Picture Bible* and read the story using the puppets.

☐ Have several students who really enjoy working with puppets and art practice with you or another helper to perform the story for the whole class. An artistic student can help color the different wardrobes needed for Adam and Eve—first the sacks should be plain, then covered with leaves, and finally animal skins. You might want to use real leaves and fake fur to do this. (See *THE Idea Book*, page 19, for instructions on making a puppet stage.)

☐ If you are going to perform last week's choral reading, "In the Beginning," before an audience, you might use this time for the children to rehearse it.

☐ Don't forget to consider starting (if you haven't already) the yearlong project of the Old Testament picture time line.

EXPLORING THE BIBLE

Pleasing God is the aim of today's session. We want the students to understand ways four people in our story did or did not do this. We are looking at the stories of Adam and Eve and Cain. They displeased God because they disobeyed Him. We also look at Abel because he pleased God in the way he worshiped Him.

You might introduce today's lesson like this:

Last week you drew a picture of your favorite thing that God created. The favorite thing that God created is people—every person, you and me. In spite of being God's favorite creation, each of us can displease Him.

Since Adam and Eve disobeyed

God by giving in to temptation, we will start this section by helping the students consider temptations that they have.

Temptation is the desire to do something wrong.

• What are some temptations you face at home or school? List these on the board or newsprint. Make sure the answers fit the definition of temptation. Eating two desserts may be temptation to some children because they have been told they shouldn't; other children may not find this a temptation. We want to help the children see that any temptation that suggests we do things that displease God is wrong to give in to. We want to say no to those temptations.

• What is the hardest temptation you or your friends face?
• Why is temptation a problem?
• What happens if you give in to temptation? (Giving in to temptation is sin.)

Have the special group of puppeteers perform the story for the whole class. When they have finished, these questions help the students understand the meaning of the story.

• What is the temptation in the story?
• Why was it a temptation?
• Adam and Eve gave in to the temptation. What were the results of doing what they were told not to do?
• How did their relationship with God change because they disobeyed? God had just created them. They were His favorite creation, but now He was very displeased about what they had done.

The Picture Bible on pages 10, 11 shows Adam and Eve and their sons living outside the Garden of Eden. Discuss the fact that, in spite of

Adam teaching his sons about God, before long, one of them sinned.

• What was Cain's sin?
• How did God feel about Cain's sin?
• How did Adam and Eve and Cain feel after they sinned?

Have the children name sins that people do today. Make a list of these sins on the chalkboard or newsprint.

• What is God's reaction to these sins?
• After talking about so many things we can do that displease God, what can we do that pleases Him?

Make another column that says "God is pleased when I . . ." List these answers.

To help the students relate the importance of the Bible story to their lives, have them put their puppets back on and pretend that the characters entered a time machine and are here with them right now. Call on a puppet character to give advice to the children based on what happened to them in today's story. For example, Eve might say, "I made a big mistake by giving in to the temptation of the serpent. You should try to learn from my mistake. If you ever can't think of the right answer on a test and are tempted to look at your neighbor's paper, don't do it!" Call on as many children as possible to have their puppet characters speak. You might want to let the children who are more creative thinkers respond last.

EXPLORING WORSHIP

In this section we want to emphasize the way we please God in worship. We are also helping the children understand the Call to Worship and Invocation in the five

lessons of this unit. This will help prepare them to meaningfully participate in adult worship services.

Adam taught his sons about God. But God was not pleased with the way one of them worshiped Him. Page 11 of the Picture Bible shows that Cain was angry at his brother while he was worshiping.

• What kind of bad attitudes could affect you and me during worship? (Too tired, mad at someone, etc.)
• What could be done to have a better attitude during worship?
• Have any of you ever thought worship was boring? Why might it seem boring? (Maybe it seems boring because we don't understand what's going on or what's being said.)
• What could we do that would please God so we wouldn't be bored in worship? (Learn about what is happening in the service so we can understand it better. Sometimes the sermon may be hard to understand, so we could read a hymn or a psalm to ourselves and worship Him that way.)
• What kind of attitudes do you think God would want us to have when we come to worship Him? (Joyful, thankful, etc.)

Review the meanings and purposes of the Call to Worship and Invocation from last week. We hope

If we're looking for transformation of life, we'll teach for transformation, we'll pray for transformation . . .

the students remember that a Call to Worship could be a responsive reading, a Scripture passage, a song, or a reading given by the worship leader.

Give each child a copy of today's In Worship. Point out that this Call to Worship is a passage from Psalms. You'll need four or five volunteers to read the Call to Worship. Whisper to each one a feeling like happy, sad, mad, enthusiastic, bored. Have the student read the first few lines expressing one of those feelings in his or her tone of voice and facial expression.

• **What emotion was being expressed?**

• **How did you feel as the Call to Worship was read in different ways?**

Talk about words or phrases in the Call to Worship that might not be understood such as "enter his gates with thanksgiving."

• **When we worship, how does Psalm 100 tell us to be?**

Practice the Call to Worship expressively with the boys. Tell them to take a breath where they see a punctuation mark.

• **What part of a worship service is just like an invitation?** Invocation. **What is it for?** Inviting the Lord to join us.

Review and explain the Invocation

. . . and we'll not cease our efforts until we see transformation.
—Lois E. LeBar

in the same way that you did the Call to Worship.

Rehearse the Invocation with the girls.

WORSHIPING TOGETHER

Here we are at the high point of the session when students actually participate in worship. Use the Worship Questionnaire from last week to find out in what way each student would like to participate. A child might want to play the hymns, or you might assign some roles to teen or adult helpers. In this way, you will show your confidence in the helpers as spiritual leaders.

In keeping with this week's worship aim—pleasing God—choose songs that focus on joyfully praising God, such as "Joyful, Joyful, We Adore Thee" from your hymnal, or "God Is Great," page 6, and "I Was Glad," page 3, in *Worship Time Music Book.*

RESPONDING PERSONALLY

Now that students have worshiped together, we want them to leave our time today realizing that there are many things they can do that please God. To help them, we have planned a gift exchange which will give them a daily reminder of how they can please God.

Give each of the children seven jelly candies (not to be eaten now, of course), seven toothpicks, and seven small strips of paper. On each strip of paper have them write a different thing a child can do to please God. You might suggest things like "Offer to help Mother" or "Read and think about Psalm 23" or "Tell your

brother or sister something you like about them" or "Pray for a friend at school." Glue or tape the strips of paper to one end of the toothpick. Stick the toothpick into the candy. Gift wrap and tie each of these sweet "pleasing God" messages.

Have the children place all seven of their gifts in the plastic bag. When everyone has finished preparing his or her presents, have the children exchange bags with each other. This way each child will have a bag full of surprise messages.

Open one gift every day next week. The surprise message will tell you just one special thing you can do to please God that day. We know you will want to do many others. Don't peek ahead at the messages. Keep them as surprises to be opened every morning when you wake up. You might want to save the candy to eat after supper. Then it can remind you to think back over the day about the things you did that would please God.

Before leaving, have the children put puppets in their worship journey notebooks. ■

IN WORSHIP
WE PLEASE GOD

1. Call to Worship—from Psalm 100:1-4 *(boys)*
Shout for joy to the Lord, all the earth. Worship the Lord with
   gladness; come before him with joyful songs.
Enter his gates with thanksgiving and his courts with praise;
   give thanks to him and praise his name.

2. Invocation—From Psalm 4:1, 3 *(girls)*
Answer me when I call to you, O my righteous God.
Know that the Lord has set apart the godly for himself;
   the Lord will hear when I call to him.

3. Hymn

4. Scripture Reading—Genesis 3:1-13

5. Prayer—
   Leader: For giving us rules to follow,
   Children: We thank You, God.
   Leader: For loving us, even when we do wrong,
   Children: We praise You, God.
   Leader: For forgiving our sins in Jesus Christ,
   Children: We love You, God.

6. Hymn

7. Student Worship Talk—*Complete the following
sentences.*
   I. Read Genesis 2:8, 9; 3:2, 3.
      A. God made a wonderful place for Adam to live. The only
         thing God told him not to do was _____.
      B. I live in a nice house and go to a good school. Some of
         the things I cannot do at home or school are _____ .
   II. Read Genesis 3:6-12.
      A. Eve gave in to the temptation to eat the fruit of the tree
         of knowledge of good and evil because _____.
      B. Sometimes I'm tempted to do something I'm not
         supposed to because _____.
      C. After Adam and Eve ate the fruit, they felt _____
         and hid from God because they _____.
      D. When I've done something wrong, I feel _____.
   III. God was very disappointed when Adam and Eve
      disobeyed Him.
      A. I feel good about God and myself when I please Him.
      B. Some things I know I can do that please Him are
         _____.

9. Benediction—May God help us to want to please Him more
and more every day. ■

**UNIT 1
WORSHIP
SERVICE
FOCUS:
INVOCATION,
CALL TO WORSHIP**

*B*ut to each one of us grace has been given as Christ apportioned it. It was he who gave some to be . . . teachers, to prepare God's people for works of service, so that the body of Christ may be built up until we all reach unity in the faith and in the knowledge of the Son of God and become mature, attaining to the whole measure of the fullness of Christ.
—Ephesians 4:7, 11-13

**SESSION 3
WORSHIP AIM:**

*T*HANKING OUR CARING GOD

Journey into Genesis 6—10: God saves Noah and his family (pp. 15-22).

Special Things You'll Need:

☐ "Make a Relief Map," page 50 in *THE Idea Book*. All special materials you'll need are listed there.
☐ Copies of "Animals in the Ark," page 100 of *THE Idea Book*
☐ Copies of "An Archeologist's Findings," page 99 of *THE Idea Book*
☐ Worship Journey Notebook, artwork from last week
☐ Large balls of twine or string (approx. 1200')
☐ Roll of white shelf paper
☐ Tape recorder with blank tape
☐ Stamped postcards addressed to people in the church family who are away or unable to attend, like shut-ins, missionaries, or college students (Optional)

GETTING STARTED

As the children arrive today, you and your helpers will want to try to learn something new about as many of them as possible. This helps the students feel important and know that you care about them.

Here are some activities for the students. They provide different ways for students to think about the story and helps for understanding the worship focus.

☐ Weather permitting, take the children outside and help them measure off the dimensions of the ark in the church yard, parking lot, or other open area. Outline the area with string—450' x 75'. This will help them see how huge the assignment was that God gave Noah.
☐ A group of children can begin to make a relief map of Abraham's world. This project may take several

weeks, but it will be useful during many lessons.
☐ Children who will have special parts in the worship service can spend this time preparing.
☐ Have a group of children draw and color "Animals in the Ark," for use later in the session.
☐ Other children can draw "An Archeologist's Findings." This will also be used later.
☐ This time may be used to bring worship journey notebooks up to date.
☐ Add this week's story to the Old Testament picture time line (optional).
☐ Rehearse "In the Beginning" choral reading (optional).

EXPLORING THE BIBLE

Before beginning this lesson, you may want to review last week's lesson by playing Bible Basketball, page 95 in *THE Idea Book*.

In today's lesson we want the children to see that we have a caring God and to thank Him for that. Here are some questions to help the students start thinking about our story.

● **How do you know when someone cares about you?**
● **How does that make you feel?**
● **What would it be like if you did everything you could to let someone know you care about them, but they didn't care for you?**

This is how God must have felt in Noah's day. God had created everything, but Noah and his family were the only people on earth who cared for God. God showed His care for them in a very special way. Let's look in a fun way at the care God showed to Noah.

You'll want to make the events of pages 15-22 in the *Picture Bible* come alive for your group. Here are some ideas.

☐ Have several students who enjoy doing drama read the story as if they were portraying the characters. You or a helper might be the narrator.

For fun, add sound effects. You might begin the reading with the music of "Arky, Arky, (Rise and Shine)." What sounds might be in the background as the ark was being constructed? Or when Noah lead the animals into the ark? Someone might make the sound of a sheep or an elephant. Have children think of ways to make the sound of rain. They might hit their pencils on chairs or pat their legs. Can they imitate the sound of thunder? What sounds might be in the background when Noah's family steps on dry land once again? Explain that you will cue sound effects to start and stop by raising and dropping your hand.

You might tape-record this activity to be placed in the church library for other classes to check out or to be played for the parents at a junior church open house.

☐ Talk about an archeologist, the kind of a scientist who digs up ancient ruins to learn about life long ago. Have the children imagine that they are part of a famous team of archeologists who are exploring the Middle East. One day on a tall mountain called Ararat, they find an ancient ruin of what looks like a huge boat. Remind them of the size of the area of the ark that they marked off earlier. If a child has drawn "An Archeologist's Findings," show it to the class. Explain that the team of archeologists races back to their tent and digs out some ancient scrolls, much like pages 15-21 of the *Picture Bible*. They must get news of their discovery to the TV networks and newspapers. They dig into their baggage and pull out report forms. Have them complete the report in pairs or small groups. Include some of the pictures "Animals in the Ark." Afterwards, have them read what they want to have broadcasted and printed in the newspaper. These reports and activity pieces can be included in their worship journey notebooks or part of them can go on the Old Testament picture time line.

Help the children to see the significance of this story.

● **How was Noah different from the other people living at that time?**
● **How did Noah show that he loved God?**
● **This Bible story has a sad and a happy ending. How is it sad?** (Many people and animals died because of the people's sins.)
● **How is it happy?** (God protected Noah and some animals from death.)

God, our Creator, cares about all His Creation, especially people. He is pleased when we obey Him, just as He was pleased with Noah. But God has promised to punish those who sin or disobey Him.
● **How did Noah please God?**
● **How did Noah know God cared about him?**
● **What are some ways we know God cares about us today?**

EXPLORING WORSHIP

As we help the children worship today, we want them to praise God that He cared for Noah and He cares for them. But we also want them to keep learning about the Call to Worship and Invocation.

● **In today's story, how did Noah worship God?** In Old Testament times, people built an altar when they wanted to worship God. They heaped up rocks into a pile and built a fire on top. Then they killed an animal, usually a sheep, and offered it to God.
● **How did God show that He had accepted Noah's sacrifice?**
● **What sign did God give Noah of the promise He made to him?** Like Noah, we believe that God keeps His promises. When we see a rainbow in the sky, we remember the terrible flood and God's promise never to send another one like that. When we come to church, we worship God for keeping all His promises to us.

Review the purpose and meaning of the Call to Worship. By now many of the children should be familiar with the fact that it tells the people that now is the time for worship to begin. Give each student a copy of today's In Worship.

The Call to Worship for today is "A Mighty Fortress Is Our God," a famous hymn by Martin Luther. We have chosen this hymn because it shows a way God cares for us. We sing it so everyone knows now is the time to come to worship. It was written long ago, so it has some words that we don't use very often.

The goal of Old Testament education was the shaping of a person who was committed to God and to modeling His holiness. . . .

- **What is a fortress?** (A fort or castle.) People used to hide behind the walls of a fortress so that their enemies couldn't kill them. It also can be called a citadel.
- **Who do we hide behind, according to this hymn?** God is a "bulwark," a strong wall or barrier who keeps the enemy away.
- **Who was Noah's helper in the terrible flood?** These words tell us that God is our helper, too. Sometimes we get caught in a flood of "mortal ills." When we have problems or tough situations, God helps us.
- **The "ancient foe" is Satan.**
- **What does it mean that Satan keeps on trying to "work us woe"?** (Satan tries to make life miserable for us.) We might use this hymn to say, "Come and give praise and thanks to our powerful, strong God who cares for us!"

Have the music to the hymn played so children will be familiar with it. Sing it together as a rehearsal for In Worship.

We have taken this same hymn and written words that also make it appropriate to use as the Invocation, to invite God to join us in our worship of Him.

- **How do these words show us this is the Invocation?**

> *. . . Then—and now—to reach that goal, our education programs must be lifelong.*
> —Lawrence O. Richards

- **Why is it included in our worship service?** (To invite God to come to our worship service in His honor.) Ask a volunteer to put the Invocation in his or her own words.

Sing through these words so the children will become familiar with them.

WORSHIPING TOGETHER

Now is the time when students will actually worship together. Today we are thanking God for His care for us. The children who are taking part should be becoming more comfortable in leading the worship time.

Since the children will be singing a rather difficult hymn two times during today's worship, try to also include a more active song geared to their age, such as "My Deliverer," page 9, or "Sing for Joy," page 18, in *Worship Time Music Book*.

The Scripture reading for today can be done responsively. You or another helper should read each verse of the passage. The children should respond after each verse saying, "Thank You, God, for Your care." Explain this to them before beginning In Worship.

RESPONDING PERSONALLY

☐ In advance so that you are ready for this activity as soon as the worship time is over, cover the bulletin board with plain white shelf paper, and using a thin-tipped marker and yardstick, draw lines so that the bulletin board looks like lined stationery. Label the top of the board, THANKS, GOD, FOR YOUR CARE.

Explain that the children have heard about some ways that God cares for members of the group. He has given each of them special things, people, and experiences that shows He cares for them. As a group, write a thank-You note to God on the bulletin board. Serve as secretary, and begin the letter, "Dear God, thanks so much for . . ." Have each child sign his or her name to this giant thank-You note.

☐ You might choose to have the students write postcards to church family members who are away, telling them that they are remembered and that God cares for them. The students can mail their cards. ∎

IN WORSHIP
WE THANK GOD FOR HIS CARE

1. Call to Worship—*Sing ''A Mighty Fortress Is Our God''*
A mighty fortress is our God, A bulwark never failing;
Our helper He amid the flood Of mortal ills prevailing.
For still our ancient foe Doth seek to work us woe—
His craft and power are great, and, armed with cruel hate,
On earth is not His equal.

2. Invocation—*Sing special words for ''A Mighty Fortress''*
Come, hear our praise, O mighty God!
Come, join our joyful celebration.
Long, long ago You sent the Flood
To wash away a sinful nation.
But You saved Noah's life, his children and his wife,
The animals as well, the ark their citadel;
Your power is great, O holy One.

3. Scripture Reading—Psalm 103:1- 4, 11-13
*This is a responsive reading. After each verse is read, say
together:* Thank You, God, for Your care.

4. Prayer—Dear Father, thank You for the Bible which teaches
us about You. We praise You because You cared for Noah. We
thank You for all the ways You show us Your care. Help us to
remember all You give us. In Jesus' name. Amen.

5. Hymn

6. Student Worship Talk—*Complete the following sentences
with your own words.*

  I. Read Genesis 6:8.
    A. Some of the ways Noah pleased God are _____.
    B. I try to please God by _____.
  II. Read Genesis 6:18-21.
    A. Some ways that God showed He cared for Noah are
    _____.
    B. Three ways I know God cares for me are _____.
  III. Read Genesis 8:20-22.
    A. Noah thanked God for caring for him by _____.
    B. Two ways I thank God for His care for me
    are _____.
  IV. Read Genesis 9:13-17.
    A. The rainbow showed Noah that _____.
    B. Whenever I see a rainbow, I am reminded that God
    cares for me and _____.

7. Benediction—May the Lord help us to remember to thank
Him for the many ways He shows us that He cares for us. ■

23

**UNIT 1
WORSHIP
SERVICE
FOCUS:
INVOCATION,
CALL TO WORSHIP**

**SESSION 4
WORSHIP AIM:**

FOLLOWING GOD

Journey into Genesis 11—14:
Abraham learns to trust God's guidance (pp. 23-38).

Special Things You'll Need:
☐ Copies of "Can You Do This?" activity piece 1B in the back of this book
☐ Student report on "Life in Ur"
☐ Dark-colored construction paper and 2″ x 4″ pieces of paper
☐ Worship Journey Notebooks
☐ "Make a Relief Map," on page 50 of *THE Idea Book* (Optional continuing project)

GETTING STARTED

Following God—what an important theme! We want this time to really help students look forward to the lesson and the rest of the session. This time needs to be active and fun since most of the children have just come from Sunday school and need an exercise break.

Two activities introduce the lesson. The others depend on the needs of your class and the time available. Don't forget the importance of also using this time to get better acquainted with each child.

☐ As the children arrive, play a fast-moving game of "Simon Says." This can be a fun way to introduce the theme of following directions. You might change the name from Simon to your name or some other name that's significant to the kids. Be sure to include a lot of strenuous exercise in your instructions. As students are caught not following directions, they must stop participating in the game.

☐ A few minutes before Exploring the Bible, have students sit at their

tables to fill out "Can You Do This?" Tell them not to talk with each other because you want to see how quickly they can do this exercise.

☐ If children have made the relief map of Abraham's world, have them paint lakes, seas, rivers, and land. After the paint dries, have them locate Ur, Haran, and Egypt.

☐ If you are performing "In the Beginning," continue rehearsing.

EXPLORING THE BIBLE

Review previous lessons by pointing out significant events in the Bible stories for the past three weeks as well as the worship aims. We want to emphasize the chronology of these events and the greatness of our God. As the class makes the Old Testament picture time line, it can remind the children of earlier lessons and make the reviewing process easier.

Ask if any student would like to share a way God has recently cared for him or her, or a new way a student found to please God, or something in Creation to praise Him for.

At this time, help students see the significance of the Getting Started activities.
● **Why was it hard for most of you to follow the directions in "Simon Says"?**
● **What happened in the "Follow the Directions" exercise? Why was it tricky?**
● **Has there ever been a time when you or someone you know should have followed directions but didn't?**

Today's session is about following God. We will look at times Abraham followed God's instructions and a time when he did not.

Have the children silently read pages 32-38 in *Picture Bible.* Ask a volunteer to briefly tell the story in his or her own words.

● **What instructions was Abraham given?**

● **How would you have felt if you were given those directions? To know how it must have been for Abraham, we need to know more about what life was like back then.**

Have the student whom you have asked in advance and who is interested in history present a brief report of what life for ten-year-old children would be like in Abraham's day. What would they play? How would they dress? What about food, travel, chores, religion, etc.? Any general or Bible encyclopedia would provide this information. You might look up Ur, Babylon, or Abraham. He or she might be dressed in a period costume and give the report in the first person. For example, "I am ten years old and live in Ur . . ."

Now that we understand more about life in Abraham's day, let's look more closely at the story.

● **What does it mean to follow God?** (Do what pleases God.)

● **Does Abraham always follow God?**

● **When does it seem that he stopped following God?** (When he told Sarah to say that she was his sister.)

● **How do you know this?**

● **What happened to Abraham after this?** (He asked God and Sarah to forgive him, and then he followed God once again.)

● **Do people follow God today?**

● **Why is it important to follow God?**

● **How can we follow Him when we can't see or hear Him?**

● **Do you remember a time when**

you didn't follow God? What happened?

● **When that happens to us, what do we need to do to follow God again?**

EXPLORING WORSHIP

Today we will see that one way we can worship God is by following Him. Also we will continue to emphasize the purpose of the Call to Worship and the Invocation.

Ask children to find a picture in the *Picture Bible* of Abraham worshiping God (see page 33). Explain that in Old Testament times when people worshiped God, they heaped rocks into a pile called an altar. Then they built a fire on top, killed an animal, and offered it to God.

Christians do not build fires and offer sacrifices, but we meet on a regular basis to praise and thank God for His goodness to us. Usually we begin our worship service with a Call to Worship. In the past few weeks, we have learned how to use a responsive reading, a Scripture passage, and a hymn. Today we are going to read a couple of verses that tell us to start praising God.

Distribute copies of In Worship to the students and practice today's Call to Worship. Everyone will read it together clearly three times, each time getting a little louder.

● **How does the Call to Worship prepare us to worship?** (By telling all the people that now is the time to get ready for worship.)

● **What does it tell us to do?**

● **What is an Invocation?** (A special invitation to God to come to the worship service. Even though God is always with us, the Invocation reminds us of that.)

Invocations come in several forms: prayer, responsive reading, Scripture reading, or a hymn.

● **What kind of Invocation is planned for today's worship?**

WORSHIPING TOGETHER

We want today's worship service to help the students worship God by following Him. The more you involve your students and helpers in the service, the more they will enjoy it. So why not divide the responsibilities among a number of people? Ask or phone children well in advance to suggest songs they might play or sing. For smaller parts, such as handing out songbooks or reading Scripture, advance notice may not be necessary.

The following worship plan includes suggestions that adult or student worship leaders can follow. Select hymns that are in keeping with this week's worship aim—to worship God with a desire to follow Him. You might begin with a praise hymn like "Praise to the Lord, the Almighty." "I Was Glad," page 3, and "You Know, Lord," page 19, in *Worship Time Music Book*, will also fit this worship theme. You may want to substitute songs from other hymnals

We are teachers, too. We know that Sunday after Sunday commitment to a class is hard work. Don't be discouraged . . .

or children's songbooks. Use your church's order of worship wherever possible. Other liturgical elements, such as singing the Doxology or praying the Lord's Prayer, should be added in their customary place. This approach should help children to participate meaningfully when they join the adults in congregational worship. If your congregation follows the order of worship in a printed bulletin, you may want to print or type a similar worship outline and duplicate enough for the children in place of the In Worship page.

Encourage students to participate in the prayer time by sharing sentence prayers. Help them to think of different ways they might finish the prayer for today's worship service.

RESPONDING PERSONALLY

To conclude this session, give children an opportunity to personalize what they have gained from the worship experience. Have each child cut three tracings of one of his or her footprints from construction paper. Each child should also have three 2″ x 4″ pieces of paper that he or she will write on and fasten to each footprint.

Tell children that two of the footprints may be taken home and put up in their rooms as a reminder to follow God. The other footprint will go in their worship journey notebooks. Let the students choose what to write on their footprints. One footprint could have a special reminder like "I will follow God when . . ." Another might contain a Scripture verse like Proverbs 3:5, 6, or Psalm 25:4. The footprint that goes in the notebook might state an important event from today's lesson. ■

. . . *You are one in a multitude of people who is giving time and energy to train children. We are praying for you.*
—the Editors

IN WORSHIP
WE ARE FOLLOWING GOD

1. Call to Worship—From I Chronicles 16:23, 24
Sing to the Lord, all the earth . . .
Declare his glory among the nations.
(*Read together three times, getting louder each time.*)

2. Hymn of Praise

3. Invocation—Dear God, we invite You to be with us as we worship You today. Help us to understand how we can follow You better every day. Amen.

4. Scripture Reading—Psalm 25:4, 5

5. Prayer—Dear God, I want You to show me how to
_____ .

Many of you will want to stand and finish this sentence prayer.
Leader: Dear God, we have just heard in Your Word that You
   will teach us how to live. You have also promised to give us
   good direction. We are thankful that You watch over us.
   Help us to be willing to follow You. Amen.

7. Hymn

8. Student Worship Talk—*Complete the sentences below with your own words and ideas.*
  I. Read Genesis 12:1.
    A. Abraham obeyed when God told him to _____ .
    B. I need to obey God when He tells me to _____ .
  II. Read Genesis 12:11-13.
    A. We know that one time Abraham stopped following
      God's direction because he _____ .
    B. One time I stopped following God's direction when I
      _____ .
 III. Read Genesis 13:3, 4, 18.
    A. We know that Abraham worshiped God because he
      _____
    B. Some ways I can worship God are to _____ .

9. Benediction—May the Lord help you to follow Him in everything you do. May the Lord help you to obey His directions so that you will make wise decisions. ■

UNIT 1
**WORSHIP
SERVICE
FOCUS:
INVOCATION,
CALL TO WORSHIP**

SESSION 5
WORSHIP AIM:

TRUSTING GOD

Journey into Genesis 16—25:8
God blesses Abraham because of his faith (pages 39-57).

Special Things You'll Need:
☐ Worship Journey Notebooks
☐ Strips of cloth suitable for blindfolds like men's old ties
☐ "Make a Relief Map" project, page 50 of THE *Idea Book* (Optional continuing project)

GETTING STARTED

The following activities are designed to prepare students for the Bible lesson and worship time. You may use all activities or select one activity that meets the needs and interest of your entire group.

☐ Take the children on a trust walk. Arrange a simple and safe obstacle course in another area, maybe even outside. Have a helper take five or six children at a time to this area and blindfold them. They should join hands and be led around and over several obstacles. The leader should talk to the children, giving verbal instructions as well as leading them through the course.

☐ While one group of students is on the Trust Walk, the other students can read today's story from the *Picture Bible.*

☐ One student could be responsible for keeping the Old Testament picture time line up to date.

☐ Put final touches on "In the Beginning" if you are performing it.

EXPLORING THE BIBLE

Today we want the students to experience what it means to trust and to see how Abraham trusted God.

Trust can be a difficult concept to understand. Here is a way you might want to explain it to the students.

We depend on a lot of things, don't we? We depend on our parents to take care of us when we're sick. We depend on our car to get us to school or church. We depend on our friends to have fun with. The word we use to describe our belief that people or things will be there when we need them is trust. We say, "I trust my mom to wake me up in the morning" or "I don't trust you to keep a secret." God wants us to trust Him. Another Bible word for trust is faith. God wants us to have faith in Him, to depend on Him, to believe in Him. Today's Bible lesson is all about trusting God.

The trust walk helped the students experience trust and prepared them to identify with Abraham's situation.
● **What were you thinking while you were on the trust walk?**
● **What did it feel like?**
● **Did anything concern you during the walk?**
● **Have you ever had those same kind of feelings? What happened?**

Help students to explore these feelings by creating figures of speech like, happiness is like a bowl of chocolate ice cream, or being lonely is like one puppy in a pet shop window. Ask the them to finish this sentence in as many ways as they can. "Not knowing where I'm going is like . . ." They might answer ". . . being a car without a steering wheel" or ". . . trying to catch a bouncing superball."

You might want to review other lessons at this point by having the students think about promises God made to people or when they needed to have faith in someone or something.

• What are some situations where people that we have studied needed to trust, like Adam and Eve, Noah, or Abraham?

Let's look at today's story and see that Abraham had a similar experience. Briefly review pages 39-57 in the *Picture Bible* with students. Point out the important people in the story—Abraham, Sarah, Hagar, Lot, Abraham's servant, and Rebekah. List the situations in the story where they had to trust. For example, Abraham was told that his descendants would number as the stars. Have the students explain why that situation required trust.

Abraham took a trust walk on pages 49-51.
• How was his walk like our trust walk?
• How was it different? Would it have been easier or harder to be on Abraham's kind of trust walk than our trust walk?

Now have the children find situations where people did not trust, like Sarah giving Hagar to Abraham as his wife because she thought she would never have a child.

When you really believe God will keep His promise, you have faith in God. You trust Him to keep His Word. Today's Bible story puts Abraham's and Sarah's faith to the test.
• Have you or someone you know ever had his or her faith tested?
• What do we need to do to be sure we will keep our trust in God when we are tested? (Learn to know Him better and better through the Bible, and remember how God has kept His promises in other situations.)

To help your students visualize the Bible story, pages 39-57 of the *Picture Bible*, try one or more of these suggestions.

☐ On the children's relief map of Abraham's world, have them draw a dotted line with a felt-tipped marker to show Abraham's travels from Ur to Haran to Canaan. Then draw another dotted line to show his travels from Canaan to Egypt. Locate important points where the events in today's Bible story took place by checking a Bible dictionary or encyclopedia. For example, locate Bethel and Sodom (where Abraham was living at the time of this story). Students will relate to these events with more understanding if you help them find the modern names for these locations.

☐ Have a group of children look up Sodom and Gomorrah in a Bible dictionary and report on their findings.

EXPLORING WORSHIP

This is the last session of the unit focusing on the Call to Worship and Invocation. We want to be sure students understand these two elements of worship as well as keeping the aim of this session in mind.

Help students think about the purpose of worship.
• Why do we worship God? (Because we want to praise Him and tell Him He is worthy of our worship.)
• Do we always have to come together at church when we worship?

Explain to the children that we can worship God formally, when we all come together for a worship service, and informally, when we are by ourselves. Remind them of times when Abraham worshiped God formally in his day by building an altar. Other times he prayed informally without an altar.

Today we want the children to create a Call to Worship and an Invocation to use in our worship service. It is also important to help the students understand the worship aim of trusting God.

Abraham, Sarah, Hagar, Lot, Abraham's servant, and Rebekah all trusted God. When people in our church worship together, we are remembering that we worship a God we can trust. God provided for Abraham, Sarah, Hagar, and you and me. We tell Him how much we trust Him. We ask for His guidance in our lives. And we sing praises to Him.

Many worship services begin with a Call to Worship. Show Calls to Worship from previous weeks, and have the children tell whether each is a responsive reading, a Scripture passage, or a hymn. Then have the children help you write their own Call to Worship. Write it on the board or newsprint so they can read it easily. Suggest that they think of some reasons they trust God.

You might write something like this:

Leader: God is great, and He has made us,
Children: Come and worship God!

I am just a little pencil in God's hands. . . doing something beautiful for God.
—Mother Theresa

Leader: God keeps all His promises to us,
Children: Come and worship God!
Leader: God can help us solve hard problems,
Children: Come and worship God!

● **What is an Invocation?** (An invitation for God to come to the worship service. We want Him to hear everything we are saying to Him, so we ask Him to be with us. Of course, God hears and sees everything anyway, but we want God to be our special Guest at the celebration.)

Have the children help you write a simple prayer of Invocation. Again, write it clearly. It might include ways they plan to celebrate. Their prayer might look something like the following:

Dear God, Today we are worshiping You. We want to sing and pray and talk about how great You are. Please come to our worship service. Amen.

WORSHIPING TOGETHER

Here we are at the high point of our session when everyone takes part in worship. Our celebration will be extra special today because the students created the Call to Worship

Teach me your way, O Lord, and I will walk in your truth.
—Psalm 86:11

and Invocation. We also will worship God because we can trust Him.

In advance, decide which children might be willing to take part, and ask for their participation. You might ask a teen or adult helper to also take part. For small reading parts, a day's notice is usually sufficient. However, musical presentations require at least a week's notice, possibly more. Children are usually enthusiastic about playing the numbers they learn in music classes during the worship service.

Today's worship service will not require each student to have a copy of "In Worship."

You might select a hymn for today like "Trust and Obey" from your hymnal or "I Was Glad," page 3, or "Psalm 100," page 5, in *Worship Time Music Book.*

RESPONDING PERSONALLY

To conclude this session, give the children an opportunity to personalize what they have gained from the worship experience. Have them write a cinquain (SIN-kane), a short poem of only five lines. Divide the students into groups of three. Give each group paper and pencils. Explain that the first word of the cinquain is the title. Print GOD on the board. The next line has two words that describe God. Have children brainstorm and select two good adjectives. For example, they might select POWERFUL, KIND.

The third line describes what God does. These words should end in ING. Have children brainstorm and pick three words, for example, LEADING, PROTECTING, LISTENING. Line four should be a four-word sentence that tells how we

respond to God: I WILL TRUST YOU. The last line is one word that describes God. You might choose GUIDE or some other word:

God
powerful, kind
leading, protecting, listening
I will trust You.
Guide

Adjust activity to the time remaining. After groups finish their poems, have each group read the poem. You might also ask children to print their poems on white paper and illustrate them before putting them in their worship journey notebooks. ■

WE ARE TRUSTING GOD

1. Call to Worship—*Read responsively what was written earlier.*

2. Invocation—*Prayer composed earlier, read by leader.*

3. Hymn

4. Scripture Reading—Proverbs 3:5, 6

6. Prayer—*Share sentence prayers thanking God for ways we can trust Him. Think of some of God's promises—like, He will always be with us; He helps us in time of trouble—and thank Him for keeping that promise. Close by asking God to help the group trust God in all things.*

7. Hymn

8. Student Worship Talk—*Complete the outline below with your own words and ideas.*

  I. Read Genesis 15:3-6.

   A. Abraham trusted God in many different situations. Two of them were _____.

   B. An important time I trusted God was when _____.

 II. Read Genesis 18:9-15.

   A. Sarah didn't believe God when He said she would have a son. She did not trust God. Another person in this lesson who did not trust God was _____ because _____.

   B. Sometimes I find it hard to trust or believe God when _____.

III. Read Genesis 22:9-12.

   A. God was pleased with Abraham because he showed God that he trusted Him completely by _____.

   B. Three ways that we can show God we trust Him are _____.

9. Benediction—May the Lord grant you much trust in Him. May you learn that God keeps all His promises. May you keep your promises to God, too. ∎

31

SESSION 6
WORSHIP AIM:

AGREEING WITH EACH OTHER

Your students have begun a yearlong adventure to help them grow in their appreciation of God's greatness and, thus, in their ability to worship Him. This journey moves straight through the Old Testament and, at the same time, through the various parts of your church's order of worship. But the purpose of this journey is more than sightseeing. We want your students to learn *about* God and worship. We want them to be excited participants, caught up in the drama of God's unfolding story and in the joy of worshiping Him.

Unit 1 focused on beginnings—on God's earliest dealings with people, on the call to worship and invocation that start each service, and on the right attitudes we should have for worship.

In Unit 2, our Old Testament journey followed the adventures of Abraham's immediate descendants. Though far back in time, the family problems of Jacob and Joseph should seem familiar to your students.

They will see that worship is a family time, too, when brothers and sisters in Christ gather in their Heavenly Father's presence. Our communication is not just with God but also with fellow worshipers: we teach, exhort, forgive, and encourage one another. This unit gives special emphasis to the common beliefs that help to unite members of your church as you worship. If your order of worship includes the recitation of a statement of faith (such as the Apostles' Creed), this will be a good time for students to learn it. ■

Journey into Genesis 25—28: Esau and Jacob disagree over who will get the inheritance (pp. 58-68).

Special Things You'll Need:
☐ "Bible-Time Meal," page 54 of THE Idea Book
☐ Copies of "Abraham's Family Tree," activity piece 2A in the back of this book
☐ Tent and supplies for Isaac's campsite
☐ Copies of "Help Stamp Out Fights," page 102 of THE Idea Book
☐ Copies of "We Believe It!" activity piece 2B in the back of this book. Insert part of creed before copying.
☐ "Old Testament Picture Time Line," page 7 in THE Idea Book
☐ Bible costumes and props (bowl of food, fur, bow and arrows) (Optional)
☐ Tape recording of Bible story (Optional)

GETTING STARTED

This time allows you to get to know your students individually. Ask about their week at school—favorite subject, a special friend, etc. You also will want to create interest in what will take place in today's session. Choose one or more of these activities.
☐ Simulate Isaac's campsite by setting up a tent and some large stones with a pot for a cooking area. Children can sit around this area as the story is told. If a real tent is not available, how about a blanket draped over a line of rope?
☐ Serve a Bible-time snack the way Jacob and his family might have eaten it. The directions for preparing and serving the meal are on page 54 of THE Idea Book. As you eat,

students may tell other things they know about the way people lived in early Bible times.
☐ Play a pantomime game to remind each other of things God wants us to do. Start by naming a category, such as "Things we should do to help at home (to help our teacher, to be a good friend, etc.)." Then let students take turns pantomiming a task in that category. (Take out the trash; pick up scraps; wash dishes; share toys or sports equipment.) The rest of the children try to guess what is being acted out. Whoever guesses right gets to pick the next category and act out a good deed.
☐ The "Help Stamp Out Fights" will help children begin to think of ways to be peacemakers. After they design covers for a book, have them cut them out to display on the bulletin board. Save these pictures to be used with next week's lesson.
☐ Keep Old Testament picture time line up to date. It can help the children see the chronology of the events and review earlier lessons.
☐ Have five students who enjoy drama volunteer to present pages 60-65. You'll need a Narrator, Isaac, Rebekah, Jacob, and Esau. Use this time for them to rehearse. Encourage them to use as many props as they can find.

EXPLORING THE BIBLE

Today we look at the conflict that develops between Jacob and Esau. We want the students to realize that this story about God and His people is important for them today because all of us can be involved in conflict.
● **What kinds of things make the people in your family angry with each other?**

List all responses in a column on the board or newsprint. This might include lying, taking each other's things, playing favorites, jealousy, etc.

● **What happens in your family when someone is angry?**

● **How do you feel when that happens?**

Let's look at the people in Isaac's family to see if any of them had conflicts.

Have students gather around the campsite they created earlier. Students who rehearsed pages 60-65 will present this part of the story.

After the presentation have students suggest things that caused conflict in Isaac's family. Make a list of these things beside the first list.

● **Do some of the wrong actions that caused problems in Isaac's family also cause problems in your family?**

Today families with problems often go to their pastor or counselor for advice.

● **What do you think a counselor would say to the people in Isaac's family?**

Divide the children into four groups, one to counsel each Bible character. A group should discuss what was wrong with its character's actions, what that person could have done instead, and what he or she could do next to get Isaac's family back together again.

After discussing what the Bible people could have done next, the children will want to know what actually happened next in Isaac's family. Read together or provide a summary of pages 66-68.

The ending for this story was both sad and happy.

● **How was it sad?** (Esau lost the blessing and hated his brother; their family was broken up when Jacob left; Rebekah never saw Jacob again.)

● **How was the ending sort of happy, too?** (God spoke to Jacob and promised to take care of him.) **Even when we do wrong, God still loves us and helps us, just as He did Jacob. Next week we'll see what happened to Jacob after he ran away.**

● **Can you think any of the advice you would give to Isaac's family would help with problems in your family?**

● **What can you do to help make family problems better?**

EXPLORING WORSHIP

In this unit the aspect of worship on which we will focus is the doctrinal creeds—a statement of faith on which a group of people worshiping together can agree. We can easily see how this unit focus fits with the aim of our worship today—agreeing with each other.

In today's story we have learned that after Jacob lied to his father and cheated his brother, Jacob probably thought God would stop loving him. But Jacob was wrong. God promised He would always be with Jacob. Because God said this, Jacob knew it was true and believed it for the rest of his life. Being sure that God loved him made Jacob want to worship God.

Like Jacob, we believe what God tells us. We hear it in His Word, the Bible. When our church meets, we remember the things we believe. We worship God for letting us know what is true.

Discuss with the children how your church declares its beliefs as part of the order of worship. If your church regularly recites a creed or statement of faith (such as the Apostles' Creed), make a copy of it for each student to use throughout this unit. (Even if a recitation of a creed is not a regular part of your worship services, it is still helpful for the students to know a creed as basic as the Apostles' Creed.) Read this statement aloud together.

● **Why do you think we say this together in the worship service?**

During the five weeks of this unit, help your children understand and memorize this creed or statement of faith. This will move them one step closer to one of the goals for this program—enabling children to be intelligent, enthusiastic participants in worship.

Divide the creed into five parts and cover one each week. Use activity 2B entitled "We Believe It." Prepare and copy a different version of this work sheet for each session. Before making copies, fill in the first blank section of the dialogue which tells what part of the creed children are learning this week. Leave the last section blank. A sample of a complete work sheet based on the first section of the Apostles' Creed follows. What appears on the work sheet is in heavy type; what you add is in italics; what students write is in regular type.

So much that passes for education takes away the wonder of life.
—Daniel L. Marsh

WE BELIEVE IT!

BUDDY: Hey! Listen to what I just learned. *I believe in God the Father Almighty, Maker of Heaven and earth: And in Jesus Christ, His only Son, our Lord.*

PAL: People say that in church every Sunday. What does that mean anyway?

CHUM: Our church believes that God made everything, and Jesus—God's only Son—is our Savior.

BUDDY: How do we know that's true?

CHUM: Because the Bible says so.

PAL: But why do we say it every week?

BUDDY: Because these things are so important. We don't want anyone to forget them.

CHUM: Well, I might forget if we don't practice some more. Let's say all we know so far.

ALL: *I believe in God the Father Almighty, Maker of Heaven and earth: And in Jesus Christ, His only Son, our Lord.*

WORSHIPING TOGETHER

You've come to the focal point of the session when students actually participate in worship. Adapt the following plan to parallel your church's order of worship. In keeping with this week's worship aim—to remind each other how God wants us to get along—choose songs such as "We Are One in the Bond of Love" from your hymnal or "God's Way, the Best Way," page 20, and "The Church Is God's People," page 24, from *Worship Time Music Book.*

Where Our Statement of Faith is indicated, children should recite the creed or confession they are learning this month; they can read it until they learn it by heart. If your church includes other liturgical elements, such as singing the Doxology or praying the Lord's Prayer, these should be added in their customary place. This approach should enable the children to participate more fully in church services when they no longer attend this program. The worship plan included with each of these sessions may be photocopied.

Give students leadership responsibility in the worship time. You might identify roles that roughly parallel those of your church's worship leaders (song leader, lay reader, etc.). Different students could fill these roles each week, or the same student could fill a role for a longer period of time, say a month. The latter arrangement makes it easier for you to choose students whose talents fit a role.

RESPONDING PERSONALLY

To conclude this session, give children an opportunity to personalize what they have gained from the worship experience. Tell the children to write an acrostic based on the theme of this session. Write sample acrostics on the chalkboard or newsprint. Children can select their own words to make an acrostic poem to remind them how God wants us to live. They might want to use words like PEACE, GETTING ALONG, or FAMILY, etc. Some children might want to make an acrostic of their names. A simple alphabetical acrostic would be:

Always

Be

Considerate of others.

Here is an example of an acrostic based on a short word:

Give to others.

Let others know I like them.

Always be kind.

Do what pleases God.

Children may work individually or in pairs to create their acrostics. Give volunteer poets an opportunity to read aloud what they have written. Or, have children neatly copy their acrostics (you may want to check spelling) and display them for others to read on a bulletin board. Children would also enjoy illustrating their acrostics with pictures they have drawn or cut from old magazines. ■

IN WORSHIP
WE ARE AGREEING WITH EACH OTHER

1. Call to Worship—Psalm 95:1, 2

2. Invocation—Dear Lord, we are together here today to worship You. Let our thoughts be at peace as we praise You. Help us teach each other what You want us to learn. In Jesus' name we pray. Amen.

3. Hymn

4. Our Statement of Faith—*Read together your church's statement of faith or repeat it phrase by phrase after the leader.*

5. Scripture Reading—Genesis 28:10-22

6. Prayer—*Complete the following sentences:*
Dear God, we praise You because You are _____.
We admit that sometimes we don't please You when
_____.
We are sorry and ask You to forgive us. We're thankful that You love us even when we don't please You. Help us get along each other especially at home.
We know that You hear our prayers and will answer them in the best way. In Jesus' name, we pray. Amen.

7. Hymn

8. Student Worship Talk—*Complete the sentences below with your own words and ideas.*
  I. Read Genesis 28:13-15.
    A. In these verses God made a promise to Jacob. He has made promises to me and my family, too. Two of my favorite promises are _____.
    B. God keeps His promises even when we do things to disappoint Him. Jacob disappointed God when he
_____.
    C. I disappoint God when I _____.
    D. Instead God wants me to _____.
  II. Read Genesis 28:16 and 17.
    A. It is wonderful to be in a place where God is because
_____.
    B. I know God is with us here in this church because
_____.
    C. To please God this week, I will _____.

9. Benediction—May the Lord help us to be at peace with others and to be more like He wants us to be. May we live in a way that pleases Him. Amen. ∎

**SESSION 7
WORSHIP AIM:**

MAKING PEACE

Journey into Genesis 29—35: Jacob raises his family and makes peace with Esau (pp. 69-77).

Special Things You'll Need:

☐ Copies of "Abraham's Family Tree," activity piece 2A in the back of this book

☐ A variety of magazines that have lots of pictures

☐ Copies of "We Believe It," activity piece 2B in the back of this book

☐ Copies of "Peace Survey" activity piece 2C in the back of this book; insert parts of creed before copying

☐ "Make a Relief Map," page 50 in *THE Idea Book* (Optional)

GETTING STARTED

This time enables you to get to know your students better and also involve them in activities that prepare them for today's session.

☐ Have children make a "Peace Is . . ." collage. Have them cut pictures from magazines showing people with peaceful, happy expressions. As the students are working, walk among them, asking them why they think the people look peaceful. Then have the students imagine what might make the people unhappy. Glue the pictures on a three-foot strip of butcher paper. Mount the collage on the bulletin board.

☐ Hand out copies of "Peace Survey." Ask children to mark the best answer. If no answer seems good, have children write an answer beside Other. Collect surveys. Have a helper tally the results and put them on the chalkboard.

☐ Divide students into groups of five or six. Have them discuss what causes the most fights at school.

EXPLORING THE BIBLE

We want the students to see how making peace, today's worship aim, can be experienced in the lives of God's people. Discuss peace with the students.

● **What does peaceful mean?**

● **When do you feel most peaceful?** Make a list of all responses on the board.

● **When are you least peaceful?** Put these answers in a second column. Notice if student responses involve other people.

Go over the results of "Peace Survey" with the students. The items on this survey involve other people who feel angry or unhappy.

● **What can we learn from looking at the results of this survey?**

Erase the earlier lists. Make a new heading on the chalkboard, "Ways to Make Peace." Help the students to think of real-life situations and brainstorm lots of possibilities for making peace. Save this list.

From the list on the board, have the children vote on the best ways to make peace. Underline the most popular choices.

To help students see how today's Bible story continues from last week's lesson, distribute "Abraham's Family Tree" to the group. Provide extra copies for those who might not have attended last week. Have a volunteer read aloud the promise God made to Abraham. Ask another student to explain what it means in his or her own words. Have the children fill in the names of the unidentified people.

Today we're going to see what Jacob learned about making peace with his relatives.

To make events on pages 69-77 of the *Picture Bible* come alive for your

students, try some of these ideas.

☐ Help children locate in a Bible atlas or Bible dictionary Jacob's trip from Beersheba to Laban's home in Padan-Aram (or Haran). If children are developing the relief map, have them draw on the map a line to show Jacob's travels. Also mark Bethel on the map.

Assign roles of Jacob, Rachel, Laban, and Extras (there are several one-line parts). Read aloud the story on pages 69-77 of the *Picture Bible*. You, another leader, or a group of children might take the Narrator's role.

Stop the presentation at the following points and discuss the ways that Jacob tried to make or keep peace. Write children's responses on the other half of the board under the title, "How Jacob Made Peace."

• **What difficulty happened on page 71? How did Jacob handle it?**
• **Why was Laban angry with Jacob on page 72? What did Jacob do?**
• **Why didn't Laban get into a battle with Jacob on page 73? How did Laban and Jacob settle this dispute?**
• **What things on pages 75 and 76 did Jacob do to try to avoid a problem with Esau?**
• **How did Jacob feel when he was able to keep peace with Esau?**

Compare the two lists on the board to see if the children and Jacob have any peacemaking strategies in common. Then have children vote on Jacob's best strategies and underline those ways.

• **What poor peacemaking strategies did Jacob use?** (He ran away from the problem; he gave his brother big gifts.)

Sometimes it helps to cool off if we have a problem with a friend, but running away usually doesn't help solve anything. It is better to talk with someone about a problem rather than giving him or her a gift.

This story shows us how Jacob's problems helped him to grow into a better person. At the beginning of the story Jacob was forced to leave home because of the trick he had played on his brother. He should have relied on God to gain his father's blessing. When Jacob lived with Laban, he had to deal with someone who was tricky, too. Jacob could have become even trickier, but he chose to follow God's way. By the time Jacob had returned home to Canaan, he was a more honest and loving person.

Help the students see the connection between the Bible story and their own situations.

• **How does our peace strategy list compare with Jacob's?**
• **Could we become better peacemakers by adding some of Jacob's ways of making peace to our list?**
• **If a friend tries to start an argument with you at school tomorrow, what would you do?**

Close this section with prayer, asking God to help each student be able to help make peace in at least one situation next week.

EXPLORING WORSHIP

We want students to realize that a creed or statement of faith helps keep peace among people who worship together. It helps Christians realize that they agree on important truths about God.

• **What are some reasons that congregations would recite a creed or confession of faith?**

During the five weeks of this unit, we want the students to understand and memorize your church's statement of faith. This will help them to participate in worship with more meaning and enjoyment.

If you have divided the creed into five parts, this week's session should deal with the second part. Use the work sheet entitled "We Believe It." Before you make copies, fill in the first blank section of the dialogue which tells what part of the creed children are learning this week. Then fill in the last blank section with the part of the creed they learned last week.

WORSHIPING TOGETHER

You have arrived at the focal point of the session, when children participate in worship. The active involvement of the students will help them appreciate worship.

Return Worship Questionnaires that children filled out several weeks ago and have them decide whether they would like to volunteer for other worship roles. If so, have them mark appropriate boxes. Provide questionnaires for newcomers, too. Collect questionnaires and plan weekly services based on the results. Every week invite different children to take leadership roles. At first some

He (Jesus) often used questions to get His learners personally involved in the teaching situation and to lead them on into the truth. . . .

might be more comfortable handing out songbooks or reading Scripture. Those with more self-confidence might lead in prayer, play a musical instrument, or sing a solo. Allow at least a week of practice time for those who present musical numbers. Others might be contacted a day in advance. If you ask a child to present the student worship talk, arrange to have him or her practice with you during the week. You may also ask a teen or adult helper to take this responsibility.

Adapt the following plan to parallel your church's order of worship. Select hymns that are in keeping with this week's worship aim—making peace. You may want to use "Joyful, Joyful, We Adore Thee." Also consider "I Need You and You Need Me," page 15, and "Working Together," page 16 in *Worship Time Music Book*. If you'd like, add special emphasis to today's Call to Worship by singing "I Was Glad," page 3, *Worship Time Music Book*, right after the reading.

Children should recite the creed or confession they are learning this month where Our Statement of Faith is indicated. You may also want to include other liturgical elements, such as singing the Doxology or praying the Lord's Prayer. By using

the customary worship outline that your church follows, children will learn to participate fully when they join the adults for congregational worship. If your church provides a printed bulletin, you may want to distribute something similar each week.

RESPONDING PERSONALLY

We want students to apply what they learned today to their own situations. Last week they drew a cover for a book entitled "Help Stamp Out Fights." Return the pictures to them. (Provide extras for any children who don't have them.) On the back of the page have each student write a way they can help make peace in a specific situation. They should name the problem and the people involved. Then they should list the steps they can take to help make peace.

The students should take these papers home to put up in their bedrooms as reminders that they can be peacemakers and to pray for this specific situation.

For next week: If a family or group of children enjoys acting, have them make a tape recording of Joseph's story. You'll find complete directions for "Joseph, This Is Your Life," on page 20 of *THE Idea Book*. ■

. . . He often answered a question with a question in order to make the learner think for himself.
—Lois E. LeBar

GOD HELPS US BE PEACEMAKERS

1. Call to Worship—

Reader 1: Come and worship God!

Readers 1, 2: Come before Him with singing!

Readers 1, 2, 3: Shout out His greatness!

Readers 1, 2, 3, 4: Bow down and worship,

Readers 1, 2, 3, 4, 5: For He is our God and we are His family.

Reader 1: I was glad when they said unto me, Let us go into the house of the Lord.

2. Hymn

3. Invocation—*Leader:* You are our great God!

   People: There is no one greater than You.

   Leader: You are our loving Lord!

   People: There is no one more loving than You.

   Leader: Come and hear our joyful praise!

   All: Come and be joyful with us, God.

4. Hymn

5. Statement of Faith—*Read this aloud together.*

6. Scripture Reading—Genesis 35:1-3, 9-15

7. Prayer—Dear God, we want to be peacemakers as we worship You. We want to welcome everyone and help them feel accepted. Help us worship You with joyful praise. Amen.

8. Hymn

9. Student Worship Talk—*Complete the following sentences.*

  I. Read Genesis 35:3.

    A. Several times Jacob needed God's help because he had lots of difficult times. Two of those were when
_____.

    B. I have a difficult time and need God's help when
_____.

    C. We know that God was with Jacob when he met with Laban and Esau again because _____.

    D. Two ways I know God is with me are _____.

  II. Read Genesis 35:14, 15.

    A. Jacob wanted to remember the spot where God had been with him.

    B. I feel happy when we worship together here because
_____.

10. Benediction—Praise and glory and thanks and honor be to our God for ever and ever. May God help each of us to be peacemakers this week. Amen. ■

SESSION 8
WORSHIP AIM:

BEING CONFIDENT

Journey into Genesis 35—42:
Joseph trusts God while in slavery
(pp. 78-87).

Special Things You'll Need:
☐ Construction paper name tags
☐ "Weave a Swatch of Joseph's Coat," page 72 in *THE Idea Book*; construction paper in bright colors
☐ Copies of "We Believe It" activity piece 2B in the back of this book; insert parts of creed before copying
☐ Tape recording of "Joseph, This Is Your Life," prepared in advance, page 20 of *THE Idea Book* (Optional)

GETTING STARTED

The following activities will help your students become involved with learning experiences that introduce today's lesson. Choose one or more to do with your group.
☐ Have each student draw a picture on newsprint or art paper of what he or she does best, like doing gymnastics, playing the piano, skateboarding, or reading.
☐ To help the students identify with the characters in today's story, have them roleplay Joseph's brothers. In advance, make name tags of Jacob's sons:
Joseph
Simeon (SIM-ee-un)
Judah (Jew-duh)
Zebulun (ZEB-yuh-lun)
Naphtali (NAF-tuh-lie)
Asher (ASH-er)
Reuben (ROO-ben)
Levi (LEE-vie)
Issachar (ISS-uh-car)
Dan
Gad
Only one Joseph name tag is needed, but make enough of the others so every student has one to wear.

(Benjamin is not part of this activity.)

You or another adult or teen helper will be Joseph. (You might want to wear a beautiful robe.) Remind everyone that your father, Jacob, loves you most and does special things for you. The students, pretending they are your ten older brothers, will act angry towards you, call you names, and plan to do bad things to you. You may want another helper to assist the students in how they should be acting toward you.
☐ Assign one student to keep the Old Testament picture time line current. (Optional)
☐ Review last week's lesson by playing "Bible Basketball," page 95 of *THE Idea Book.*

EXPLORING THE BIBLE

Begin the lesson time by picking up on the challenge given to the students last week.
● **Is anyone feeling especially happy because you were able to help make peace with someone last week? Tell us about it.**
Earlier today the children were asked to draw a picture of something they are good at. This activity introduces the worship aim of being confident—if I am good at something, I feel confident about it. Ask volunteers to explain their drawings. These questions may help the discussion.
● **How long have you been doing this?**
● **How did you feel the first time you did this?**
● **Do you do this often?**
● **How do you feel when you do it now?**
When we practice something, we

get better and better at it. We begin to feel confident about doing that thing. You feel confident about doing what you do best.

Introduce the Bible lesson by explaining that confidence in God grows from experience just as confidence in riding a bike grows from practice.

Today's story is about a man named Joseph. Joseph had confidence in God. This confidence was tested many times throughout his life. The first test came when Joseph was a teenager. We want to help students understand how Joseph was able to develop such confidence when he was put in so many difficult situations.

To see how this story follows from last week's story, talk about "Abraham's Family Tree." God kept His promise to Abraham that his descendants would be as many as the stars in the sky because all Jewish people have descended from him, including Jesus. Joseph was the son of Jacob, the grandson of Isaac, and the great-grandson of Abraham.

Earlier in this session we roleplayed Joseph's family.
● **How would you feel about yourself if you had been Joseph?**
● **Who would you believe—your father who says he loves you most or your brothers who say they hate you?**

For Joseph to have had confidence in God and feel good about himself, he must have heard many wonderful things about God, and he must have listened to his father more than his brothers. These things helped Joseph have confidence in God.

Play the tape recording of the story that has been prepared in advance. Stop the tape at the end of "The King's Dream."

Divide children into three groups.

Have a scribe (secretary) volunteer for each group. The first group will read "Into the Pit," pages 78-80, the second group, "Slave Train to Egypt," pages 81-84, and the third group "The King's Dream," pages 85-87. Each group is to write a summary of events in that section stating when it might have been hard for Joseph to keep trusting God. Each group will share its summary with the class.
● **When do you think it is easier to have confidence in God—during easy times or difficult times? Why?**
● **Can anyone share a time when you or someone you know found it hard to have confidence in God?**
● **What things can we do to help us to have more confidence in Him?**

EXPLORING WORSHIP

As the students focus on your church's creed or statement of faith throughout this unit, the aim of every lesson will help them understand the importance of a creed. Our confidence in God is increased when Christians are agreed on the important beliefs of our faith.

By the end of this unit, children should be able to say your church's creed or the Apostle's Creed. Their understanding of this important statement should help them to become informed, enthusiastic participants in worship.

If you have divided the creed into five parts, this week's session will deal with the third part. Use the work sheet entitled "We Believe It." Fill in the first blank section of the dialogue, which tells what part of the creed children are learning this week. Also fill out the last blank section, which tells what they have learned in previous weeks. Then make enough

copies for everyone. (Refer back to Session 6 if you would like more directions.)

(If your class is learning the Apostle's Creed, the third section contains a difficult passage. If someone asks why Jesus went to hell, explain that it is the place where people go who are separated from God because of their sins. Since Jesus died for the sins of the whole world, He took the penalty for sins, the consequence our sins deserved. While this phrase from the Apostles' Creed is based on certain interpretations of Acts 2:27; Ephesians 4:9; and I Peter 4:6, not all orthodox Christians hold to this particular phrase in the Creed.)

WORSHIPING TOGETHER

You have arrived at the focal point of the session when children participate in worship. Enhance their appreciation of this experience by involving them in every phase of the service. In advance, check Worship Questionnaires to see what leadership roles children have volunteered to take. Plan for the children to play musical instruments and sing an occasional solo, but be sure to give at least a week's notice for practice.

. . . *When the teacher is in total control of the class's activities, his or her ego may be the only growing thing in the classroom.*
—Marlene LeFever

Small parts, like handing out songbooks, reading Scripture, or leading the Call to Worship, require less notice. You can ask a child to take part the morning of the service, but, children asked in advance often show greater enthusiasm and self-confidence.

Adapt the following plan to parallel your church's order of worship. Select hymns and songs that are in keeping with this week's worship aim—being confident in God. You may want to use "To God Be the Glory" from your hymnal or "God Is Great" or "Lord, I'm Crying" from *Worship Time Music Book*. This last song contrasts musically to praise hymns. If you wish, introduce it to the students as a song the Hebrews might have sung at times while they were slaves in Egypt.

Children should recite the creed or confession they are learning this month where Our Statement of Faith is indicated. You may also want to include other liturgical elements, such as singing the Doxology or praying the Lord's Prayer. By using the customary worship plan that your church follows, children will learn to participate fully when they join the adults for congregational worship. If your church provides a printed bulletin, you may want to duplicate

and distribute something similar to the children.

RESPONDING PERSONALLY

Joseph is an example to us of someone who had confidence in God. Many of us remember Joseph and the wonderful coat his father, Jacob, gave to him. Let the children personalize this session by weaving a construction paper "swatch" of Joseph's coat. After weaving the paper, the children may decorate it like the fabric in Joseph's coat may have been.

Have each student write and complete this sentence on his or her weaving: I need God to help me have more confidence when I _____. They might also want to include a Scripture reference like the first part of Proverbs 3:26, "For the Lord will be your confidence."

Children may take their weavings home for a reminder to have confidence in God or place them in their worship journey notebooks.

For next week, ask two adults to come to the session and share with the class a personal experience of forgiveness. ■

. . . A child can learn only when he is valuing himself and feeling valued.
—Virginia Satir

IN WORSHIP
WE HAVE CONFIDENCE IN GOD

1. Call to Worship—Psalm 29:1, 2

2. Invocation—Dear God, be present in our worship today. We praise You because You are worthy of our confidence. Learning how Noah, Abraham, and Joseph trusted You, helps us to have more confidence in You. In Jesus' name we pray. Amen.

3. Hymn

4. Our Statement of Faith—*Read this aloud together or repeat it, phrase by phrase, after the leader.*

5. Scripture Reading—Genesis 39:2- 6, 20-23

6. Hymn

7. Prayer—*Leader begins with* "Dear God," *and then all repeat in unison* "Let our church be . . ." *After each introductory phrase, leader says,*

   . . . people who make You happy.

   . . . people who love each other.

   . . . people who serve You.

   . . . people who agree on what we believe. In Jesus' name, we pray. Amen.

8. Student Worship Talk—*Complete the following sentences with your own words.*

  I. Read Genesis 39:2.

    A. Joseph had confidence in God because God had been with him when _____.

    B. One special time God was with me was when _____.

  II. Read Genesis 39:20, 21.

    A. Two situations when Joseph really needed confidence in God are _____ and _____.

    B. I need more confidence in God when I _____.

 III. Read Genesis 39:22, 23.

    A. God showed Joseph that He was worthy of His confidence because God was always with Joseph.

    B. God is worthy of my confidence because He _____.

9. Benediction—May our God, who is always with us, help us to have more confidence in Him every day. ■

**SESSION 9
WORSHIP AIM:**

BEING FORGIVEN

Journey into Genesis 42—45:
Joseph forgives his brothers (pages 88-99).

Special Things You'll Need

☐ Shelf paper, letter patterns on page 120 of THE Idea Book, 4" x 6" pieces of dark-colored construction paper

☐ Sack, eraser, trash bag, bar of soap, the word "forgiveness" in large letters on a piece of paper

☐ In advance, ask two adults to come to this session and share with the children a personal experience of forgiveness.

☐ Camera and film

☐ Worship Journey Notebooks

☐ Copies of "We Believe It" activity piece 2B in the back of this book; insert parts of creed before copying

☐ Rolls of butcher paper, soft chalk (pastels) or tempera paint and brushes

☐ Flood or spotlight or slide projector

☐ Sandals, bathrobes, dish towels, sashes (Optional)

☐ Tape recording of "Joseph, This Is Your Life," used in last week's lesson (Optional)

GETTING STARTED

As children arrive today, make a point to converse with several of the quieter students or ones that you don't know very well.

Introduce the aim for today, being forgiven, by one or more of these activities.

☐ Cover the bulletin board with shelf paper. Using letter patterns on page 120 of THE Idea Book, tack up the title, I NEED FORGIVENESS. Give children a 4" x 6" piece of colored construction paper and

crayons or markers. Have each of them write a wrong thing he or she has done on one side of the paper. (You and your helpers may want to join in this activity.) As each person finishes, he or she should tack his or her paper to the bulletin board.

☐ Give groups of four or five children a sheet of paper and appoint a secretary. Pass around a sack containing an eraser, a trash bag, a bar of soap, and the word "forgiveness" on a piece of paper. Ask children to think of ways the objects in the bag are alike. The secretary should write down all responses.

EXPLORING THE BIBLE

The students today will discuss what it means to forgive and to be forgiven by listening to testimonies of adults and by looking at the story of Joseph and his brothers. We will help students understand the two aspects of forgiveness—to forgive and to be forgiven—by using the bulletin board to represent the need to be forgiven and the chalkboard to represent the need to forgive.

Help students to focus on the aim of this session.

● **What does forgiveness mean?**
Allow time for explanations from several students.

Introduce the two adults you asked to share an experience of forgiveness. We want students to hear personal illustrations from people they know. (Let speakers decide if they should share a time when they have been forgiven or when they needed to forgive someone else.) To help the children identify more personally with you, you might want to add an experience of your own at this time.

Point out the bulletin board entitled "I Need Forgiveness." Now write on the chalkboard "I NEED TO FORGIVE."

Look at the difference in the two titles.

● **If the papers we put on the bulletin board contain things we have done wrong, things that need forgiveness, what kind of things would we write on the chalkboard?** (Wrong things people have done to us that we need to forgive.)

Fill the chalkboard with things for which we need to forgive others. Start by listing anything that was just shared by the guest speakers. Then have the class suggest things people have done to them that need forgiveness.

Let's look at the story of Joseph and his brothers to see how forgiving and being forgiven were important in it.

To help review last week's lesson and identify places where forgiveness was needed, ask volunteers to share with the class the important events that happened to Joseph (pages 78-87 in the *Picture Bible*).

● **Whom did Joseph need to forgive?** (His brothers for throwing him into the pit and selling him into slavery; Potiphar's wife for lying about him so he would be put in prison.)

If you have asked a family or group of children to make a tape recording of the story of Joseph, play the second part of the tape taken from pages 88-99.

Another option is to ask volunteers to help you read the story aloud. Provide readers with simple costumes—sandals, bathrobes, and dish towels for head coverings. Encourage readers to be expressive, to try to feel they really are the people they're portraying.

To be able to forgive his brothers for the wrongs they had done to him, Joseph must have trusted God and known that God loved him.

● **Besides telling them, how did Joseph show his brothers that he forgave them?**

● **What can we do to show someone we forgive them?**

● **Did Joseph wait for his brothers to say they were sorry before he forgave them?** Help the children to see that Joseph's acts of forgiveness came before his words of forgiveness and before his brothers asked for forgiveness.

● **What can we do to show someone that we forgive them?**

● **When we forgive someone for doing wrong to us, what happens? It's as if it was erased.** Erase from the chalkboard all the wrong things that had been done to people in the class.

● **What must I do if I am the person who did the wrong thing?** Allow time for several to respond. **I need to be forgiven by the person I wronged. That person is always God, but most of the time it is God and someone else. When I go to God and that other person and say, "Please forgive me," it makes everything okay again.**

Take from the bulletin board all the colored papers on which the class had written the wrongs they had done, tear them up, and put them in the trash bag.

Get one of the sacks used earlier containing the soap, eraser, trash bag, and the word "forgiveness." Conclude this section by asking someone to tell you again how all those things are alike.

EXPLORING WORSHIP

One of the most special and personal reasons that we worship God is because He forgives us for our wrongs. We become aware of forgiveness when we tell Him we are sorry that we sinned. Many creeds include forgiveness of sins as an important part of the Statement of Faith. (If you are using the Apostle's Creed, that phrase occurs in the portion to be learned in next week's session.)

Joseph's brothers were afraid that Joseph would hate them for selling him into slavery, but they were wrong. Joseph forgave them. In this way, Joseph was doing what God has done for us.

● **Why is forgiveness important?** Every person does wrong things. If God didn't forgive us, we could never be close to Him; we could never be His friends. The same is true of people. If we do not forgive those who sin against us, we can't develop a close relationship with them.

Forgiveness of sin is one of the most important of all Christian beliefs.

● **How does our church show its belief in forgiveness as part of the order of worship?** (Through hymns,

. . . *I began to allow more and more time during the school day for my students to talk to and do things with each other. . . .*

45

prayer, Scripture reading, the sermon, and the statement of faith.)

- **Why do we repeat our Christian beliefs during the worship service?** (Because we don't want to forget the important beliefs that we agree on, and we want other people to know what we believe.)
- **Why are we memorizing our Creed or Statement of Faith?** (So that we can thoroughly know what we believe and participate in worship better.)

Use the work sheet entitled "We Believe It." You'll prepare the fourth version of this work sheet for this session. Before making copies, fill in the first blank section which tells what part of the creed children are learning this week, and the last blank section telling what they have learned in previous weeks. (For more instructions, see Session 6 in this unit.)

WORSHIPING TOGETHER

The student worship time is the primary activity of each session. To enable the children to participate fully, decide in advance how each child can contribute to the service. If two friends have volunteered to read Scripture, you might have them read

> . . . *They had to teach me before I could begin to teach them.*
> —John Holt

a passage responsively. One might read the Scripture and the other provide an example to show what the passage means. Two or more children from a neighborhood might sing together or play musical instruments. You might also ask one child to take a leadership role (such as Statement of Faith leader) for a month.

Adapt the following plan to parallel your church's order of worship. Select hymns and songs in keeping with this week's worship aim—being forgiven. From the hymnal you could sing "Praise Ye the Triune God." "I Was Glad," page 3, and "I Can Join," page 31, from *Worship Time Music Book*, would fit in nicely as well.

Where Our Statement of Faith is indicated, children should recite the creed or confession they are learning this month. Perhaps a child could lead them in reading it until they learn it by heart. Singing the Doxology or praying the Lord's Prayer may be added if the usual order of worship at your church includes these elements. This approach should encourage the children to participate knowledgeably and confidently when they join the adults for congregational worship.

RESPONDING PERSONALLY

This time is especially important in today's session. We want the children to have the opportunity to realize their need to be forgiven and then to express how that forgiveness feels.

Read Psalm 51:10 to them. Have them close their eyes and think about what that verse means. Read it again as a prayer asking the children to pray it silently with you.

Children usually express their

emotions freely. Help students express the feeling of being forgiven in a tangible, personal way by making silhouettes of joy. Fasten strips of butcher paper together (about four feet high) and mount them on a blank wall. Focus a light source directly on the paper. Have children pose in a position expressing happiness (like when their favorite team is winning) and stand in front of the light, projecting a shadow onto the paper. You or a helper can outline each child's shadow. Everyone can cut out his or her silhouette and color it with chalk or tempera paint. The finished silhouettes of joy can be mounted around the room.

Because of the emphasis on forgiveness, this lesson provides an opportunity to explain salvation. Some may be ready to make this commitment. You will want to follow the leading of our Master Teacher in this regard. We have provided a section on how to lead a child to Christ in the introduction to this guide. ■

IN WORSHIP
WE PRAISE GOD FOR FORGIVING US

1. Call to Worship—from Psalm 32:1, 2, 11

Reader 1: Blessed is the person whose transgressions are forgiven, whose sins are covered.

Reader 2: Blessed is the person whose sin the Lord does not count against him or her and in whose spirit is no deceit.

All: Rejoice in the Lord and be glad, you righteous; sing, all you who are upright in heart!

2. Invocation—Dear God, be present with us in our worship service. We praise You and thank You because You forgive us when we do wrong. Bless us as we worship You. In Jesus' name, we pray. Amen.

3. Hymn

4. Our Statement of Faith—*Read this aloud together.*

5. Scripture Reading—Genesis 45:3-7, 14-18, 25-28

6. Prayer—*Several of you may finish this sentence prayer.*

Dear God, I thank You that Your forgiveness is like (pick one: an eraser, a bar of soap, a trash bag) because _____.

7. Hymn

8. Student Worship Talk—*Complete the following sentences.*

I. Read Genesis 45:4, 5.
  A. Joseph was glad to see his brothers because he had forgiven them. If he had not forgiven them, he probably would have felt _____.
  B. When I forgive someone for doing wrong to me, I feel

  _____.

II. Read Genesis 45:3.
  A. Joseph's brothers were terrified of him because they had not yet asked him to forgive them.
  B. Once when I had not yet said I was sorry for something I had done, I felt _____.

III. Read Genesis 45:7.
  A. God took the wrong things that were done to Joseph and brought good from them. Two good things that came from Joseph's troubles are _____.
  B. One time someone I know did something wrong to me (or someone else). God helped me show forgiveness when I _____.

9. Benediction—May God help each of us accept His forgiveness. May God help us to be willing to forgive others as Joseph did, and be willing to say we are sorry when we do wrong. Amen. ■

47

SESSION 10
WORSHIP AIM:

BEING BLESSED

Journey into Genesis 46—50: Joseph helps his family in Egypt (pp. 100-106).

Special Things You'll Need:
☐ Tape recording, "Joseph, This Is Your Life,"(Optional)
☐ "Joseph's TV Special" page 21 in *THE Idea Book* (Optional)
☐ Copies of "We Believe It," activity piece 2B in the back of this book; insert parts of creed before copying
☐ Large poster-size paper
☐ Letters cut from large sheets (18″ x 24″) of bright-colored construction paper to spell THANKS, GOD
☐ Contact a church leader or member of long standing to participate in the worship time

GETTING STARTED

The following activities are suggested to provide your students with productive learning experiences while everyone arrives.
☐ Have children create a poster showing times when they have gotten together with relatives for a party—parents, grandparents, aunts, uncles, and cousins. The occasion may have been a wedding, funeral, birthday, holiday celebration, or family reunion. Have children color a poster showing what happens at a family party involving the extended family. Have them try to picture several different age groups as well as family activities. Title the poster TOGETHER WE'RE BLESSED! Display poster on the wall. If your group of children is large, several posters can be made. During this activity, visit with the children about their families and the occasions they are drawing. Also talk about what

the word "blessed" means.
☐ Play "Superhelpers." Divide children into teams, and give each team a piece of paper and pencil. Have each group think of all the ways they help their families. After two minutes, call time and have each group read the list. Winners are those who have the most items. For a second round of the game, have them think of all the ways they might help their families when they have their own children and their parents are old. Afterwards, explain that being part of a family is a blessing, and in a family, everyone works together.

Although the students might not think they contribute much to family life, actually they can help in many ways even while they are young.
☐ Have students begin researching and preparing "Joseph's TV Special." Have students select the part they would like to have in the presentation. If the class enjoys this type of project, they may want to present it to another group after students feel comfortable with it.

EXPLORING THE BIBLE

The aim for today is to realize how we have been blessed. We will look at the lives of Joseph and his relatives to see how they were blessed as the family helped each other.
● **How many of you do things to help around the house?**
● **How do you feel about doing those things?** Allow several children to respond.

The word "blessed" may be unfamiliar to children this age. Discuss the word with the students to be sure all of them understand what it means.
● **What does it mean to be blessed?**

(Enjoying happiness, receiving pleasure or contentment.)
- **How have we been blessed?** Make a list of responses on the chalkboard or newsprint.
- **Could it ever be a blessing to help your family? How?**
- **What do you do to help your family that you enjoy most?**

Let's see how Joseph's family was blessed by his help.

☐ Review the life of Joseph by listing on the chalkboard the following chapter titles as clues to the events in Joseph's life. Then call on volunteers to tell one way that Joseph helped his family or the people he was living with in each chapter of the story. If children have difficulty, have them check the *Picture Bible.*
1. Into the Pit
2. Slave Train to Egypt
3. The King's Dream
4. Trouble in Egypt
5. The Stolen Cup
6. Joseph's Secret

Today's story shows how Joseph continued to help his family throughout his life, even when some of his family didn't realize it.

The students will relate to the events in Joseph's life more fully if they are able to be actively involved with the story. Select one or more of these activities to help stimulate learning.

☐ If a family or group of children has made a tape recording of the story of Joseph, play the last part of the tape, "South into Egypt," and "Death Sentence" (taken from pages 100-106). Have children listen for ways that Joseph continued to help his family.

☐ Have children present "Joseph's TV Special." This program might have been on television if the ancient Egyptians had had TV sets.

☐ If children have made a poster of a family gathering, discuss what was drawn. Then tell the group to pretend to be the grandchildren of Jacob sitting around at a family party telling stories about how they were blessed (even in the hard times). After the presentation, discuss Joseph's influence on his family.

At the beginning of his life, Joseph's family was full of jealousy and resentment. But instead of contributing to their bad feelings, Joseph made peace with his brothers. Not only did he protect them from famine and help them to find good pasture land in Egypt, but even more importantly, he helped his brothers to be more loving toward each other. You may never be rich or powerful like Joseph, but you can still be a great help to your family and help them to realize how they are blessed.

If children have listed ways they help their families, read over the list and ask children to point out which things are most helpful. Explain that children have already learned some ways to assist other family members. God wants them to continue helping their families throughout their lives.

Take several minutes to let the students share ways their families have been blessed by their help. (Review definition of "blessed.") Encourage students to think of future things they might do that could continue to bless all of them.

EXPLORING WORSHIP

Today we have been talking about blessings—how Joseph's life was blessed as he helped his family, and how each of us can bless our families by helping them. Now, in worship, we want to focus on how God blesses us. One of the things that helps us to remember all that God has done for us is to recite our creed or statement of faith. This statement contains many of the important things that God has done for us.
- **Why do you think we say this statement together during the worship service?** So that we will remember it, so that visitors will know what the church believes, because these are the church's most important beliefs, etc. Explain that for the last several weeks, you have been memorizing this creed or statement of faith. We want everyone to learn it so we will be more knowledgeable participants in worship.

The creed has been divided into five parts, and one part is covered each week. Use the work sheet entitled "We Believe It." Before copying it for the group, fill in the first blank section of the dialogue, which tells what part of the creed children are learning this week, and the last blank section telling what they have learned in previous weeks. (More instructions can be found in Session 6 of this unit.)

To be able to play with ideas is to feel free to throw them into new combinations, to experiment, and even to "fail."
—Elliot Eisner

WORSHIPING TOGETHER

Today the worship aim is to praise God for blessings or memories of wonderful things He has done for us. We want as many students as possible to participate in this worship celebration. You might begin preparing them throughout the session.

In advance, assign students various sections of the service (refer to the Worship Questionnaires that they filled in at the beginning of this course). Also contact a longtime member of your church to share with the students ways he or she has seen God bless the church in a special way over the years. (This will come under point II in the worship talk.)

If you wish, adapt the following plan to parallel your church's order of worship. Be prepared to assist the students who have been assigned responsibilities. Help them make transitions from section to section so the worship time flows smoothly. Select songs such as "God Is So Good." You might want to use "The Lord Is My Shepherd," page 28, or "God's Way, the Best Way," page 20, in *Worship Time Music Book*. This music stresses the goodness of God and all that He has done for us.

May the words of my mouth and the meditation of my heart be pleasing in your sight, O Lord, my Rock and my Redeemer.
—Psalm 19:14

Where Our Statement of Faith is indicated, children should recite the creed or confession they have been learning all month. If your church includes singing the Doxology, praying the Lord's Prayer, or other liturgical elements, add these in their appropriate places. Spend a few minutes before the worship service preparing the children to participate in the responsive prayer (section 6).

RESPONDING PERSONALLY

Children need to be encouraged to think about all the different blessings they have from God. In advance, cut out large, fat letters (from 18″ x 24″ colored construction paper) that say THANKS, GOD. Scatter the letters throughout the children's work area. Let them personalize what they have gained from the worship experience by writing words or coloring pictures of God's blessings on each letter. On the letter T, children should write or draw blessings that begin with T, like friend Tom or the Trip we took. Children may move to different letters writing or drawing blessings beginning with that letter.

As the session closes, mount the letters on the bulletin board so they spell THANKS, GOD. This will be a visible reminder to the children of all that God has blessed them with. ◼

IN WORSHIP
WE THANK GOD FOR BLESSING US

1. Call to Worship—Psalm 119:1, 2

Reader 1: Blessed are they whose ways are blameless, who walk according to the law of the Lord.

Reader 2: Blessed are they who keep His statutes and seek Him with all their heart.

2. Hymn

3. Invocation—You are the Lord who made everything. You have blessed us in many ways. We bow down before You and thank You for Your blessings. Amen.

4. Hymn

5. Our Statement of Faith—*Read or say this together.*

6. Prayer—Dear Heavenly Father,

Leader: For Your love,

Children: Thank You, God.

Leader: For the world,

Children: Thank You, God.

Leader: For our parents,

Children: Thank You, God.

Leader: For all the good things you give us,

Children: Thank You, God.

7. Scripture Reading—Genesis 46:1-4; 48:15, 16; 50:15-21

8. Student Worship Talk—*Complete the sentences below with your own words and ideas.*

  I. Read Genesis 48:15, 16.

  A. Jacob blessed Joseph and his sons just as Abraham and Isaac had been blessed. God stills blesses His people today.

  B. I have been blessed by God because He _____.

 II. Read Genesis 48:16. *(A person who has been a member of your church for a long time will do this section.)*

  A. This church has needed God's help when _____.

  B. God has especially blessed this church by _____.

III. Read Genesis 50:18-20.

  A. Joseph's brothers meant to harm him by _____, but God used that for good because _____.

  B. A time I know about when God took something bad and made it be for good was when _____.

9. Benediction—from Psalm 115

The Lord remembers us and will bless us. He will bless those who fear the Lord—small and great alike. May you be blessed by the Lord, the Maker of Heaven and earth. ∎

SESSION 11
WORSHIP AIM:

PRAISING OUR PROTECTOR

As we continue this yearlong spiritual pilgrimage through the Old Testament and your church's Order of Worship, we want this adventure to encourage your students to grow in their appreciation of God's character and in their expression of worship and adoration.

The stories of the Old Testament are presented in chronological order. By using the Old Testament Picture Time Line (*THE Idea Book*, page 7), the students will be able to see the sequence of God's acts.

In the first two units, students explored Genesis. They witnessed the power and work of God in Creation, the Flood, and the lives of patriarchs Abraham, Isaac, Jacob, and Joseph. In addition, students explored the reasons Christians meet together for worship as well as the attitudes they should have in approaching their Creator. They focused specifically on three aspects of corporate worship: the Call to Worship, Invocation, and the church's doctrinal creed. Through these experiences, they have learned that true worship means more than simply saying words and singing hymns. It requires proper attitudes.

In Unit 3, our Old Testament journey follows the story of Moses: his birth and protection from Egyptian persecution, his call from God to lead his people out of Egyptian bondage, his struggles and final victory over the Egyptians, and his leadership of the Israelites in the wilderness. At the same time, students will explore the way hymns serve as a form of praise and adoration to God. ◼

Journey into Exodus 1—2: God saves baby Moses (pp. 107-112).

Special Things You'll Need:
☐ Wood dowels 1/2″ x 36″ (enough for all children), hand saw, sandpaper, liquid brown shoe polish, permanent felt-tipped markers, aluminum pie tins, handbells
☐ Box or paper bag, goblet, picture of a rainbow, envelope or bottle of sand
☐ "Build a Pyramid," page 103 of *THE Idea Book*
☐ One envelope containing tangram for each student, page 73 of *THE Idea Book*; construction paper for mounting tangrams

GETTING STARTED

These activities will help prepare students for today's session. This time also provides an opportunity for you to interact with the students.
☐ Make musical instruments. In advance, mark wood dowels so that children can cut them into three equal parts. Show children how to use a hand saw, and help them cut dowels. They can stain sticks with liquid brown shoe polish and decorate them with permanent felt-tipped markers. Have children experiment with sounds—dowel sticks beating against books, chair seat, pie tins, handbells (purchased at a craft store), etc. Directions for making other musical instruments are found on page 11 of *THE Idea Book*.
☐ Have a group of children complete the "Build a Pyramid."
☐ Have a couple of students who enjoy doing research look up slaves and pyramids in a Bible encyclopedia and be prepared to share brief reports with the class.

☐ Assign students the responsibility of keeping the Old Testament picture time line and class worship journey notebook up to date.

EXPLORING THE BIBLE

Today's lesson shows the students how God protected baby Moses. We want to help the children see that they can trust God to protect them as well.

Take a few minutes to review in a fun way how this unit follows from the last. Place the three items listed below inside a Mystery Box (or bag). Ask a volunteer to take an object from the Mystery Box and recall what part the object played in a Bible story previously studied. After his or her turn, have the student pick another contestant.

1) Envelope or bottle of sand. (God's covenant with Abraham)

2) Picture of a rainbow. (The sign of God's promise to Noah)

3) Goblet. (Joseph had a guard place it in Benjamin's sack when he was leaving Egypt.)

Briefly review our worship journey thus far by emphasizing the chronology of events.
● **What does chronology mean?**
● **What is the order in which we have studied the Bible characters?** (Adam and Eve, Noah, Abraham, Isaac, Jacob, and Joseph) **Today we begin looking at the story of Moses.**

God protected Moses as a baby, and we want to discover ways that we need God's protection today.
● **What are some things that your friends at school are afraid of or worry about?** List responses on the chalkboard or newsprint.
● **Do some of those same things bother you?**

- **What does it mean to protect someone?** (To keep free from injury or harm.)
- **What kind of things protect us every day?** (Many rules are for our safety; policemen and firemen, etc., are for our protection.)
- **What would it be like without this protection?** Spend a few minutes helping the students explore what life would be like without any of these protective measures.

Students should now read pages 107-112 in the *Picture Bible* to discover the conditions under which the Hebrew people were living.

Have children locate (on the map included with this material) the Land of Goshen where the Hebrews were living. Have them identify that area by its current name.

Students who prepared the reports on slavery and pyramids should share them with the class to help everyone realize how hard life was for the Hebrews. Some volunteer students who colored "Build a Pyramid" can explain their pictures to the class and then mount them on the bulletin board.

- **From what did the family on page 109 need protection? Why?**
- **How did they get help in this situation?**
- **Did the rest of the Hebrews need protection?**

God's answer to the Hebrew's prayer for help may have seemed helpful to Moses' family, but the rest of the Hebrews probably didn't even realize that God was working to lead them out of Egypt.

Next week we will learn more about the little boy who was protected from death because his mother floated him on the Nile River in a basket.

- **Do any of you know of a**

situation where God was working to protect people even though sometimes it didn't seem like it?
- **What can you and I do when we need protection from something?** We can follow the example of Moses' mother—she prayed for God's guidance.

EXPLORING WORSHIP

Throughout this unit, as the students study the life of Moses, they will also focus on the purpose and meaning of hymns in our worship services. Since today we have seen how God protected baby Moses, show students that we have selected hymns that praise God, our protector—such as "O Worship the King" or "A Mighty Fortress."

In today's worship we also use hymns or songs as the Call to Worship and Invocation. This will help the students to see different uses for music in worship depending on the lyrics or words and rhythm of the melody.

Make a list on the board of all the hymns that will be used to see if students can tell you what the purpose of that hymn will be. Help students understand more difficult

words and phrases found in the hymns.

Explain that God's people have used musical instruments in worship for many thousands of years.
- **Why did they use instruments?**
- **What kind do you think they used?**
- **Would you always use the same instruments for every song? Why or why not?**

Have children experiment with various rhythms and sounds the dowels and aluminum tins can make. Discuss the type of music that would go well with this sound.

Have children beat out the rhythm of "My Deliverer," page 9 of *Worship Time Music Book*. "Praise the Lord," page 4, is another song that they could sing today that fits the theme and also allows students to use instruments. Help them appreciate the kind of sound that is most appropriate for each song.

WORSHIPING TOGETHER

As we worship together, we want the students to praise God for being our Protector and to see the important place that music has in the worship service. Spend a few minutes before beginning the worship time

Scripture has clearly established music as a link between the intellectual and emotional levels— between thinking and doing.
—Connie Fortunato

explaining to the students what will take place. Decide together when it will be appropriate to use the rhythm instruments and how they should be played.

If children play musical instruments or sing, discuss the songs they are learning in their music classes. You might use one of these songs, even if it does not fit the worship theme. The experience of playing at church usually strengthens children's loyalty to the group and develops their confidence.

Where Our Statement of Faith is indicated, ask two children to recite the creed or confession they memorized in the previous unit. If your church includes other liturgical elements, such as singing the Doxology or praying the Lord's Prayer, add them to the order of service.

RESPONDING PERSONALLY

We want the students to use their imaginations to creatively construct a picture of a way God provides protection for them. They will do this with a tangram, a series of geometric shapes cut from a square.

Have each student work with the shapes until he or she fashions a picture of one way God protects. Have them mount the pieces on contrasting construction paper. Title the tangram "God, You Provide Protection." These pictures may be taken home as a reminder of God's protection.

As the session ends, students may place their drawings of pyramids in their worship journey notebooks. ■

IN WORSHIP
WE PRAISE GOD, OUR PROTECTOR

1. Call to Worship—*Sing hymn, "O Worship the King."*

2. Invocation—*Sing hymn, "Come, Thou Almighty King."*

3. Hymn—*Sing "My Deliverer."*
Play instruments to the rhythm of the music.

4. Our Statement of Faith—*Two children will recite this.*

5. Scripture Reading—Exodus 1:22; 2:1-10

6. Prayer—Dear God, thank You for the protection You gave to baby Moses. We want to thank You for the ways You are our Protector today, too. Help us to recognize ways that You do that so we can praise You. In Jesus' name, we pray. Amen.

7. Hymn—"A Mighty Fortress Is Our God"

8. Student Worship Talk—*Complete the sentences below with your own words and ideas.*

  I. Read Exodus 1:22.

    A. The families of the Hebrew people needed God's protection because _____.

    B. One time I (or someone I know) needed God's protection was when _____.

  II. Read Exodus 2:1- 4.

    A. God protected Moses as a baby by _____.

    B. God protected me when I needed it by
_____.

  III. Read Exodus 2:5-10.

    A. God's plan brought protection for baby Moses because
_____.

    B. Some plans that God gives us that can protect us are
_____.

9. Benediction—May God help each of us to understand His protection of us during this next week. May we thank and praise God for that protection. ■

SESSION 12
WORSHIP AIM:

PRAISING OUR LORD

Journey into Exodus 2—4: God calls Moses to lead the Hebrews (pp. 113-118).

Special Things You'll Need:

☐ Crown pattern on page 23 of *THE Idea Book,* red and yellow (or gold) construction paper, paper cups
☐ Grocery and medium-sized sacks, construction paper
☐ Plastic plates or bowls, rice or beans, tape, colorful stickers, trim from a fabric shop, and other ornaments
☐ Musical instruments (made by children)
☐ Recording or tape of "Moses" by Ken Medema (WORD Records) (Optional)

GETTING STARTED

As children arrive, involve them in one or more of these activities. Don't forget to talk with them about special things that may have happened during the week.
☐ Make musical shakers. Have children tape together two plastic plates leaving a hole at one end. Pour in beans or rice and finish taping shut the plates. Decorate shakers with stickers and other trim. Directions for making other musical instruments are on page 11 of *THE Idea Book.*
☐ Have half the children cut crowns from yellow or gold construction paper. Have the rest cut armbands out of red construction paper. Children will wear the item they have made. (Divide students arbitrarily.) The children wearing crowns are masters; those wearing armbands are slaves. Slaves must sit on the floor at the feet of their masters. Slaves must obey their masters and ask permission before

they speak. Before the activity begins, have students help set guidelines for jobs that slaves will do. Slaves might get cups of water for their masters to drink, help to seat them in chairs, etc. (Explain to students that throughout today's session you will use lord/master and slave/servant interchangeably.) Continue the slave/master activity until In Worship time begins.

EXPLORING THE BIBLE

In today's lesson, we want the students to realize what it means to obey a lord or master. They will see that this can be a good or bad thing depending on the nature of the master. The Hebrew people were slaves for Egyptian masters; God was Lord or Master for Moses. As you discuss this lesson, be sure to enforce the rules of the slave/master activity—slaves obey their masters and must ask their permission to speak.

Have students read pages 113-118 in the *Picture Bible.* You might want slaves to get the book and read to their masters. Discuss with the students the kind of masters the Egyptians were.

Discuss the slave/master activity with students even though it has not been going on very long.
● How does it feel to be a master? To tell someone else what to do? To have someone obey you?
● How does it feel to be a slave? To always follow orders? To have to ask permission to do what you want?
● How might you feel about yourself if you were a slave or a master all of your life?

Help students realize that God's people, the Hebrews, were slaves to the Egyptian people who worshiped different gods.

- **What did God do about this situation?** (God asked Moses to obey Him and lead His people out of Egypt.)

Help the students to see that Moses needed to have God be his Lord if Moses was to lead the Hebrews. It is interesting to see what kind of man Moses was—a perfect, obedient servant of God or someone who made mistakes and didn't feel he was the right person for the job?

To give the children an optional, creative look at Moses, play Ken Medema's song, "Moses." Ask the children to listen carefully for how Moses felt about the job God was asking him to do. (Optional)

- **Why was it hard for Moses to accept the job God wanted him to do?**
- **Would you have picked Moses to lead God's people out of Egypt? Why or why not?**

When we read about all the great things Moses would do in the future, it's easy to forget that Moses also made some mistakes. He killed a man, and when God asked him to do an important job, Moses was so scared that he made excuses. But God used Moses to lead the Hebrew nation in spite of Moses' weaknesses.

Have children turn to pages 117 and 118 in the *Picture Bible*.

- **Which people on these pages want God as their Lord? How do you know that?** (Moses obeyed God, and the Hebrew slaves and Aaron are praying for God's help.) **When we pray for God's help, God promises to be our Lord and to lead us if we obey Him. God spoke to Moses and Aaron, telling them what to do.**
- **How did God help the Hebrew**

slaves? (God did not speak to them directly.)

God sent Moses and Aaron to help them. God was answering their prayers, but the Hebrews didn't realize it at the time. It's like He was telling them, "Wait, and see what I'm going to do." God wanted to be their Lord, but He wanted them to obey Him by waiting.

- **Which kind of direction from God do you think would be harder to get—to obey something He tells us to do, or to wait? Why?**

Through this Bible story, we see that God, as our Lord or Master, can give us a command to do something, or He may command us to wait.

We want to conclude this section by helping students see important characteristics for a good lord and a good servant.

On the chalkboard make four columns. Title them Good Masters, Bad Masters, Good Servants, Bad Servants. Have students vote to see how many kids, during the slave/master activity, fit into each of the categories. In each column have students list what made the slaves or masters seem to be good or bad.

- **Those of you who were servants, did you feel your masters treated you as if you were special or important? Or did they give orders just to make life easier for themselves?**
- **Would you want to serve that kind of lord for the rest of your life?**
- **Masters, did you feel that your servants served you willingly and cheerfully?**
- **Would you want that servant for the rest of your life?**

We want to be certain that every student realizes the connection between the activity and his or her relationship to God. Students should

know that God is the best possible Master; they also should know what He expects from His servants. We don't want to tell them this; we want to help them figure out these conclusions themselves.

- **What kind of Master would God be, good or bad?** Have students name additional qualities for you to list in the proper column (which, of course, will be the Good Master column).
- **Would you want to be God's servant? Why?**
- **What kind of servants would God want?** Add responses to the Good Servant column.
- **What would a Bad Servant for God be like?**
- **Would God be pleased with your obedience to Him? Why?** To help students feel comfortable answering this question, you might want to share your response first.

EXPLORING WORSHIP

Today's lesson and discussion has been aimed to help students see what a wonderful Master God is. He is worthy of our service and obedience. During In Worship, we want to praise Him for being our Lord.

- **How would good servants praise their good Lord?**

Show me your ways, O Lord, teach me your paths; guide me in your truth and teach me, for you are God my Savior, and my hope is in you all day long.—Psalm 25:4, 5

Let them suggest a variety of ways.

One special way we can praise our Lord is through hymns and music. Singing is often enhanced by using instruments. Scripture, especially the Book of Psalms, is full of occasions where singing and various instruments are part of worship.

Have students volunteer to look up the following passages: Psalms 33:1-3; 92:1-4; 95:1, 2; 96:1, 2; 98:1, 4-6; 150. Have them read the verses that refer to singing, and make a list on the board of all instruments mentioned. From these Bible verses we see that music is one of the best ways to help us praise the Lord.

● **What kind of music would be indicated in these verses? Fast or slow, soft or loud, sad or happy?**

Discuss with students how music expresses our feelings or emotions. Have them give examples of music that express different feelings. You might suggest feelings: happy, lonely, excited, needing help, etc.

● **Can you think of a song you would like to sing that tells how you feel about God as your Lord?**

WORSHIPING TOGETHER

To make the worship service as effective as possible, discuss with the children what type of music should be part of our worshiping God because He is our Lord. Let them decide where and how the instruments will help them praise God better. Rehearse the songs that will use instruments so everyone will be prepared for the worship time.

Assign various parts of the worship time to students or helpers. You will want to be prepared to help the service flow smoothly. Select hymns in keeping with this week's worship

aim—praising God, our Lord. The call to worship almost demands that a rousing hymn of praise follow it. Consider using "Praise to the Lord, the Almighty" from your hymnal. Other pieces from *Worship Time Music Book* that fit with the theme are "The Lord Is My Shepherd," page 28, and "Praise the Lord," page 4.

RESPONDING PERSONALLY

Children learn better if they have something they can see to remind them of an important truth. Have the students create a way they can identify themselves as servants of their Master, the Lord God.

Have a supply of various sizes of paper sacks, as well as construction paper. Explain that they are to make something they can wear, such as a vest from a grocery sack, a hat from a smaller sack, a badge, a patch, or an apron. Then they should label the item with a phrase that identifies who their master is. They might write "Servant of God" or "The Lord Is My Master." Encourage them to come up with their own ideas.

Explain that just like Moses carried a rod that probably became a reminder that God was with him, the

children can have a reminder that God is their Lord. Have the children wear the item home and explain its meaning to their families. ■

IN WORSHIP
WE PRAISE GOD, OUR LORD

1. Call to Worship—Read Psalm 95:1, 2.

2. Hymn

3. Invocation—*Sing to the tune of "God Is So Good":*
Lord, hear our praise,
Lord, hear our prayer.
Grant us Your peace,
Visit us today.

4. Our Statement of Faith—*You should be familiar with this from the last unit. Read it together, or one person can say it.*

5. Hymn

6. Scripture Reading—Exodus 3:7-12; 4:27-31

7. Prayer—*Several of you finish this sentence.*
Thank You, God, for being my Lord, for helping me follow You when _____.
(The Lord's Prayer may also be prayed together.)

8. Hymn

9. Student Worship Talk—*Complete the sentences below with your own words and ideas.*

I. Read Exodus 3:9, 10.
  A. We know that God wanted to be Moses' Lord because God asked him to _____.
  B. I know God wants to be my Lord because God wants me to _____.

II. Read Exodus 3:11.
  A. When God gave Moses a job, Moses made excuses to God saying, _____.
  B. One time I made an excuse to not do what God asked me by _____.

III. Read Exodus 3:12; 4:29-31.
  A. Moses showed us he chose to have God be his Lord by obeying Him. Moses, Aaron, and the Hebrew people saw that God was a good Lord and Master because God _____.
  B. I want God to be my Lord because _____.

10. Benediction—May God help us to want to serve Him more every day because He is a good Lord. May we see His goodness through His Word, through people that love us, and through things that happen in our lives. ■

UNIT 3
WORSHIP
SERVICE
FOCUS:
HYMNS

SESSION 13
WORSHIP AIM:

PRAISING OUR SAVIOR

Journey into Exodus 5—15: God miraculously frees the Hebrews from slavery (pp. 119-130).

Special Things You'll Need:
- ☐ Eight soda pop bottles
- ☐ Pitcher of water
- ☐ Current newspapers and news magazines; construction paper; shelf paper
- ☐ Flashlight, piece of rope, key, paper bag
- ☐ "Shapes of Praise," page 74 in *THE Idea Book*; aluminum foil, cardboard squares for mounting foil sculpture
- ☐ "Egyptians into Sea" page 104 of *THE Idea Book*

GETTING STARTED

As children arrive, start them thinking about what it means to be saved or rescued. (Explain to students that, throughout this session, rescue and save mean the same thing.) The theme for today praises God as our Savior. Select one or more of these activities for the children to do.

☐ In advance, cover a bulletin board with shelf paper. Title the board "They Need to Be Saved from . . ." Have students look through newspapers and magazines for clippings or pictures of people that need to be saved or rescued from something. Suggest natural or man-made disasters, political injustices, problem situations like abuse, drugs, etc. Mount clippings on construction paper. Write what the people need to be saved from under each clipping.

☐ Put a rope, flashlight, and key into a paper bag. Have a group of students think of a situation in which each object might be used to save someone from harm. Have students write their responses for use later. Have other students draw a picture of a situation when they needed to be rescued or saved.

☐ Have children add water to soda bottles to make the tones of a scale. Kids can experiment to determine the proper amount of water for each tone—the more water poured into the bottle, the higher the tone will be. Tone is produced by blowing across the top of a bottle. Eight students will pick one bottle to "play" at the proper time for that note in a melody. You might challenge some of your more musical students to see if they can "blow" a melody like "Clap Your Hands." Or they may want to create their own simple melody. Explain that for many centuries, musicians have praised God by creating melodies in God's honor. Directions for making other musical instruments are found on page 11 of *THE Idea Book*.

EXPLORING THE BIBLE

Through the story of God using Moses to rescue the Hebrews from slavery in Egypt, we want children to recognize that God uses people and circumstances to work in the same way today. We want to help children reflect on times when they needed to be rescued so they can praise God for His part in saving them.

Discuss the activities of Getting Started. Have students who wrote about items in the bag—the rope, flashlight, and key—share with the class things they thought of. Give children who drew pictures opportunity to relate the time they needed someone to save them. Guide the discussion with these questions:
- **How did you feel while you were**

waiting to be rescued? What was it like?

• After you were rescued, how did you feel?

• How did you feel toward the person that rescued you?

• How was your experience alike or different from those on the bulletin board?

• How are the situations on the bulletin board like the situation of the Hebrews in Egypt? How are they different?

Remind students of last week's exercise when they roleplayed slaves and masters. Briefly discuss what they remember most. Locate on the map, included in this material, the path the Hebrews took from Goshen to the Red Sea. Help students realize how far the Hebrews walked by comparing that distance (approximately 70 miles or 110 kilometers) to the distance between two cities with which the kids are familiar.

Divide children into three groups. Each group will dramatically present a section of the story from the *Picture Bible*. Have one group read "Plague of Death," pages 119-123, and look up Plagues in a Bible encyclopedia or dictionary. Have a second group read "Trapped," pages 124-127, and look up Passover. Have a third group read "Crossing the Sea," pages 128-130 and look up Red Sea. Set up three centers or areas in the room where each group may perform for the rest of the class. The centers will be Pharaoh's throne room, the Hebrew's camp, and the Red Sea. Have the students improvise props and costumes or help them indicate imaginary props, like Moses' rod or the walls of water in the Red Sea.

After each group presents its section of the story, students should share any important facts they learned from their research and answer these four questions:

1. Who needed to be saved?
2. From what did they need to be saved?
3. Who is the savior or rescuer?
4. How were they saved?

The third group may want to use "Egyptians into the Sea" to help visualize the crucial point in the story when the Pharaoh's troops were defeated by God.

Hopefully these presentations have shown the students that even though Moses led the Hebrews out of Egypt, it was really God that saved them.

• How do you think the Hebrews felt about their Savior, God?

• What have you learned from this story about God's ability to save?

EXPLORING WORSHIP

The lesson emphasizes God as Savior because He rescued the Hebrews from difficult situations. This theme presents a logical opportunity for you to talk about the importance of being saved from sin. At this time you might want to take several minutes to present the plan of salvation and allow children to accept Jesus, God's Son, as Savior. For information on presenting the salvation message to a child, see the introduction of this book.

During this session of In Worship, we will continue our unit-long focus on hymns. The hymns we want to select will praise God for being our Savior. We want students to know that wonderful music has been written to help us worship our saving God. A wonderful hymn, like "O for a Thousand Tongues to Sing," is a good way to sing praise to our God.

Some of the words and phrases in these hymns is abstract and may be difficult for some children to understand. Take a few minutes to discuss it with them.

Kids love music, rhythm, and, yes, even noise—happy noise. As additional instruments have been made each week, allow students plenty of opportunity to use them with their singing. The *Worship Time Music Book* includes several songs telling the story of Moses and the children of Israel. Help students to enjoy music and the sounds they have made. Allow them to be creatively expressive now; then when it is time to worship through music, they are likely to make appropriate sounds.

WORSHIPING TOGETHER

As we emphasize through hymns and music that we are praising God who saves us, we want to be sure the students are prepared for worship. Have them review for you different parts of a worship service and the attitudes that please God.

There is lots of music available that praises God as Savior as well as many choruses that tell the story of the Hebrews deliverance from Egypt.

No matter how much we love a person, accept him, give him support, have warmth and affection for him, unless we actually call him forth . . .

Here are some ideas from which you can select songs familiar to your group or ones that you want them to learn. It is best to mix songs that are unfamiliar with ones they know well. How about "O for a Thousand Tongues to Sing," or, from *Worship Time Music Book*, "Lead On, Lord," page 10, and "Moses," page 11. The Scripture chorus, "Horse and Rider," is taken directly from Exodus 15 and allows for enthusiastic use of rhythm instruments. See if you can find it in a recently published chorus book. Kids love it.

If children have created a bottle melody during Getting Started, remind them that they will perform it at the beginning of the worship service. The Call to Worship would be fun for the children if you sing the chorus, "Clap Your Hands," after reading the verses from Psalms.

RESPONDING PERSONALLY

To help students think about how a person responds after being saved, we want them to sculpt out of foil the figure expressing that response. Have them think about a way that an Israelite may have expressed joy and praise to God for saving him or her and then fashion aluminum foil into

that shape. Maybe they would rather sculpt themselves in a position that shows themselves expressing how they feel about God's salvation. Have the students mount their sculptures on a square of cardboard. They can take their work home to keep as a reminder to praise their saving God.

For next week:

Ask three or four students to bring a possession from home that is very special to them.

A Seder meal will be an important part of next week's session. Read the explanation on page 55 of *THE Idea Book* so you can get the necessary supplies in advance.

Ask students to bring an item of food that won't spoil (canned goods, etc.) with them next Sunday. Items will be donated to a food pantry for the needy. You might want to include (or have students write) a note of explanation to parents. ∎

. . . so that he is himself exercising the uniqueness God gave him, then the love is incomplete; he is not free, he is less than human.
—Gordon Cosby

IN WORSHIP
WE PRAISE GOD, OUR SAVIOR

1. Call to Worship—Psalm 47:1, 2
Clap your hands, all you nations;
    shout to God with cries of joy.
How awesome is the Lord Most High,
    the great King over all the earth!
Sing together "Clap Your Hands."

2. Invocation
    Girls: Dear God, we know You love us.
    Boys: Come and hear our songs of praise.
    Girls: You protected the Hebrews from the Pharaoh's army.
    Boys: Come and hear our words of praise.
    Girls: You take care of us, too.
    Boys: Come and hear our prayer of praise.

3. Hymn

4. Our Statement of Faith—*Read this together.*

5. Scripture Reading—Exodus 15:1-5, 11-13, 17-21

6. Prayer—Dear God, thank You for being a Savior for the
Hebrew people by rescuing them from slavery. We know You
are our Savior and that we can count on You to help us when
we are in trouble. In Jesus' name, we pray. Amen.

7. Hymn

8. Student Worship Talk—*Complete the sentences below.*
 I. Read Exodus 15:2.
    A. Moses and the Hebrews sang this song. God had saved
        them from _____ because _____.
    B. One time I (or someone I know) needed to be saved
        from _____ because _____.
 II. Read Exodus 15:3-5.
    A. God used Moses to lead the Hebrews out of Egypt. God
        saved the people by causing things to happen to
        Pharaoh and the Egyptians and to the Egyptian army.
        Three of those things are _____.
    B. God saved me (or someone I know) by _____.
 III. Read Exodus 15:11, 13, 17, 18.
    A. Moses and the children of Israel (Hebrews) realized that
        God was a wonderful Savior. When He saved them,
        God showed the people that He was _____.
    B. When God saved me, I realized that God was
        _____.

9. Benediction—May we be aware that You, God, are our
Savior and want to help us when we have trouble. ■

SESSION 14
WORSHIP AIM:

PRAISING OUR PROVIDER

Journey into Exodus 15—17: God provides food and water for the Hebrews (pp. 131-135).

Special Things You'll Need:
☐ Instructions and supplies for Seder meal on page 55 in *THE Idea Book*
☐ In advance contact several students to bring a special possession from home.
☐ Metal coat hangers, thread, 3" squares of tagboard or heavy paper
☐ Copies of "My Favorite Hymn," page 105 of *THE Idea Book*
☐ Musical instruments made by children
☐ Camera, film, class Worship Notebook

GETTING STARTED

The worship theme for today is praising God our Provider. The major way this theme will be emphasized is through the celebration of a Seder meal. Because of the extra preparation that is necessary, we are not suggesting the usual number of activities for this time. Take advantage of the opportunity to get better acquainted with your students as you work together to prepare things for the meal.

☐ Since the worship service focus for this unit is on hymns, have students complete the activity on page 105 of *THE Idea Book*. Have them draw the way their favorite hymn makes them feel. Mount the pictures on the bulletin board until next Sunday. Then students may put them in their worship journey notebooks.

☐ Have children take snapshots for their worship journey notebooks. Pictures might include visitors, children preparing for the Seder

meal, a special program or activity, someone working on the bulletin board, etc. Art and written work from previous sessions might also be labeled and placed in the notebooks.
☐ Have students help with preparations for the Seder meal. They can arrange tables and chairs, help with food preparation, etc. Some who enjoy research could look up information on the Feast of Passover and Seder meal and share it with the class.

EXPLORING THE BIBLE

In the affluent materialistic society in which we live, most of us have never had to do without things that we need to survive. In fact, many of us are even able to get the things we WANT, which is so different from things we NEED. For this reason, we tend to take God's provisions for us for granted.

● **Have you ever had to go without something you needed?** Help students to understand the difference between wants and needs.

In last week's lesson, the Hebrews celebrated the Feast of the Passover in their homes before leaving Egypt. Discuss with the students why the Hebrews had this feast and what it meant. Let them tell you what they know. This helps you see their understanding of the story. You can also find out if they are confused or if they have forgotten some of the significant facts.

As the students read pages 131-135 of the *Picture Bible* about the Hebrews' journey through the wilderness, we want them to try to imagine what it must have been like on that journey.

● **What things did the Hebrews**

have to do without until God provided for them in a special way?

Discuss how the people might have felt—the children, the mothers with babies. Have the students tell you about the travel conditions—how long was the journey, over what kind of terrain? Have them pretend they are on the journey.

● **What would you have complained about to Moses?**

We want the students to appreciate how marvelous God's provision was for His people. The Hebrew people, also called the children of Israel, are known today as Jews. God's provision for those people is still celebrated thousands of years later during Passover at a Seder (SAYD-ur) meal. This reminds them to praise God for what He did and for the way He continues to provide for them.

Much of what is done during this feast is symbolic. Be sure students understand that a symbol is a representation of the real thing. Many of our churches have a cross in or on top of them. This cross represents that Jesus died at Calvary for our sins, but it is not THE cross on which He was crucified—it is a symbol. A wedding ring is a symbol or represents the fact that two people were united in marriage. Ask students to give examples of other symbols.

Some symbols in a Seder do not taste very good because some of the things that happened to the Hebrews were not pleasant. Some symbols were to remind them of the difficult things God brought them through.

Now the children should be prepared to understand the Seder meal as you lead them in it. Don't rush this special activity so they can realize it is a significant event for all Jewish or Hebrew people.

After the meal is completed, try to

determine the significance it had for the students.

● **What have you learned about God or the Hebrews that you didn't realize before?**

Help make the symbolism of this event personal for your students.

● **If you were creating your own Seder meal, what kind of symbols would you use? What would they mean?** List responses on the board.

Conclude this section by helping students see that God provides for us, but that doesn't mean we can sit back and relax. God provided for the Hebrews, but every time they had to take some action.

● **What different things did God expect the Israelites to do so they could enjoy His provisions?** List responses like "catch and clean the quail," "gather the manna following God's directions," and "fight back when attacked."

● **What are some things God expects us to do in order to enjoy His provisions for us?** List these as well. (Making lists of responses helps the students remember what has already been said and also stimulates them to think more creatively.)

EXPLORING WORSHIP

It is wonderful to worship and give thanks to God when we are aware of all the ways He provides for us. We want your students to sense that wonder today as they prepare to worship Him.

Provide opportunities for the children to express gratitude to God. One way they can do this is by giving to people who are needy the foodstuff they brought from home. Point out that by doing this, God is providing for others with their help.

Have children who brought special things from home explain what they brought, who provided it for them, and why it is special to them. Help them to see that even though a friend or relative gave it to them, ultimately all things have been provided by God.

Since this unit focuses on hymns, we want the students to be familiar with music that praises God for His provision. One familiar hymn that does this is the Doxology. Discuss the meaning of the words. Have students tell you in what part of a worship service this hymn might be used. If your church sings the Doxology after receiving the offering, help children

I will sing of the Lord's great love forever;
with my mouth I will make your faithfulness known through all generations.
—Psalm 89:1

recognize we sing it because we recognize that God has given us so much that we're praising Him as we give some back to Him and to others.

Once again, this week, allow the kids to enthusiastically sing and praise God with the rhythm instruments. You might want to repeat some songs used last week.

WORSHIPING TOGETHER

We are continuing to emphasize the importance and value of music in worship. Many of the liturgical elements of today's In Worship will be through music. We will use the familiar "Doxology" for the Call to Worship and then put different words to the same tune for the Invocation.

Other musical selections you might use are "Now Thank We All Our God" and, from *Worship Time Music Book*, "God Gave Them Everything," page 8, or "Sing for Joy," page 18. These songs are especially appropriate for this session. The rhythm instruments will add to this piece.

Because of the grateful attitude that today's worship theme provides, you might want the children to end the worship time, following the Benediction, with an enthusiastic statement of musical praise.

RESPONDING PERSONALLY

Help the students think about how God has provided for them by having them make a mobile of "Great Gifts from God."

Have them bend a wire coat hanger into a desirable shape. Have them draw, color and cut pictures out of the tagboard of things God has provided for them. Fasten thread of different lengths to each picture. Tie or tape the thread to the bent hanger so the mobile will balance. They can hang the mobile in their bedroom to help them remember that God provides for them. ■

IN WORSHIP
WE PRAISE GOD, OUR PROVIDER

1. Call to Worship—
Reader 1: Dear God, You take care of me every day.
Reader 2: I praise You in the morning.
Reader 3: I praise You in the evening.
Reader 4: I will sing praises to You all my life.
Reader 5: Come, everyone, let's praise our God!
Sing together: "Doxology"

2. Invocation—*Sing the following words to the tune of "Doxology."*
Come, Lord, and hear our grateful praise,
We give to You our years and days,
Help us to give our best to You,
And to Your Word be always true.

3. Hymn

4. Our Statement of Faith—*Recite this aloud together.*

5. Scripture Reading—Exodus 15:22-26; 16:2-11

6. Prayer—*Offer sentence prayers thanking God for the special thing you brought and how He provided it.*
Bring the item of food from home forward and place it on a table as a way of saying "Thank You" to God for all He has given you.

7. Hymn

8. Worship Talk—*Finish these statements in your own words.*
I. Read Psalm 111:2-6, 8.
  A. In the story of Moses leading the Hebrews out of slavery in Egypt, God provided for them in wonderful ways. Three of those ways are _____.
  B. Three ways God has provided for me are _____.
II. Read Exodus 16:8.
  A. In spite of God's wonderful delivery of the Hebrews out of Israel, the people still complained and grumbled because _____.
  B. Sometimes, when I don't have something that I think I need, I complain because _____.
III. Read Exodus 16:11, 12.
  A. God wanted the Hebrews to know who He was, so He met their needs because _____.
  B. It is important for me to know what God has done for me so that I can _____.

9. Benediction—May the Lord help us realize all that He has provided. May we joyfully praise our great Provider. ■

UNIT 4
WORSHIP
SERVICE
FOCUS:
SCRIPTURE
READING

The fourth section of our yearlong worship journey focuses on Scripture reading. This important part of a worship service may be done in various ways. Some churches read a portion from both the Old and New Testament. In some services Scripture is read by the pastor, in others by lay leaders, or the congregation may do a responsive reading.

Students will learn that Scripture readings help the whole congregation worship God. In this unit they will remember God's power, God's laws, God's promises, and God's heroes. We want students to realize that they, too, can worship God when they enter fully into the reading of the Scriptures.

This unit will focus on a key event—the giving of the Law. Students have been following the Israelites as they travel through the wilderness. Now the powerful story of the Ten Commandments will unfold. Through these Old Testament stories students will learn that God gave His people rules so that they could lead good lives.

There are several optional ideas contained in *THE Idea Book*. A group of children may enjoy putting up a bulletin board display called "God's Hall of Fame." Other children will enjoy making "Tribal Banners" and carrying them into their worship service. Still others may choose to make a model of the Tabernacle.

Your love for God's Word will be a model for your students. They will read and enjoy God's Word if you do. As you read Scripture to them with enthusiasm and meaning, may you be blessed by it. ∎

SESSION 15
WORSHIP AIM:

Remembering God's Power

Journey into Exodus 17—19: God gives the Hebrews victory (pp. 136-138).

Special Things You'll Need:

☐ Copies of "Psalm 100," activity piece 4A in the back of this book.
☐ Blocks or shoe boxes suitable for stacking
☐ Slips of paper
☐ Travel poster (Optional)

GETTING STARTED

Use this time to prepare students for what will take place during this session. We've included activities that introduce them to the Bible story. This is also a great time to interact with your kids—get to know them and let them get to know you.

☐ Divide the class into two groups. Let the first group create a travel poster for Rephidim or the Valley of Sin. You may need to provide a travel poster as an example. Have a pictorial Bible encyclopedia available for them to consult. They can also look at page 136 in the *Picture Bible*. Have the other group create a travel poster for the Promised Land. They will need to use their imaginations to some degree, but you can also provide them with encyclopedia pictures of beautiful areas in Israel. These posters will be used later in the Exploring the Bible section.

☐ Write the following statement on the chalkboard: "The time in my life when I was most discouraged was . . ." Students of this age should know what "discouraged" means, but, to be sure, help them to define it. Share a time when you were discouraged. Then ask for volunteers to share their stories.

EXPLORING THE BIBLE

The aim of this session is to remember God's power. The Israelites experienced God's power at a time when they were especially discouraged. Since children of this age can also be discouraged, we want them to realize that this story about God's power relates to them.

Today we are going to read about a time when the Israelites had every reason in the world to be discouraged.

● **Where were the Israelites in Exodus 17?**

Using an NIV Bible, have a student or students look up Exodus 17:1. Have another group of students find Rephidim on the "Wandering in the Wilderness" map.

● **What was it like in Rephidim and the Desert of Sin?**

Let the students who researched this tell what they found. If students prepared travel posters on Rephidim and the Promised Land, let them present these at this time. If the children did not do these opening activities, show them pictures from Bible encyclopedias or other reference books. The pictures should show the contrast between the desert characteristics of Rephidim and the lush vegetation of Israel.

● **Which place would you rather go on vacation?**

● **How would you feel if you were stuck in Rephidim when you thought you were going to the Promised Land?**

That must be what the Israelites were feeling. Then on top of everything else, they were attacked by fierce tribesmen. Let's see how they reacted.

Assign the various parts and let the

children read pages 134-136 of the *Picture Bible*. The first part of this story is review from last week, but the students should read the whole thing to get the flow of the story.

- **Who won the battle?**
- **What was their secret weapon?**

The rod itself did not help the men win. It reminded them that God was on their side. It helped them to have faith. When they had faith, God helped them win the battle.

Have one student read the bottom of page 136 to see how the Israelites felt about God's power after they won the battle.

- **What did the Israelites do after God helped them?**
- **What should we remember from this story when we feel discouraged?**

Guide the students to think about the stories they shared in the Getting Started section about times of discouragement.

- **Did you ask God for help when you were discouraged? If so, how did God help?**

Summarize ways that God has helped members of the group overcome discouragement. You might list these on the board.

We have these things to thank God for, don't we?

EXPLORING WORSHIP

Today the worship aim builds on the Exploring the Bible section. The transition need not even be noticeable. Help students see the need to praise God for His mighty deeds in their lives just as the Israelites did after He helped them win the battle.

After the Israelites won the battle against their enemies, Moses built an altar and prayed a prayer of

thanksgiving to God. In the Old Testament, people often built altars. The altars reminded the people of God's mighty acts.

Today one way that we can be reminded of God's mighty acts is through reading the Bible as we have just done. The Bible tells us of the things God has done in history. It reminds us that God can still help us. When we hear the words of the Bible, we remember that we do not need to be discouraged. Then we can pray a prayer of thanksgiving to God.

In our worship service, we think of times when God has helped us. Then like Moses, we thank God for His help.

Distribute copies of the worship outline and hand them to the group.

- **What Scripture verses will we read in the worship service this morning?**
- **Why do we read verses like these?**
- **Why do you suppose some people don't get anything out of reading Scripture?**
- **How can we make Scripture reading a meaningful activity so that it helps us and pleases God?**

Distribute copies of the "Psalm 100" and ask students if they have ever joined the adults in reading

something like this during a worship service.

- **This is a responsive reading. Why is it called that?**
- **Why do you suppose church people like to have responsive readings?**

Read half of the psalm in a flat, bored voice.

- **I need help! Can you give me some tips to improve my Bible reading?**

Follow kids' instructions, and read the entire psalm. Then repeat several phrases, and ask kids what they mean. You might also discuss the meaning of words such as "endures," "faithfulness," and "generations." Explain that kids will read this psalm as a responsive reading during the morning worship.

Ask a volunteer to lead and have the rest of the students read their parts. If they read without emotion, stop them and ask for more expressive responses.

WORSHIPING TOGETHER

During In Worship, we want to praise God for His power. Students will relate to the way the Israelites worshiped by enacting what they did.

As today's worship begins, your

students can build an altar as Moses did. The altar can be made of blocks, shoe boxes or anything else that is available and sturdy enough to stack. Let the students go forward, one at a time, and name one act of God that they are thankful for as they add their item to the altar's construction. Tell the students ahead of time to be ready to read the Call to Worship from Exodus as soon as the altar is complete.

Select music for In Worship that speaks of God's power. From the hymnal, you might sing "To God Be the Glory." "God Gave Them Everything," from *Worship Time Music Book*, page 8, or "My Deliverer," page 9, would also work well.

RESPONDING PERSONALLY

Choose one or more of the following activities to help the students apply what they have learned this week.

☐ Distribute wire hangers to the students and help them cover the hangers with paper so that the hangers resemble the paper-covered hangers that come from the dry cleaner. On the paper the students can write the words, "Hang in there. God's power will help you." They can take the hanger home and use it as a wall hanging to remind them of God's power when they are discouraged.

☐ Have the children make a "God's Power Booklet" which they can use as a journal this week to record examples of God's power. After they have designed covers from construction paper, help them to do the first entry from today's lesson. Their entries may be evidences of God's power in Scripture or in their own lives. For instance, "God helped the Israelites win the battle. God helped me when I was discouraged about having too much homework." This journal can be a way to encourage your students to read the Bible during the week in keeping with this unit's emphasis on Scripture reading. ■

IN WORSHIP
WE PRAISE YOU, GOD, FOR YOUR POWER

1. Call to Worship—Exodus 19:4-6a

2. Invocation—Heavenly Father, be with us as we worship You. Thank You for this time that we can come together to worship. We praise You for the mighty things You have done in history and for the things You do for us every day. Amen.

3. Hymn

4. Our Statement of Faith—*Recite together.*

5. Prayer—Dear God, we thank You for being powerful. Thank You for showing Your power to the Israelites when they were so discouraged. Help us to turn to You when we need help. In Jesus' name, we pray. Amen.

6. Scripture Reading—*Read the "Psalm 100" responsively.*

7. Hymn

8. Student Worship Talk—*Complete the following sentences.*

I. Read Exodus 17:9.
   A. When the Israelites were fighting their enemies, Moses held the rod of God in his hand. This reminded the people that God _____.
   B. When the men in Israel's army saw the rod, they knew _____.
   C. The Israelites won the battle against their enemies because _____.
   D. One time I (or someone I know) needed help. God showed His power by _____.

II. Read Exodus 17:15.
   A. When the battle was over, Moses built an altar because _____.
   B. The altar Moses built reminded the people that _____.
   C. Sometimes we do things in our worship services to remind us that God has done powerful things. One of the things we do is _____.
   D. We all get discouraged. A time when I was discouraged was _____.
   E. God encouraged me because _____.
   F. When we are discouraged we should remember the mighty acts God has done.

9. Benediction—May you remember this week that God has done mighty things in the past and that God is still able to do things for you today. ■

**UNIT 4
WORSHIP
SERVICE
FOCUS:
SCRIPTURE
READING**

SESSION 16
WORSHIP AIM:

REMEMBERING GOD'S LAWS

**Journey into Exodus 20—40;
Leviticus 1—10:** God gives the
Hebrews His laws (pp. 139-146).

Special Things You'll Need:
☐ Copies of reading (from page 139
of the *Picture Bible*) for students
without *Picture Bibles*
☐ Construction paper

GETTING STARTED

☐ On a chalkboard or newsprint,
make a heading which reads "Rules
That I Would Like to Change." As
your students enter today, let each
one add a rule to the list. These can
be rules from home or from school.
☐ Encourage your students to think
of what it would be like to live in a
world with no rules. Tell them about
a town called Looneyville where
there are no rules at all. Give them
several minutes to write or talk
through a story telling what they
think it would be like to live a day in
Looneyville.
● **What would happen at school?**
● **What would the traffic be like?**
● **How would you get along with
your brothers and sisters?**
   Some children will only think of
the fun they would have. Help them
to think about the consequences of
playing football or soccer without
rules. What would they do if a big
kid started to bully them? Continue
to help children brainstorm until
they begin to see what chaos there
would be without rules.

EXPLORING THE BIBLE

   Our session today focuses on God's
laws or rules. We want students to

see how important these rules are for
all of us.
● **Why are rules necessary?**
   If children have made a list of rules
on the board, discuss the
consequences of doing away with
each rule. For example, ask the
children what would happen if their
parents let them eat six desserts every
night? What would they feel like at
school the next day if they were
allowed to watch TV till 3:00 a.m.?
**It looks as though we need rules to
make life enjoyable for everyone.
God knew that when He gave the
Israelites rules. Let's read the rules
that Moses wrote down for them.**
   (Explain to students that we will
be using the words rules, laws, and
commandments interchangeably.)
   You may wish to read the Ten
Commandments in a creative way
with your students. Kids should be
divided into eight groups. If you do
not have enough students for eight
groups, some groups may take more
than one part, or individuals may
read the group parts. Make copies of
page 139 from the *Picture Bible* for
students who do not have one.
Assign parts and read from the *Picture
Bible* as follows:
Teacher: While the people of Israel
stood before Mount Sinai, God spoke
from the mountain and gave them
the Ten Commandments.
All Students: I am the Lord thy
God. Thou shalt have no other gods
before Me.
Group 1: Thou shall not make unto
thee any graven image.
Group 2: Thou shalt not take the
name of the Lord in vain.
Group 3: Remember the Sabbath
day, to keep it holy.
Group 4: Honor thy father and thy
mother.

Group 5: Thou shalt not kill.
Group 6: Thou shalt not commit adultery.
Group 7: Thou shalt not steal.
Group 8: Thou shalt not bear false witness.
Group 9: Thou shalt not covet anything that is thy neighbor's.
Teacher(s): Amen!
Students: Amen!

Explain phrases students may not know, such as "Thou shalt not," "graven image," "in vain," etc. Discuss the meaning of each rule.

Let students suggest what they think each Commandment means. (Watching students learn can be exciting for you. During discussions, kids often help each other learn. Of course, you'll need to explain any Commandment they don't understand and also make sure their conclusions are right.)

Let's read more about the Israelites' adventures and find out if they obeyed these rules. Read through the story of the golden calf. You may wish to assign parts to different students.

Point out that the Israelites had just promised to obey all God's rules. But very soon afterwards, they broke the First Commandment.
● **What was the First Commandment? How do we know it was really important, and why?**
● **Why do you suppose the Israelites disobeyed so quickly after they promised to obey God's Commandments?**
● **How might they have felt when Moses showed how angry and disappointed he was?**
● **Can you think of times when you disobeyed your parents?**
● **How did you feel when you knew you had hurt them?**
● **What did you do?**

Let several students share examples from their lives. You may want to share an example from your own childhood to get them started.
● **What usually happens when parents find out that their kids have disobeyed?**
● **Why do you think parents punish their children?**

Continue reading through page 146.
● **How did Moses punish the people?** Have students turn to the top of page 144, which pictures Moses punishing the people by making them drink the water with the crushed idol in it. Remind the students that this water did not taste like the clean, clear ice water we have. Explain that it was warm. Ask them to close their eyes and imagine how it would smell with ashes and burned metal in it. Ask them how gritty it would feel. Let the whole class comment on the taste of the water as if they were the Israelites.
● **Do you think the people learned their lesson? Why or why not?**
● **Moses prayed that God would forgive the people. How can we be forgiven today?** As you read the rest of the story, have volunteers show how the Israelites might have expressed their joy when they saw Moses coming down from the mountain with his face glowing from seeing God, the relief that they had been forgiven, and their eagerness to bring offerings and build a place to hear God's laws. Discuss how the Israelites must have felt when they gathered at the Tabernacle to hear God's laws.
● **Do any of you feel differently about rules now since we've looked at this story? Why or why not?**

EXPLORING WORSHIP

Since we wanted students to realize the importance of God's rules, we also want them to praise Him for these rules.

The Israelites learned that God's rules are wise. They also learned how important it was to obey them. They built the Tabernacle as a place to hear God's laws being read and discussed. Every year the high priest called the people to the Tabernacle. There the high priest read God's laws out loud to the people. Together they promised to obey them.

We have churches instead of a Tabernacle, but we still gather to learn God's rules for us. God's rules are something to celebrate because they help us to live together peacefully. Can you imagine what life would be like without God's rules? It might be a lot like Looneyville.
● **When in the worship service do we remember God's rules?**
● **How do we show God that we want to obey His rules?**

*J*esus said to them, "Therefore every teacher of the law who has been instructed about the kingdom of heaven . . .

WORSHIPING TOGETHER

Today your students have heard how God gave the Israelites good rules to follow. They have heard how the people disobeyed God, and what God did to teach them the importance of obeying His rules. They have learned that today we also recall God's good rules when we worship God, and we agree to follow them.

● **Why might it be good to read aloud the Ten Commandments in our worship time?**

Begin reading the Ten Commandments in a tired voice. Yawn several times. Read more and more softly.

● **Do you think I'm getting much out of the Scripture reading?**

● **Do you think God is enjoying my reading?**

● **How can I make our Scripture reading meaningful?**

Help students suggest ways to read Scripture effectively. You might have a student volunteer to be director for the reading.

You may wish to have the students write their own invocation or other prayers for today's service. A prayer outline is provided in the Order of Worship for a student or group of

students to complete. The students may have other creative suggestions to aid in your worship celebration. Remember that the more input they have, the more the worship service will mean to them. You might let them select songs to go with today's theme. Suggestions might be the hymn, "Joyful, Joyful, We Adore Thee" or "Psalm 119" and "Moses" from *Worship Time Music Book*, pages 27 and 11.

RESPONDING PERSONALLY

Use the following activity to help your students apply today's lesson to their lives.

Cut construction paper into 11" x 4" strips and have the students design bumper stickers. The slogans should be taken from the Ten Commandments, but they can be put in modern language. You may wish to make a sample which says, "No other gods B 4 Me!"

These bumper stickers may be taken home to be put up in students' bedrooms as reminders to praise God for His laws. ■

. . . is like the owner of a house who brings out of his storeroom new treasures as well as old.''
—Matthew 13:52

IN WORSHIP
WE THANK GOD FOR HIS LAWS

1. Call to Worship—Psalm 119:30-32.

2. Invocation—Thank You, Father, for giving us laws to follow and directions for how we should live our lives. Help us to do what You would have us to do. In Jesus' name we pray. Amen.

3. Hymn

4. Our Statement of Faith

5. Scripture Reading—*Read the Ten Commandments, page 139 of the* Picture Bible *as a special reading.*

6. Prayer—Dear Heavenly Father, we praise You because You made us. We are sorry for the times we have not followed Your laws, and we ask for Your forgiveness. We thank You for giving us rules like _____. We thank You for giving us Jesus' life on earth to show us how to live. Thank You that we are healthy and strong. Be with those around us who are sick or hurt. Especially be with _____. Thank You for hearing our prayers and always being here for us. In Jesus' name we pray. Amen.

7. Hymn

8. Student Worship Talk—*Complete the following sentences with your own words.*

I. Read Exodus 19:17-19.
   A. God gave Israel the Ten Commandments and other rules to live by. God knew that people could not live without rules because _____.
   B. Israel disobeyed God's rules by _____.
   C. When Israel disobeyed God, Moses punished them by _____.
   D. I'm glad there are rules for me to obey at home and at school because _____.
   E. Even though I don't like to be punished, the punishment that helps me most is _____.

II. Read Psalm 119:11.
   A. We cannot obey God's rules unless we know what they are. We can learn God's rules by _____.
   B. One way that we can celebrate God's rules is _____.
   C. God's rules are great because _____.

9. Benediction—May God help you to know and obey His laws this week in everything you do. May we thank Him for the laws He has given us to help us know how to live. ■

**UNIT 4
WORSHIP
SERVICE
FOCUS:
SCRIPTURE
READING**

*H*ear, O Israel: The
Lord our God, the Lord is
one. Love the Lord your
God with all your heart
and with all your soul and
with all your strength.
These commandments that
I give you today are to be
upon your hearts. Impress
them on your children.
Talk about them when you
sit at home and when you
walk along the road, when
you lie down and when
you get up.
—Deuteronomy 6:4-7

SESSION 17
WORSHIP AIM:

REMEMBERING GOD'S PROMISES

Journey into Numbers 10—16: God
leads the Hebrews despite their
disobedience (pp. 147-160).

Special Things You'll Need:
☐ "Manna by Kids," recipe on page
59 of *THE Idea Book*, one or two
pieces for each child
☐ Cooked quail or chicken in bite-
size portions, one bite for each child
☐ Copies of "Gripe Session,"
activity piece 4B in the back of this
book
☐ "Popcorn Promises Game,"
activity piece 4C in the back of this
book
☐ Poster board
☐ Popcorn, ready to eat; bowl or
popcorn box (Optional)

GETTING STARTED

Choose as many of the following
activities as time permits to help
introduce students to the aim of
today's session. Don't forget to use
this activity time to get to know your
students better. Share with them
things that happened during your
week.
☐ In advance, set up a table or
booth so that it looks like a familiar
TV taste test. The students will be
acquainted with taste tests from
commercials for peanut butter or soft
drinks. On one side of the table,
place samples of "Manna by Kids."
(Divinity without nuts will also
work.) On the other side of the
table, place a plate of bite-size
portions of quail. If quail is not
available, prepare bite-size pieces of
chicken. A sign may be displayed
which reads, "Which Would You
Rather Eat?"
Stand behind the table and play
the role of a salesperson.

• If you were going to eat this for
many days on a camping trip, which
would you choose?
• If you could only have one of
these foods on your table, which
would it be? You can have it
whenever you want, as much as you
want. The quail needs to be caught,
cleaned, plucked, gutted, washed
and then baked or fried. You can't
save any because it spoils easily. To
eat the manna, you just pick up and
eat as much as you want of it. There
is a fresh supply every day.
After they have tasted both items,
the students may vote on slips of
paper or sign their names to lists
beside the manna or quail.
In today's lesson you will talk about
the foolishness of grumbling and
complaining instead of believing
God's promises. Take the students by
surprise in this early part of the
lesson by encouraging them to whine,
grumble, and complain while they do
these starting activities. Lead the
way by doing your own share of
whining and fussing. This will be fun
for the children and will help them
to understand how unpleasant it was
in the Israelite camp when everyone
was grumbling instead of trusting in
God's promises.

EXPLORING THE BIBLE

We want students to see the
importance of remembering God's
promises. God always keeps His
promises to us, but the Israelites
seemed to forget that, so they
complained, complained,
complained.
Begin this section discussing with
students the meaning of a promise.
Have volunteers give examples of
promises made to them.

- How would you feel about someone who always kept promises to you?
- What if that person said you would get something special, but you've waited a long time for it, and nothing has happened. How would you feel about that person now?
- Do you think you would grumble if you had to eat manna or quail for a long time? What would you say? The Israelites grumbled a lot. Today we are going to hear several stories of the way they grumbled and disobeyed God.

Tell today's stories to the children. Be sure that you are well prepared so that you can tell the story without holding the *Picture Bible*. Gestures and facial expressions make a story much more exciting. When you come to places where the people grumbled, let the class grumble out loud. Encourage them to think of things they would say if they were there. You can do this when the people complain about the manna, when they get sick from the quail, when Miriam and Aaron complain because they cannot be as important as Moses, and when the people do not believe that they can conquer Canaan.

When you have completed the stories, hand out copies of "Gripe Session." The students can write in the left-hand column the things that the Israelites complained about in each pictured situation. On the right, they can draw pictures of bad things that happened because the people did not believe God. The Israelites' tents caught on fire. They got sick. Miriam got leprosy.

This activity serves two purposes. It reinforces the students' understanding of the events of the story, and it shows them that there are always consequences for disobeying God.

- What is the difference between the ten spies and Joshua and Caleb?
- Why weren't Joshua and Caleb afraid? Help the students to see that believing in God's promises kept these two men from being discouraged.

As you make the transition to worship time today, tell the students that you need to enlist their help as spies. **Twelve pieces of paper have been hidden in our room. When I say "Go," see if you can find the papers. If you find one, do not open it. Bring it to me. Remember that you are spies. You must search silently or you will be captured.**

When all 12 pieces of paper have been found, let the students who found them open them one at a time. Some will say, "There are giants in the land," or "The city walls are very high." Two of the twelve papers should have Bible promises printed on them. These two students will get to present the Call to Worship today by reading the verses they have found.

EXPLORING WORSHIP

Discuss with students the importance of remembering God's promises. We all need to remember God's promises just as Joshua and Caleb did. If we learn God's promises, then we will not need to be afraid as the other ten scouts were. One of the things we do in our worship services is listen to God's promises from the Bible. Sometimes these are read to us; other times we read them in a responsive reading. Reading God's promises can encourage us.

- Have you ever had to do something scary? Remember how good you felt when one of your friends agreed to come along? All of a sudden, things were not quite as frightening. It is the same way when God promises to be with us. When we hear God's promises in worship, we walk away feeling stronger than before.

This unit's worship emphasis is on Scripture readings. We want our students to recognize the importance and place of Scripture readings in worship so that they can enter into them wholeheartedly. Today take time before the worship service to go through the Scripture reading from In Worship. Let the students pick out the promises. List them on the board. Talk about times when it would be helpful to remember these things. Practice reading the passage in unison.

- How do you think Joshua felt when he heard these words?
- Which promises are most helpful to us today?

WORSHIPING TOGETHER

Today's worship service will emphasize God's faithfulness in keeping His promises. You may wish

The educator should be the "leading learner."
—Thomas Groome

to incorporate testimonies from children or to give your own testimony of how the Lord has kept His promises to you. Choose Scripture choruses, if possible, so that the children can actually sing God's promises. You also might consider songs in keeping with this theme, such as "Great Is Thy Faithfulness" and "Standing on the Promises" from your hymnal. From *Worship Time Music Book* you might sing, "God's Word for Us Today," page 25, and "Joshua and Caleb," page 12.

RESPONDING PERSONALLY

Today students have learned about God's faithfulness in keeping His promises. They have seen the results of not believing God's promises. They have thanked the Lord in their worship time for the promises He has given. In the final moments of children's church today, choose one of the following activities to help students discover many promises they may apply to their lives.

☐ Have the students make promise posters. They can choose several favorite promises from God's Word and write them on poster board with colored markers. As the students work on these posters, interact with them individually. Ask them why a certain promise has meaning for them. Point them to other related promises in the Bible.

☐ Play the "Popcorn Promises Game." Pass around a popcorn box or bowl filled with promise reference papers. Each student will get two or three of these promise papers. Students will need Bibles that contain the Old Testament. Tell students not to look at their papers until you say "Go."

In a minute when I say "Go," we are going to become a popcorn popper. You have all seen popcorn poppers. The popcorn pops slowly at first, but it gets faster and faster. Look up the references on your pieces of paper. When you find one of the promises in your Bible, pop up and read the verse. Once we get going, there may be times when several of you pop at once. When that happens, read your verses one at a time. Then sit down again and find your next verse.

When your students finish this game, you may wish to serve them real popcorn for a special treat.

For next week: Contact some students who are avid readers to see if they have read some biographies recently that they would be willing to share with the class. ■

IN WORSHIP
WE PRAISE GOD FOR HIS PROMISES

1. Call to Worship—*Students who found the promises in the spy game will read them now.*

2. Invocation—Lord, be with us today. We praise You for the promises You have given to us. Thank You for always being with us to help us and to guide us. Amen.

3. Hymn

4. Statement of Faith—*Recite our creed together.*

5. Scripture Reading—Joshua 1:1-9
Leader, read Joshua 1:1-4, then worshipers read verses 5-9 in unison.

6. Hymn

7. Student Worship Talk—*Complete the following sentences with your own thoughts and words.*

  I. Read Numbers 14:1, 2.

    A. The Israelites did not always believe God's promises. Instead they grumbled about _____.

    B. Joshua and Caleb did believe God's promises. When they returned from spying out the land of Canaan, they said _____.

    C. Sometimes I forget that God is helping me, and I grumble like the ten spies. One thing I grumbled about this week was _____.

  II. Read Joshua 1:9.

    A. The Lord has promised to be with us. One time when the Lord took care of me this week was _____.

    B. We need to remember that God's promises are true. My favorite promise from God's Word is _____.

8. Benediction—May the Lord remind us this week of His great promises. May He help us not to grumble and complain or to be afraid, but to remember that He is with us. ■

UNIT 4
WORSHIP
SERVICE
FOCUS:
SCRIPTURE
READING

SESSION 18
WORSHIP AIM:

REMEMBERING GOD'S HEROES

Journey into Numbers 16—27; Deuteronomy 34: God helps Moses as leader of the Hebrews (pp. 161-172).

Special Things You'll Need:
☐ Accessories, such as scarves, bathrobes, pieces of cloth, and belts
☐ Materials for "Tribal Banners," page 60 of *THE Idea Book*
☐ Two or three students prepared to share book reports
☐ Materials for "God's Hall of Fame" bulletin board, page 123 of *THE Idea Book*
☐ Copies of "Bible Heroes T-Shirt," page 106 of *THE Idea Book*

GETTING STARTED

Today your students will be learning about God's heroes, people who are faithful in serving God. Choose one or more of the following activities to help prepare students for what will happen during this session.
☐ In advance, make one of the "Tribal Banners," and show it to the group. Explain that each Israelite tribe made such a staff and carried it when the people were traveling. These banners may be used in your worship celebration today.
☐ Provide a box full of accessories which may be used for costumes: colored scarves, bathrobes, hats, sheets, etc. Ask the children to think of their favorite Bible hero and to choose a few accessories to represent that person. Make sure that early arrivers do not use all of the props. When all of the students have gathered, have a fashion show in which the students display their costumes and tell who they have dressed as and why they admire the characters.

☐ Have the students think of people in your church who are "God's Heroes." These should be people that the students admire for their service and dedication to God. Have each student draw a picture of one of these heroes and what they do to serve God. Let the students share their pictures with the class. You can use these pictures later on your "God's Hall of Fame" bulletin board in the Responding Personally time.

EXPLORING THE BIBLE

Today's Bible lesson is the last in a series on the life of Moses, one of God's heroes. We want the students to see that God's heroes are people who allow God to direct them. Moses had been a faithful leader. However, at one point, Moses became angry and disobeyed God. Your students need to see that God's heroes are not perfect. Sometimes they disobey God, and they have to pay the consequences for their wrong acts.

Because of his disobedience, Moses was not allowed to enter the Promised Land. Yet he was still one of God's heroes because he loved and served God. He played an important part in carrying out God's plan.

Today's lesson will also introduce Joshua, the new leader of God's people.

Begin today's Bible exploration time by talking about heroes.
● **What makes a person a hero?** List student responses on one side of a chalkboard or piece of newsprint. Be sure to record what the students say instead of feeding them your definition of a Christian hero. The lesson should help the students discover the difference for

themselves. **Today we are going to study Moses one last time. See if you can decide whether or not Moses was a hero.**

Read or tell the story on page 161 of the *Picture Bible*. This is the story of the destruction of the evil people of Korah.

● **Was Moses a hero here? Why or why not?**

Next read or tell the story on pages 162 and 163. This is the story of Moses striking the rock for water.

● **Was Moses a hero here? What did he do wrong?**

● **Can a person do wrong things and still be a hero?** Help students see that one thing that made Moses a hero was that he let God guide him. Even though Moses was a hero, he still had to obey God. When he disobeyed, God punished him.

● **What kind of punishment did Moses get for striking the rock?**

● **Why was Moses punished even though he was one of God's heroes?** Divide the class into two groups. Have one group read the story of Moses' saving the people from the snakes by following God's instructions (pages 164-166 top). The other group may read the story of Moses' leading the people in battle against the Amorites (pages 166-169). Each group should prepare a report for the class.

● **What happened in the story?**

● **Who was the hero? Why?**

It looks as though Moses was an outstanding hero—even though he made mistakes and sometimes disobeyed God.

● **What made Moses a hero in these stories?** Compare this to the students' previous description of a hero on the board.

● **Is this the same as our definition of a hero? How is it different? What does it mean to be one of God's heroes?**

We want our students to see that the things that make TV characters into heroes—good looks, physical strength, power, and other externals—are not the things that make a person one of God's heroes. Help the students see that God's heroes are people who have faith in God and who serve God. They are not superhuman, and they are not perfect.

● **Should we change our definition of a hero in any way?** Have children erase or add to the old definition.

● **Do you think Joshua will be this kind of hero? Does he start out the right way?** You may wish to read to students what the Lord said to Joshua in Joshua 1:1-9.

Moses had been a great leader. When great leaders die, we remember the things that happened during their lives. Let's see if we can remember the events of Moses' life.

On the chalkboard, have students help you list these events (hiding in a basket on the river, talking to God at the burning bush, going before Pharaoh, leading the people out of Egypt and across the Red Sea, helping the Israelites win battles, going up Mount Sinai to write down God's law, etc.) Be sure to include the four events in today's story. Then let students put the events in order. At the end of the list, write "Joshua," Israel's new leader. Underneath, you may print the words, "As I was with Moses, so I will be with you." **This is the key to being one of God's heroes—God's presence and power in our lives.** If your students have been making an Old Testament picture time line, they may wish to add the stories about Moses to it today.

EXPLORING WORSHIP

In this unit, we are focusing on Scripture reading in worship. We want students to be alert to ways we use Scripture in services. In today's Order of Worship, the Scripture reading focuses on God's heroes. Several students will read verses from Hebrews 11, but first we want them to know why they are doing this.

As children enter the third and fourth grades, they begin to read biographies in school. Often they are asked to write book reports on famous people. As students read about these famous people, they decide to be like them. Call some of your students during the week, particularly any who are avid readers, and see if they have read any biographies that they would like to share with the class. Interview two or three students in front of the class.

● **Who was the biography about?**

● **What was the person famous for?**

● **What was the person like as a child?**

● **What was the best part of the story?**

● **How did the book make you feel?**

● **In what ways would you like to be like this person?**

We all have had famous people

Students need to feel that this is "our" class. "Yes, we have a leader, but without our help, this class would not work."
—Marlene LeFever

that we wanted to be like. Some of us like sports stars; others like famous scientists; others like musicians or actors. These kinds of heroes often inspire us to dream and try new things.

In the Bible we have biographies of God's heroes—people who helped God carry out His plans. We need to learn about these people, too. They show us how to obey God. That is why we read about them in our worship services.

WORSHIPING TOGETHER

The major portion of the worship service today will be the Scripture reading which highlights God's heroes. You may also wish to choose songs about these Bible characters.

Choose six students who are good readers to practice reading Hebrews 11:1-30. Each student should read five verses.

If children made banners of the tribes during Getting Started, hold some up and explain that sometimes church people carry colorful banners like these in parades or as they enter the worship service.

● **Why might carrying banners be a good way to praise God?** Explain that just before worship begins, children will line up outside and enter carrying their banners. You might have them sing a rousing hymn of praise, like "O for a Thousand Tongues to Sing." Other songs, from *Worship Time Music Book*, that are appropriate for this theme are "Moses," page 11, and "Lead On, Lord," page 10.

RESPONDING PERSONALLY

Today students have learned about God's heroes. They have seen how dedicated followers of God can show us how we can follow Him. In the final moments of class, choose one of these activities to allow students to recognize specific heroes.

Decorate a bulletin board to fit the theme "God's Hall of Fame." The students may draw pictures of Bible heroes to hang on the board. If the children drew pictures of God's heroes from your church in the Getting Started time, you may wish to hang these pictures, too.

Several students may wish to decorate medals for people in your church who are faithful servants of God. These may be made easily by covering one side of a cardboard circle with glue and then with gold glitter. On the other side, you can write the words "God's Hero." Punch a hole in the circle and place it on a ribbon long enough to hang around an adult's neck. The students may present these to the adults they have chosen after church today or in an adult service.

Hand out copies of "Bible Hero T-Shirt" and let the students design a T-shirt featuring their favorite Bible hero. They can draw the Bible hero of their choice and write a slogan to go with their artwork. ■

WE PRAISE GOD FOR HIS HEROES

1. Call to Worship—Psalm 9:1

2. Invocation—Dear Lord, today we want to thank You for the lives of men and women who have followed You faithfully in the past. Help us to learn to be like them. Amen.

3. Hymn

4. Statement of Faith—*Recite our creed together.*

5. Scripture Reading—Hebrews 11:1-30

6. Prayer—*Offer sentence prayers thanking God for one of His heroes, a person from Bible times or someone you know. Several of you may want to finish this sentence:* Dear God, I want to thank You for _____, because this person shows me _____. Help me to be like this person. In Jesus' name, I pray. Amen.

7. Hymn

8. Student Worship Talk—*Complete the following sentences based on today's Bible story.*

  I. Read Deuteronomy 34:1-8.

    A. Moses was one of God's heroes. One time he served God by _____.

    B. Moses was not perfect. One time he disobeyed God by _____.

    C. Moses had to be punished. God told Moses that he could not _____.

    D. The reason Moses was one of God's heroes was not because he never did anything wrong, but because _____.

  II. Read Joshua 1:9.

    A. God promised to be with Joshua just like He was with Moses. I know that God is with me because _____.

    B. Sometimes we become afraid or discouraged because _____.

    C. We need to remember that God was with Moses and Joshua. He will be with us the same way.

9. Benediction—May we remember this week that God has promised, "As I was with Moses, so I will be with you; I will never leave you nor forsake you." From Joshua 1:5. ■

SESSION 19
WORSHIP AIM:

OBEYING GOD'S WORD

How are your students responding to the children's church worship adventure? Hopefully many kids are responding with wholehearted eagerness and creativity. The theme that runs throughout this unit is our response to God.

In this unit your students will focus on a range of responses that can be made to God. They will learn that worship is more than passively receiving from God. True worship includes obeying God's Word, putting Him first, confessing sins, pleasing God, and relying on His strength.

Students will also explore the period of the Judges, a time when the Israelites' responses to God followed an up-and-down pattern. After Moses' death, they promised to serve God with their whole hearts. Gradually, however, they turned away from God and began to worship idols. As a result, God allowed enemies to invade their land. The Israelites then turned back to God and begged for help. God heard their pleas and chose a judge to defeat the invaders. This judge led the Israelites back to worshiping God. Eventually, however, the Israelites forgot God, and the cycle was repeated.

Children learn in different ways, so we have provided some activities in THE Idea Book that we hope they will enjoy. "Concentration" is a game that can help them review the Bible stories. Students can also follow the spiritual and physical fitness exercises in "God's Strength Booklet."

Have fun with this unit! God bless you. ■

Journey into Joshua 2—6: The Hebrews obey God's directions at Jericho (pp. 173-181).

Special Things You'll Need:
☐ Copies of puppet patterns, page 18 in THE Idea Book; materials for puppets
☐ Puppet stage (Optional)

GETTING STARTED

☐ To prepare for today's Bible story, have the children make puppets of the story's characters. Distribute copies of puppet patterns. Have the children cut out their puppet shapes, attach them to paper bags, and decorate them to make the different characters. For today's story, you will need Rahab, two spies, soldier of Jericho, Joshua, and Captain of the Lord's Army. Optional puppets you could also use are several priests and Israelites to fill out the story.

☐ As children arrive, have them list on the chalkboard all the responses they can think of to orders such as "Go to bed," "Play in your room," "Take out pencils and paper for a test."

EXPLORING THE BIBLE

Since our response is the worship service focus for this unit, we want to be sure students understand what response means. Discuss the word with them. Listen to what they are thinking. Conclude the discussion telling them that the way we act when someone tells us to do something is called our response. Read the responses on the board, and point out those that show obedience. Then have volunteers tell how they

would respond in the following situations.

1. You are eating dinner. Mom looks at your plate and says, "Eat your peas or you get no dessert!"
2. You are walking to school and a stranger says, "Hey, kid, hop in my car, and I'll give you a ride."
3. Your granddad comes to your house and says, "Come on and let me buy you some ice cream."
4. Your teacher says, "The principal wants to see you in her office."

Point out that if kids don't know or trust someone, they usually are reluctant to respond positively to that person. Even when they do trust the person, they may still give a negative response. Explore why they sometimes respond negatively.

Today, we are going to hear how a woman named Rahab, some spies, and a man named Joshua faced dangerous and confusing situations. Each of these people had to decide how to respond to God.

Guide the children in dramatizing today's section of the Picture Bible using puppets. The story should be divided into three parts:
1. Rahab and the spies (pages 173-175 top);
2. Crossing the Jordan (pages 175-177);
3. Joshua and the angel (pages 178 and 179).

Children might form three teams with each team doing one part. Or one group can do all three scenes.

Explain that everyone will help act out the fall of Jericho after the puppet play. See page 19 in THE Idea Book for directions to make a puppet stage.

Read pages 180 and 181 in the Picture Bible. Then have a volunteer find Gilgal on the "Wandering in the Wilderness" map. See if they know what that area is called today.

After the children have presented their puppet shows, list the following names on the chalkboard: Soldiers of Jericho, Rahab, Joshua, people of Israel.

● **Which of these people heard rumors about God?**

● **What were the rumors?** (That God had saved the Israelites from the Egyptians and their other enemies.)

● **How did they respond to what they had heard about God?**

Explain that only Rahab decided to help the spies. She believed that God was real and that God would help the Israelites defeat Jericho. The other people in Jericho decided to fight against the Israelites and their powerful God.

● **How did God tell Joshua to take Jericho?**

● **Is this the usual way to take over a walled city or castle? Why or why not?**

● **Why do you suppose God gave such unusual directions?**

Help kids to see that God wanted the Israelites to trust in His strength. However, God did not ask them to sit on the sidelines and only watch the destruction. God expected them to take part in the battle.

● **How did Joshua and the people respond to what God told them to do?** (If necessary, refer to pages 175 and 176 in the *Picture Bible*.)

● **How do you think the Israelites felt when the walls of Jericho came tumbling down?**

● **How does God give us instructions today?**

EXPLORING WORSHIP

In this unit, we are looking at ways of responding to God. One way to

respond is to obey God's Word. We want the children to follow the example of obedience set by Rahab, Joshua, and the Israelites.

As a way of review, have students tell you some things we do in worship. (Tell God how wonderful He is; confess our sins; thank God for taking care of us; learn about God from the Bible.)

Another important part of worship is responding to what we know God wants us to do. God told Joshua to take over the city of Jericho, and this was a tough job to do. God gives us some tough things to do, too.

On the chalkboard write, "Be good to kids who are mean to you."

● **How do most kids treat people who are mean to them?** (Ignore them; get back at them; talk behind their backs; etc.) Help children to see that God expects us to do better than that, and this command can be really tough.

● **What are some other things that God tells us to do?** Make a list of these on a chalkboard or newsprint. Encourage many responses. List them all, even though some may be quite general (Share; pray; be helpful; obey your parents; read your Bible; etc.) Keep this list on the board for the remainder of the session.

Help children to be specific by asking them when it is easy or hard to do these things. For example, it may be easy to share a bike with a friend but not easy to share it with a neighbor who breaks things.

Joshua probably found it difficult to obey God sometimes. But God helped Joshua obey. God can do the same for us. Give an example from your childhood so that kids understand how we learn to obey God's tough commands.

Then distribute paper and pencils and have the children copy from the board something tough that God expects. They can follow that statement with a sentence prayer, asking God to help them obey. The children will use these prayers during the prayer time in the worship service.

When we worship God, we hear what God expects of us. It isn't enough just to hear God's commands. True worship means obeying God, even when God expects us to do things that are tough. But God doesn't expect us to do tough things alone. God also promises to help us obey, so that makes obeying easier.

WORSHIPING TOGETHER

Today we have helped students realize that one response we can make to God is to obey His Word. Now we want them to see that by obeying His Word, we are also worshiping Him.

In Worship needs to be planned ahead of time so it will go smoothly and make it easy for children to worship God. The Scripture reading today is the fall of Jericho. Ask a student who is a good reader and

All Scripture is God-breathed and is useful for teaching, rebuking, correcting and training in righteousness.
—II Timothy 3:16, 17

enjoys being dramatic to be Reader 1.

During prayer time, the student leader will mention four areas for prayer. Have the student leader allow a brief time after introducing each prayer category, then tell students whether they should pray aloud or silently. For example, the leader will say: "Aloud, say what you like most about God." The worshipers should respond with sentence prayers. Be prepared to add your own sentence prayer, since the children might be a little embarrassed about praying out loud.

Spend a few minutes before the worship service explaining what sentence prayers are. Give the children an example. If they want to give thanks, they might say, "Thanks, God, for our parents," or "Thanks, God, for my dog." Make sure the student leader understands his or her part and other children know what they are supposed to do.

Select music that is appropriate for today's theme. You might consider "Trust and Obey" from your hymnal. "God's Message," from *Worship Time Music Book*, page 26, and "Psalm 119," page 27, are also fitting.

RESPONDING PERSONALLY

In today's lesson, the children have learned that it is important for them to obey God. They have also discussed some things God tells them to do. Use the following activity to help the children respond to what they have learned.

☐ During Exploring Worship, students listed on the board things that God expects of us. They also wrote a prayer about one thing that is hard for them. Explain that sometimes we remember only those times when we have failed God, and we forget about the times we have pleased God. Recall a time when you struggled to do something that God commands, and finally you were able to do it. Share your feelings when you finally did the right thing. Then have students close their eyes and relax. Repeat several commands listed on the board, and have kids think about times when they have done what God wants. Maybe no one else knew that they were trying to please God. How did they feel as they were deciding to obey God? How did they feel afterwards? Explain that obeying God makes us feel good about ourselves. As we acquire good habits, we gain confidence in ourselves. We learn to trust ourselves. This is a good reason to obey God.

☐ Provide paper and crayons with which children can draw a picture of themselves doing something God says to do. Remind the children about the messages they wrote to God. Encourage them to draw a picture showing their being obedient in the area with which they are struggling. Children may want to display their drawings, put them in their worship journey notebooks, or take them home. ■

IN WORSHIP
WE OBEY GOD'S WORD

1. Call to Worship—Psalm 66:1, 2

2. Invocation—God, we have come to worship You. Help us understand Your Word and have the courage to obey You. Teach us what You want us to know. In Jesus' name. Amen.

3. Hymn

4. Our Statement of Faith—*Read this together.*

5. Scripture reading—
Reader 1: Joshua 6:1-16
Reader 2: Joshua 6:20

6. Prayer—Dear God, please listen to our prayers.
● *Aloud, tell God what you like most about Him.*
● *Silently, tell God what you have done wrong this week.*
● *Aloud, tell God some things God expects us to do.*
● *Silently, tell God what kind of help you need. Include the message you wrote to God earlier.*
Thank You that You hear our prayers. In Jesus' name. Amen.

7. Hymn

8. Student Worship Talk—*Complete the following sentences with your own words and ideas.*
 I. Read Joshua 6:2.
    A. God talked to Joshua.
    B. Today, God doesn't talk to us the same way He talked to Joshua, but He still communicates with us. Two ways that God tells me what He wants me to do are

      _____.
 II. Read Joshua 6:3-5.
    A. God told Joshua what to do in order to capture the city of Jericho. He told him to _____.
    B. Two things that God tells me to do are _____.
 III. Read Joshua 6:15, 16.
    A. Joshua and the Israelites responded to what God told them by _____.
    B. When God tells me something through the Bible, I should _____.
 IV. Read Joshua 6:20.
    A. When Joshua and the Israelites obeyed God, He helped them capture Jericho.
    B. This story helps me to know that if I obey God's Word, He will _____.

9. Benediction—May God give you the power and the courage to obey His Word. ∎

SESSION 20
WORSHIP AIM:

CONFESSING OUR SINS

Journey into Joshua 6—24: Achan's hidden sin causes trouble (pp. 181-192).

Special Things You'll Need:
☐ Several sets of "Fifteen Events Cards," activity piece 5A in the back of this book
☐ Copies of "Put a Message in God's Ear," page 107 in *THE Idea Book*
☐ Puppet (Optional)
☐ Refreshments (Optional)
☐ Copies of "Concentration Game," part 1, page 88 in the *THE Idea Book* (Optional)

GETTING STARTED

These introductory activities help prepare students for the theme of this session. Choose one or more to do with your group.
☐ Have some kind of tempting refreshments set up when the children arrive. Hide napkins, cups, or serving utensils. Make sure that none of the children know where the items are hidden. Don't allow any children to have refreshments until the culprit admits to stealing the napkins, etc. Bring a puppet to class, and have him accuse leaders or other people in the church of stealing the missing items.

After several minutes of frustration and confusion, have the puppet confess to the class. Once the confession is made, serve the refreshments. Discuss with the children how one unconfessed sin can affect everyone.
☐ To help the children review last week's story, make several copies of the "Concentration Game." Follow directions provided with the game. The children can refer to the *Picture*

Bible, pages 173-181, if they are not sure if their cards match.

In *THE Idea Book*, you will find a page of cards for each lesson in this unit. You can give the children a new set of cards each week so that they are dealing only with the people and events from the previous week. Or you can add the new set to the old set and make the game cumulative.
☐ Distribute copies of "Put a Message in God's Ear." Have students write a message to God about something they would like to confess to Him—a wrong thing they have done that they want to tell Him they're sorry for. Tell students that they don't need to share this with anyone unless they want to. They may take this paper home or put it in their worship journey notebook.

EXPLORING THE BIBLE

Today's lesson teaches students how important it is to confess our sins to God. They will learn about Achan's sin, the harm it brought to the Israelites, and Achan's confession when he was caught. They will also learn about the importance of confessing our sins voluntarily instead of waiting until we are caught red-handed.

Although the *Picture Bible* doesn't cover Achan's death, the Old Testament tells us that after Achan's confession, the Israelites put him and his family to death because God commanded them to punish him in this manner. We don't want the children to draw the conclusion that if they confess they will be stoned, but we do want them to see that if Achan had confessed his sin earlier and voluntarily, the Israelite soldiers probably would have avoided death in battle.

When the puppet stole the napkins (or cups, etc.), we all were affected. We couldn't eat the delicious goodies. Today we're going to learn how one man's unconfessed sin affected all of the Israelites and caused many of them to be killed in battle.

For today's Bible story, read pages 181-187 of the *Picture Bible*. Then summarize the rest of the story (pages 188-192). Be sure to make your reading as lively and dramatic as possible.

Then use the following activity to help the children review what happened in the story. Have the children form small groups. Photocopy and cut apart a set of the "Fifteen Events Cards." You may want to mount the cards on heavy paper.

Display cards in incorrect order, and have students put them in correct order. (Refer kids to pages 181-187 in the *Picture Bible* if they get stuck.) The story events are numbered and printed in the correct order in the back of this book. You will need a copy of this page to check the children's work. Make sure that you cut the numbers off the copies of the story events that you give to the children.

● What did Achan do wrong?
● Why was it wrong?
● Why did God let the Israelites be defeated by the men of Ai?
● What did Achan do when the Israelites found out he had done wrong?
● Why do you think Achan told about his wrongdoing after the attack on Ai rather than before the attack?
● How might things have turned

out differently if Achan had told of his wrong-doing before the attack?

When we admit to God that we have done something wrong, we call it confession. God wants us to confess because we are sorry for what we have done, not just because we have been caught.
● What are some wrong things that kids your age do?
● What should we do when we do something wrong?

EXPLORING WORSHIP

In this lesson, we are looking at confession as a way of responding to God, as a step toward accepting salvation. Now is a good time to move the children toward an understanding of salvation by discussing sin and the children's need to confess their wrongdoing and receive God's forgiveness.
● **What is sin?** Do more listening than talking at this point. Help children see that sin includes not only actions but also attitudes.
● **Have you ever asked a friend not to do something and had the friend do it anyway? How did that make you feel?** Allow several children to share their experiences.
● **Was it hard to still be friends with that person? Why or why not?**

God has told us how He wants us to live. When we disobey God, when we do the things that God asks us not to do, it makes God sad. It makes Him feel the same way that we feel when our friends do things that we ask them not to do. Our sins make it difficult for us to be friends with God. But God loves us and wants to be friends with us.

God has promised that if we admit that we have done wrong and are

truly sorry, then He will forgive us.

Use the following object lesson to help children understand what forgiveness means. Give each student a blank piece of unlined paper and a pencil with an eraser. Direct the children to write the word "sin" and to imagine a wrong they have done.

Now tell them to erase the word "sin" from the paper.
● **How clean does your paper look?** Supplement students' comments with these statements. **No matter how long we work to erase the word "sin" bits of darkness or pencil eraser will remain. Our paper might even tear. But God erases our sin so cleanly that it looks like the side of the paper we have not drawn on. When we confess, our sin is all gone and we can start all over again.**

Instruct students to turn their papers over.

Did you know that *if* you have confessed your sin to God, He sees you as clean as this paper? The wrong you did is all gone. We call this forgiveness.
● **How does it feel to be forgiven?**
● **How easy is it to tell God when you have done something wrong? Even though it can be hard to tell God when we have done wrong, it's better to do that so God can forgive us.**

. . . Teachers themselves need to feel free to innovate, to explore, and to play. Teaching is not . . . a highly efficient assembly line.
—Elliot Eisner

Assure your students that no matter how hard we try, they will do wrong sometimes. **God is always ready to hear about our wrongs. He wants us to confess so He can make us clean and let us start again.**

Now that the children have learned about confession and forgiveness, give them an opportunity to actually confess some of their sins to God. Hand out another sheet of paper. Direct your students to draw a picture of a place where they disobeyed God recently. They could draw their house, school, neighborhood, sports field, or friend's house. Instruct them to include on that drawing a wrong they did in that location. At the bottom of the drawing, instruct students to write what they want to say to God about the wrong(s) they have done.

After a few minutes, lead in a prayer something like this one: **God, we are sorry for these wrongs. We realize that disobeying You hurts not only You but ourselves and our friends. We are thankful that You forgive us. Please help us to do what is right. In Jesus' name. Amen.**

Perhaps some of your students have never decided to care about what hurts Jesus. But now they want to start a personal friendship with Him. See the introductory pages of this book for help in leading a child to Christ. If a child is ready for this important step, talk and pray with him or her privately. Be sensitive. Some children may follow any suggestion you make simply to please you.

WORSHIPING TOGETHER

Now is the time for the worship service. Set the chairs in a circle if possible. Use double circles if your group is large. Be sure to sit in the circle with the children. This arrangement promotes community and helps each child feel important.

Pay special attention to the prayer time. The prayer leader will make several statements, pausing after each one. During these pauses the children will pray silently. The instructions appear in italics in the prayer section of In Worship.

Music that would be appropriate for today's session is the hymn, "Praise to the Lord, the Almighty," from your hymnal, and "I Can Join" and "Lord, I'm Crying," from *Worship Time Music Book.*

RESPONDING PERSONALLY

In this lesson, the children have learned how important it is to confess their sins to God and receive God's forgiveness. They have also confessed their sins and experienced God's forgiveness. Help the children respond to the things that they have learned by doing the following activity.

☐ Have the children write a Thank-You note to God, telling God how thankful they are for His forgiveness. Provide the children with construction paper, crayons, scissors, and glue. The children can fold the paper in half and decorate it. They may want to write "Thank You" on the outside and leave a note on the inside. They could cut the letters out of other construction paper. They could also draw pictures or cut shapes from the construction paper and glue those to the cards. Suggest ways for the children to be as creative as possible. Circulate among them and talk about their cards. Praise them for their good efforts. Encourage them to keep the Thank-You notes as a reminder of their need to confess their sins and of God's promise to forgive them. They should put them in their worship journey notebook or take them home to share with their parents. ∎

Care must be taken to make motivation spring from the person rather than be imposed upon him by others.
—John L. Elias

IN WORSHIP
WE CONFESS OUR SINS

1. Call to Worship—Psalm 32:11

2. Invocation—Dear Lord, we gather to worship You and to confess our sins. We want You to help us to be good. Be with us during this worship time. Amen.

3. Hymn

4. Our Statement of Faith—*Recite this together or read aloud a psalm of confession (such as Psalm 32:1-5).*

5. Scripture Reading—Joshua 7:19-21.

6. Prayer—*The leader will pause after each sentence for you to pray silently.*

God, thank You that Your power is big enough to help us in any situation.

We're glad that You want to know about everything we do.

Sometimes, God, we do things that are wrong.

We thank You that You forgive us when we confess our sins.

Help us to obey You all the time. We love you.

In Jesus' name, we pray. Amen.

7. Hymn

8. Student Worship Talk—*Complete the following sentences.*

I. Read Joshua 7:1.
  A. When the Israelites captured Jericho, Achan sinned by
     _____.
  B. No matter how hard we try not to, we all still sin.
  C. One thing that I have done wrong is _____.

II. Read Joshua 7:4, 5.
  A. Because Achan had disobeyed God, God allowed the soldiers of Ai to _____.
  B. This is the bad thing that happened at Ai because Achan sinned: _____.

III. Read Joshua 7:19-21.
  A. When Joshua asked Achan what he'd done wrong, Achan _____.
  B. When we do something wrong, instead of waiting until we are caught before confessing, like Achan did, we should _____.
  C. If we confess our sins to God, He promises that He will forgive us. One reason God's forgiveness makes me happy is _____.

9. Benediction—May God show His love by forgiving your sins. May you know the peace that comes by obeying God. ■

**SESSION 21
WORSHIP AIM:**

PUTTING GOD FIRST

Journey into Judges 1—13: Deborah and Gideon lead the Hebrews back to God (pp. 193-204).

Special Things You'll Need:
☐ Contemporary Christian children's music and tape or record player
☐ "God Is Number One," activity piece 5B from the back of this book
☐ Copies of "Concentration Game," page 88 of THE Idea Book

GETTING STARTED

To involve your students in learning from the moment they arrive, choose one of the following ideas. But don't forget to also visit with your students during this time.

☐ Play a tape or record of children's music. Try to find songs that praise God and tell how important God is to us. (You might try *The Kid's Praise!* album from Maranatha! Music, or one of the *Sing!* albums from Lillenas Musicreations.) Provide a long strip of newsprint on which every child can draw as he or she listens. Direct the children to draw pictures about the song and to write ideas from the song as it plays and they sing along. This activity will introduce the children to today's topic of letting God know that He is important to us.

☐ Ask at least one child to write a definition of loyalty on a large piece of paper. Provide a dictionary and assistance if needed. Spend a few minutes making sure that the children understand what loyalty means. Help them see that it includes things like being a friend even when it is difficult. This discussion will prepare them for today's story which is about

Deborah's and Gideon's loyalty to God.

☐ To help the children review last week's story, make several copies of the "Concentration Game." The children can use this set of cards alone or they can add this set to the other sets and review all the stories covered in this unit so far.

EXPLORING THE BIBLE

We are now entering the period of the Judges. During this time, the people of Israel followed a pattern. Although they promised to be loyal to God, they would gradually turn away from God and begin worshiping the idols of their neighboring countries. As punishment, God would allow their enemies to invade them. The Israelites would ask God for help. He would choose a judge to defeat their invaders. The judge would lead the Israelites back to worshiping God. Eventually, the judge would die, and the Israelites would forsake God. Then the pattern would begin again. This is a pattern none of us would want.

Remind the children of last week's story about Joshua. Using the information in the paragraph above and in the *Picture Bible* on page 193, explain what happened to the Israelites after Joshua's death. At the beginning of today's story, the Israelites were being attacked by the soldiers of King Jabin.

The Israelites weren't very loyal to their Creator. They often disobeyed God and began worshiping idols. But not all of the people were like that. Today, we're going to learn about two people who were loyal to God.

Today's story is really two stories—

the story of Deborah and the story of Gideon. Have children do a reader's theater of these stories. The Deborah story is found on pages 194-197 of the *Picture Bible*. For this story, you will need Deborah, Barak, a Narrator, and two or three extras to read the parts of Israelites and enemy soldiers. The Gideon story is found in the *Picture Bible* on pages 199-204. You will need readers for the following parts: Narrator, Gideon, Angel, and extras to read the parts of Israelites and enemy soldiers.

After the story, point out on the "Wandering in the Wilderness" map such places as Canaan, where the enemy lived, and Gilgal, where Gideon lived.

● **Why did the Israelites keep getting attacked by enemies?**
● **Are the Israelites a good example of loyalty? Why or why not?**

Help the children see that the Israelites treated themselves as more important than God. They did what they wanted to do, such as worshiping idols, instead of what God wanted them to do.

● **How did Deborah show her loyalty to God?**
● **How did Gideon show his loyalty to God?**
● **What do you think was most important to Deborah and Gideon?**

Pass out paper and crayons or colored markers. Instruct the children to draw a picture showing how Deborah or Gideon was loyal to God. The children can draw stick figures as well as a short title explaining the picture.

EXPLORING WORSHIP

As we continue our study of ways of responding to God, we want the children to learn that one way of responding to God is to let Him know that He is most important to us. We can demonstrate God's importance in our lives by what we tell God and by how we act. The children need to see that both these ways of responding are important.

In worship, we usually concentrate on verbalizing or speaking our appreciation of God. Through songs of praise, Scripture, and prayer, we tell God how important He is. We also express our desire to be loyal and obedient to God, and we ask for His power to do so.

Use today's story about the unfaithful Israelites and the loyal judges, Deborah and Gideon, to help the children see the necessity of making God most important in their lives.

Invite the children to call out items, people, events, and places that are important to them. List these on a chalkboard or newsprint.

● **What are some ways we might make these things more important than God?**
● **How can we remain loyal to God?**

Explain that one way to show our loyalty is to tell God how much we love Him and that He is important to us.

● **Why do you think God likes to hear that we love Him and that He is important to us?**

Divide children into small groups, and give each group a copy of the "God Is Number One." This sheet is a fill-in-the-blanks litany. (A litany is a prayer in which statements about God are recited or said responsively with the worship leader.)

The children can use this model to develop litanies that tell God how important He is to them. Give the children pencils and invite them to fill in the blanks with appropriate items from the list. Appoint one child in each group to keep the litanies since you will need them in the worship time.

WORSHIPING TOGETHER

As you worship together with your students, choose hymns that fit with the theme of loyalty to God and that speak of His importance. You might consider "All Creatures of our God and King." From *Worship Time Music Book*, you might use "God's Way, the Best Way," page 20, and "Praise the Lord," page 4.

When you get to the statement of faith, you will need a volunteer from each litany group to read the litany that his or her group wrote. If you have a lot of students, you may want to limit yourself to four or five litanies.

RESPONDING PERSONALLY

In today's lesson, the children have learned that they need to communicate to God how important He is to them, both by what they say and what they do. Choose one of the following ideas to help the children

Our creativity is destroyed not through the use of outside force, but through criticism, innuendo, subtle psychological means . . .
—Finley Eversole

respond to what they have learned.

☐ Provide construction paper and glue. Direct the children to make a mini-poster to hang in their rooms at home. Have the children make pictures from construction paper. Rather than cutting the paper with scissors, have them tear it into the shape they want. The children may wish to start the poster by making a large number one. Encourage them to add pictures that remind them that God is number one in their lives. You may want to post these idea starters:

● Draw a picture of yourself being loyal to God.

● God is number one at my home because _____.

● I can make God number one at school by _____.

● I show my friends that God is number one when I _____.

● When I play I show my loyalty to God by _____.

When the children are finished, have them hold up their completed posters and describe them. Each child's poster expresses something important about him or her. Remind students to say positive and encouraging things about each other's work.

☐ Guide teams of three or more children to create a cheer for God. They can set the words to a current school cheer or commercial. Give the children the following instructions. You may want to write them on chalkboard or newsprint.

A. Choose a commercial or a school cheer.

B. Write the words on paper with one blank line after each line.

C. Change the words to express praise to God, that He is number one. Write these new words on the blank lines. Cross out the old words.

Suggest that the children tell how to live like God is number one in addition to talking about it.

D. Practice singing the cheer.

E. Option: Write the words on large paper so the whole group can sing along.

Call for the teams to sing their cheers for everyone. Students will want to applaud the efforts of each group.

Close with a prayer asking God to help the children remember to obey Him in everything they do and to help them want God's guidance. ■

IN WORSHIP
WE PUT GOD FIRST

1. Call to Worship—Judges 5:3

2. Invocation—Dear Lord, we are here to express our love and loyalty to You. You are our best Friend, our loving Heavenly Father. Be with us now as we worship You. In Jesus' name, we pray. Amen.

3. Hymn

4. Our Statement of Faith—*Read litanies written earlier.*

5. Scripture Reading—Judges 6:11-18

6. Prayer—*Complete these sentence prayers.*

Dear Lord, we sometimes find it hard to be loyal to You because _____.

Thank You that You are always loyal to us. We love You. Help us to show You that You are more important to us than _____. In Jesus' name, we pray. Amen.

7. Hymn

8. Student Worship Talk—*Complete the following sentences with your own ideas.*

  I. Read Judges 4:1, 2; 6:1.
  A. Many times the Israelites stopped being loyal to God. They thought worshiping idols was more important than worshiping God.
  B. One way that I'm sometimes not loyal to God is _____.

 II. Read Judges 4:8, 9; 6:14-16.
  A. Deborah showed how important God was to her. Deborah showed she was loyal to God by _____.
  B. Gideon showed how important God was to him. Gideon showed he was loyal to God by _____.
  C. We can show God how important He is to us by being loyal to Him.
  D. Two ways we can be loyal to God are _____.

9. Benediction—May you always remember that God is more important than anything or any person in your life. May you trust Him enough to obey Him in all situations. May you be so excited about living for God that others want to be like you. ■

95

**SESSION 22
WORSHIP AIM:**

PROMISING TO PLEASE GOD

Journey into Judges 13—16:
Samson fights against God's enemies (pp.205-218).

Special Things You'll Need:
☐ A book of riddles
☐ Recorded music for the Call to Worship
☐ Materials for "Hey, Diddle Riddle," page 92 in THE Idea Book.
☐ Copies of "Concentration Game," pages 88-91 in THE Idea Book (Optional)

GETTING STARTED

☐ Bring in a book of riddles and spend the beginning of class asking the children riddles. Students will find this activity entertaining. They will also better understand the frustration of Samson's wedding guests. You might even throw Samson's riddle in at the end of your riddle time. Let them struggle with it, but don't give them the answer. Tell them that they will learn the answer in today's story. This challenge can hold their interest throughout the story.
☐ Play "Hey, Diddle Riddle."
☐ Have children recall a time when they were in charge of a younger child. Maybe they were baby-sitting a younger brother or sister; or perhaps they were helping younger kids learn to ride bikes, swim, or pitch softballs.
● **What did you like best about taking care of (or helping) a younger person?**
● **Did the child try to please you? How?**
● **If the children refused to obey you, how did you feel?**
● **Would you like to take care of a child who doesn't care about**

pleasing you? Why or why not?
● **How do you think God feels when we forget about Him or disobey Him?**
    Explain that God has feelings just as we do. Because God loves and takes care of us, God wants to enjoy being with us. It's not much fun for God to be around people who don't try to please Him.

EXPLORING THE BIBLE

    Last week we introduced the period of the Judges and looked at two judges, Deborah and Gideon. In today's story, we will look at Samson as a young man. We want to emphasize Samson's vow to God, his promise to devote himself to serve God. Through the story of Samson, we will encourage the children to promise God that they will try to do things that please God.
    Review last week's story with the "Concentration Game." The children can use this set of cards alone or they can add this set to the other sets and review all the stories covered in this unit so far.
    On the chalkboard, write "How Samson Obeyed God" and "How Samson Disobeyed God." As you read aloud the story on pages 205-218 of the Picture Bible, have the children listen for things Samson did that might belong in either category. Have children raise their hands when they want to stop the story and add something to the lists.
    After reading today's story, explain that the story of Samson will be continued next week. If the children want to find out what happens before then, encourage them to read Judges 16 or pages 219-224 in the Picture Bible.

Review the story using the questions which follow. Help the children realize that long hair didn't make Samson strong. God made Samson strong because God wanted to use Samson to deliver the Israelites from their enemies.

- **What promise did Samson's mother make to God?**
- **Did Samson keep that promise to God? How?**
- **Who were the enemies of the Israelites while Samson was growing up?**
- **Why were Samson's parents unhappy that he decided to marry a Philistine girl? Do you think God was happy with Samson's choice?**
- **Why do you think God asked Samson not to cut his hair?** (God wanted Samson to have long hair as a way of showing that he was serving God.)
- **Do you think Samson would have been strong if he had cut his hair?**
- **Would we be stronger if we let our hair grow long?**

EXPLORING WORSHIP

In our story today, we have seen how Samson kept the promise that his parents made to God. God was pleased that Samson kept the promise. We, too, can make promises to God. In worship, we often respond to God by telling Him that we want to obey and serve Him. As sinners, we often break these promises. But promising God that we'll obey Him can also help us work harder at obedience.

- **Have you ever made promises to someone? What did you promise?** Give the children some time to share the promises they have made. Discuss promises and why people make them.

We can make promises to God just as Samson did. In worship, one of the ways that we respond to God is to promise to do things that please God. Let's try to think of some things that please God.

Divide the children into teams. Challenge each team to make the longest list of actions that would please God. Provide large paper and markers. Give them five minutes before calling time. Have teams hold up their papers and read their lists. Congratulate the one with the longest list of God-pleasing actions.

Challenge all children to select one good action that they want to do this week. Next, have the group write a promise to God about this action. They can use this promise later during the worship service.

Ask volunteers to read aloud the promises that they have just made right after the worship talk.

WORSHIPING TOGETHER

To signal time for worship, play gentle Christian music on a tape or record player. Choose a song with clear words that appeal to children. Direct the children to find a seat in the worship area and quietly explain that worship is a time for focusing on God. While the music plays, encourage the children to think about God and what they like about Him.

After the music stops, ask children to share what they thought about while the music played. Close the sharing by pointing out that thinking about God is a type of praying and praising. Explain to the children that they have begun their worship.

During In Worship, you might have students sing the following: "To God Be the Glory" from your hymnal; "I Was Glad," page 3, and "You Know, Lord," page 19, from *Worship Time Music Book.*

RESPONDING PERSONALLY

The following activity is designed to help your students carry out the promise that they made to God.

- **What is a habit?**
- **How have you gotten into the habit of putting on your shoes in the morning?**

Explain that it usually takes twenty-one days of repeating the same action before we form a habit. One good way to begin to form a habit is to act it out in front of a group. Have your students form pairs.

*W*hat the pupils want to learn is as important as what the teachers want to teach.
—Lois E. LeBar

Line them up by birthday (student with birthday on January 1, would be first, etc.) and divide the line into two so students form pairs.

Direct each pair to prepare pantomimes showing the two actions they have promised God they will do. For example, if they have promised to be kind, they might perform a pantomime in which they ask a new kid at school to eat lunch with them. Encourage the children to come up with their own ideas, but be prepared to help them.

After a few minutes, play charades. Call for pairs to present their pantomimes. The other children should try to guess them. Point out that they have just acted out ways to please God. Encourage them to make their game actions a part of their real lives.

Close your eyes and think of the good action you will start doing. Tell God how much you want to obey Him. Ask God to help you. Now with His power you can do it! ■

IN WORSHIP
WE PROMISE TO PLEASE GOD

1. Call to Worship—Psalm 122:1

2. Invocation—God, thank You for this quiet time to think about You. We have enjoyed hearing the thoughts other children had about You. Be with us now as we worship You. In Jesus' name we pray. Amen.

3. Hymn

4. Our Statement of Faith—*Recite our church's statement of faith.*

5. Scripture Reading—Read Judges 13:1-7.

6. Prayer—Dear God, Samson was special to You. We are glad that each of us is also special to You. Show us how to stay away from what is bad and do what is good. We know that You love us, not because we are good, but because You created us. Thank You for loving us no matter what we do. But we want You to help us to be good. We love You. Amen.

7. Hymn

8. Worship Talk—*Complete the following sentences in your own words.*

  I. Read Judges 13:5.

    A. The angel of the Lord told Samson's mother that Samson should never _____.

    B. One reason that God wanted Samson to keep this promise was _____.

    C. God made Samson special. One way I know that I am special to God is _____.

  II. Read Judges 14:6.

    A. Samson was different from most people. He was _____.

    B. Samson got his great strength from _____.

    C. God will help us when we obey Him just like He helped Samson. One way I know this is _____.

    D. Samson didn't always keep his promise to God. Sometimes I don't keep my promises to God either, but God promised to forgive me if I confess it to Him.

    E. We all need God to help us keep our promises to Him. Have a volunteer read the promise that the children wrote during Exploring Worship.

9. Benediction—May God show you the way He wants you to live and may you be excited about living that way. May you experience the joy that comes through obeying God. ∎

SESSION 23
WORSHIP AIM:

Needing God's Strength

Journey into Judges 16: God allows Samson to regain his strength and defeat the Philistines (pp. 219-224).

Special Things You'll Need:
- ☐ Blindfolds for the children
- ☐ Rubber balls
- ☐ Copies of the "Concentration Game," pages 88-91 in *THE Idea Book*
- ☐ Container with rope, coins, scissors, a chain, and a plastic bag of whole wheat flour or wheat germ
- ☐ Copies of the "Strength Busters," activity piece 5C from the back of this book
- ☐ Copies of "God's Strength Booklet," pages 108-112 in *THE Idea Book*

GETTING STARTED

☐ Try this activity to help the children discover areas in their lives where they feel weak. Provide kids with several rubber balls. As the children arrive, blindfold some of them (this will also help them relate better to Samson when he gets blinded) and ask them to accomplish a task that is nearly impossible to do blindfolded. Have them bounce a ball with a partner, or draw a picture of themselves. When all the children have tried one of the tasks, ask them how they felt.
- ● Did you feel weak? Frustrated? Helpless?
- ● Have you ever felt that way before? When?

Help the children discover areas in their lives where they feel weak or frustrated, where they are up against a problem that they can't solve. Such problems might include school, sports, a neighborhood bully, etc. If necessary, share times from your own

life as examples to get the children started. You will use this discussion later in the lesson to help the children see their need for God's strength.

☐ Have the children draw one of their favorite superheroes. When they are finished drawing, allow them to share their pictures and tell what they like about the superhero.
- ● How are these superheroes like Samson?
- ● Where do these superheroes get their strength?
- ● Do they get their strength from the same source?

Discussing sources of strength will prepare the children for learning about God as a source of strength for Samson and for us.

☐ To help the children review last week's story, play "Concentration Game." The cards that cover last week's story are found on page 91. The children can use this set of cards alone, or they can add this set to the other sets and review all the stories covered in the unit so far.

EXPLORING THE BIBLE

Last week we started learning about Samson. We found out what made him different from other people. Today, we're going to learn about the rest of Samson's life.

Think about our discussion of how Samson was different from the superheroes in cartoons.
- ● What was the source of Samson's strength? (God)

Now, think about those times when you feel weak, when you have to do something that seems too hard to do. Wouldn't it be nice to be as strong as Samson? Well, Samson wasn't always strong. In fact once,

he was just as weak as we sometimes feel.

You can teach today's story in one of two ways. The first way is to set out a container with rope, coins, scissors, a chain, and a plastic bag of whole wheat flour (or wheat germ). Divide students into two sections. Assign part of the story in the *Picture Bible* to each half (219-221, and 222-224 are logical divisions). Have each group learn its part of the story and then select objects from the container that are found in the story. When the children have read their pages, have each group choose a volunteer to tell its portion of the story, using the objects as visual aids.

A second option is to have children read the story silently. Then play "Concentration," using the cards on page 91 of *THE Idea Book*.
● **Why did Delilah want to find out Samson's secret?**
● **Why did Samson finally tell Delilah his secret?**
● **What happened when Samson told her? Why?**
● **What job had God given Samson to do?** (God wanted Samson to defeat the Philistines.)
When God quit making Samson strong, Samson became weak just like other people. He couldn't do the job that God had given him.
● **How did Samson get his strength back?**
● **How did Samson finish his job of defeating the Philistines?**

EXPLORING WORSHIP

Explain to children that this is the last lesson in the unit on responding to God. Review ways of responding to God, such as obeying His Word, confessing sins, praising God, and promising to do things that please God. These responses to God are important, but the children can't do them without God's strength. They need to discover God's strength.

Have you ever taken a physical fitness test at school, one where you see how many push-ups you can do, or how fast you can run, or how many sit-ups you can do? These tests are used to show how strong you are. They can also be used to show areas in which you are weak. For example, you may be able to run very fast but not be able to do very many sit-ups. Today, we're going to take a different kind of test that helps us think about our lives and find areas in which we feel weak.

Distribute copies of "Strength Busters." Give the children two to three minutes to work on it. Assure them that there are no right or wrong answers. The point of the survey is to find out how they feel about different parts of their lives. The questionnaire is not a contest. Explain that we all have areas that we need to work on. Remind the children that nobody will get to look at their papers except themselves. Have them keep these sheets because they will use them during their worship service.
● **Do you think that Samson ever felt as weak as you sometimes feel? When might that have happened?**
● **What did Samson do then?**
We need God's help just as much as Samson did. Without God's strength, we cannot do what God wants us to do. But God promises to give us the strength we need to serve Him, just like God gave Samson strength. When we worship God, we need to ask Him for the strength to do the things He wants us to do.

WORSHIPING TOGETHER

This session concludes the unit on responding to God in worship. As you enlist worship leaders, remind them that worship is responding to God. Ask them to pray that each of their actions in worship will encourage the other children to worship daily by thinking, acting, and talking the way God wants them to.

In keeping with today's worship aim—asking God for His strength—choose hymns that talk about our weakness and God's power. These can be hymns that cry to God for help or hymns that praise God for His might. You might use "Great Is Thy Faithfulness" or "A Mighty Fortress Is Our God," and, from *Worship Time Music Book*, consider "You Know, Lord," page 19, and "Lord, I'm Crying," page 32.

In today's prayer time, the leader will mention to God that we have times when we feel weak. Then the leader will address the children and pause to allow them to pray silently. These instructions appear in italics in the prayer section of In Worship. Be sure the prayer leader knows what to do. Encourage the children to have their "Strength Busters"

The first step in Christian teaching is to prepare ourselves spiritually.
—Lois E. LeBar

questionnaires handy so that they can pray for the area in their lives in which they feel weak or frustrated.

RESPONDING PERSONALLY

In today's lesson the children have learned about Samson and how he was only strong when God gave him strength. They have also seen that they, like Samson, need God's strength to do God's work.

The following activity picks up on the fitness theme introduced in the Exploring Worship section. Before the session, you will need to make copies of the "God's Strength Booklet," pages 108-112 in *THE Idea Book*. Photocopy the necessary pages and staple them together. Each page contains a physical exercise and a spiritual exercise. For example, half of one page will be about push-ups, the other half about prayer push-ups. There is also a chart in the back to help the children keep track of the exercises they do.

Before distributing these booklets, give the following explanation.

If we exercise physically by running, jumping, and doing push-ups, we can make our bodies stronger. Today, we have discovered that we cannot do anything without

God's strength. But God doesn't want us to sit around waiting for Him to make us strong. God wants us to do things—kind of like exercises—that will make us strong. These can be things like praying and reading our Bibles. God uses them to give us His strength. But He wants us to remember that we aren't the ones making ourselves strong by reading the Bible and praying. Our strength comes from God.

After distributing "God's Strength" booklets, have children make and decorate covers for them. They could make these out of construction paper. The children could also try the first page of exercises.

When the children are finished, close in prayer. **Dear God, we love You. We can do nothing without Your strength. Make us strong enough to do special things for You. Amen.**

For next week: The worship focus of the next unit is on the offering. Ask students to bring some money for an offering which will be taken during In Worship. ■

This idea that children won't learn without outside rewards and penalties . . . usually becomes a self-fulfilling prophecy.
—John Holt

IN WORSHIP
WE ASK FOR GOD'S STRENGTH

1. Call to Worship—Psalm 18:1-3.

2. Invocation—God, be with us as we worship You today. Help us to see our weaknesses and Your strength. Amen.

3. Hymn

4. Our Statement of Faith—*Recite our church's statement of faith.*

5. Scripture Reading—Read Judges 16:25-30.

6. Prayer—Lord, You are so strong. We love You. Sometimes we feel weak. *(Take a few minutes to pray silently about areas of weakness in your life.)*

We need Your strength because we can't do anything without Your help. Thank You for loving us. Amen.

7. Hymn

8. Student Worship Talk—*Complete the following sentences with your own words.*

  I. Read Judges 16:8, 9.
    A. Samson had a special gift from God; he was stronger than ordinary people.
    B. Sometimes I wish I were as strong as Samson because _____.

  II. Read Judges 16:19-21.
    A. When Samson's hair was cut, God's special strength left him. Without God's help, Samson was _____.
    B. Samson needed God's strength. So do I. One part of my life where I feel weak is _____.

  III. Read Judges 16:28, 30.
    A. God didn't forget about Samson. He gave him the strength to _____.
    B. I know that God doesn't forget about me either. Two things He gives me strength to do are _____.

9. Hymn

10. Benediction—May God give you the strength you need every day. May He help you with all your problems and teach you to obey Him. Amen. ■

UNIT 6
WORSHIP SERVICE FOCUS: OFFERING

As we focus on the offering as an act of worship, we will spotlight four unique personalities: Ruth, a beautiful convert to Judaism; Samuel, a leader who had a deep love for God; Saul, a reluctant, half-hearted king; and David, a boy with great faith.

We will emphasize that giving an offering is more than merely putting money in the offering plate. God makes it clear to us in these stories that He desires offerings of love and wholehearted obedience. Monetary gifts are only one expression of our love and obedience.

God gives all things to us. We respond to His giving by giving ourselves. We want your students to look at different kinds of offerings which they may give: participation in worship, use of talents, loving service to others, as well as tithes and gifts of money. We will also look at our attitudes when we give offerings. God delights in gifts which are offered cheerfully and willingly. Our motives in giving are as important as the gifts themselves.

In *THE Idea Book,* you will find unit-long projects which your children may do for others. The "Psalm 150" bulletin board could be made for the entire church. Another option is a "Befriending the Elderly." Elderly people love visits from children. Kids who like to act might perform "WACT News" for another class. Through activities such as these, your students will discover the joy of giving.

May God be with you and in you as you give of yourself in the classroom. ∎

SESSION 24
WORSHIP AIM:

GIVING OURSELVES

Journey into Ruth: Ruth honors God by caring for her mother-in-law (pp. 225-230).

Special Things You'll Need:
- [ ] Paper streamers or other party decorations
- [ ] Recorded Jewish folk music
- [ ] Edible grains for sharing activity
- [ ] Rhythm instruments
- [ ] Balloons
- [ ] Offering plate or box
- [ ] Copies of the "Chain of Kindness," Activity piece 6A in the back of this book (Optional)
- [ ] Copies of the "Kindness Contract," activity piece 6B in the back of this book (Optional)

GETTING STARTED

As students arrive, your classroom should have a festive atmosphere, or you may have early arrivers help put up decorations. Party streamers or other decorations should be hung in the room. You are going to have a wedding celebration for Ruth and Boaz. If possible, music should be playing. Instrumental Jewish folk music would be an excellent choice.

As students enter the room, have them give you one of their shoes. Challenge the early arrivers to figure out what a shoe has to do with the lesson. For a clue, give page numbers in the *Picture Bible.* (A shoe was given to seal the marriage agreement.) As students read these pages, they will discover the reason for the celebration. After five minutes, distribute the shoes randomly and ask for silence. Students should quietly trade shoes, shaking hands on each trade until they get their own shoes. Then they may sit down.

Pass out some form of edible grain (whole wheat berries, popped corn, rice crispies, puffed wheat, roasted barley). Explain that this is like the kind of food that people ate in Old Testament times. The characters in our story today will eat grain, too. The first students may start eating theirs, but they should share when others arrive. They should continue to share with latecomers so that everyone has some. Relate this later to the "Chain of Kindness" activity piece.

When most of the class is assembled, you may wish to finish your celebration by forming a large circle and allowing the students to clap and move around the room in time to the music. Rhythm instruments may also be used. Sing lively praise choruses before returning to your seats. "King of King and Lord of Lords" would be appropriate.

EXPLORING THE BIBLE

The importance of giving ourselves to God and to others is the concept we want to communicate to students during this session. Be sure your students understand by asking them to tell you what it means. Have them tell you ways we give ourselves to God and ways we give ourselves to others.

Our purpose today is to help students realize that they can offer themselves to God as an act of worship. We will look at the story of Ruth as we show students ways they can offer themselves to God and to others.

Here is some background information to help introduce the story.

Naomi was a Jewish woman from

Bethlehem. She married a Jewish man, and they had two sons. They all moved to Moab. There Naomi's two sons met and married non-Jewish women. Naomi's husband died, and ten years later both of her sons died, too. Suddenly, Naomi and her sons' wives were left without an income. They knew that they would starve if they didn't do something. So Naomi told her sons' wives to go back to their own homes and find new husbands to support them, and Naomi started back to Bethlehem. One daughter-in-law did return to her home, but the other daughter-in-law, Ruth, decided to go with Naomi to help her—no matter what happened to them. She left the land of Moab, where she had grown up, to return to Bethlehem with Naomi.

Today's story begins when the two women arrived back in Bethlehem. Ruth soon found a way to get food for Naomi and herself. The Jews, God's people, would let poor people go through the fields after the workers picked the best grain and take whatever was left over without paying for it. This practice was called gleaning. God taught the Jews this kindness because He did not want anyone to starve, including foreigners. Ruth was a foreigner in Bethlehem; but Boaz, a rich Jewish landowner, let Ruth glean in his fields.

Read the story in the *Picture Bible* on pages 225-230. Have students take the parts of characters. These questions may be used during or following the reading:
● Why did Boaz want to help Ruth?
● What things happened that helped Ruth know that Naomi's God was alive and did great things for her?
● What things did Boaz do that showed he was a righteous man?

● How do you think Ruth felt when Boaz asked her to marry him?

At this point, hand out the "Chain of Kindness" activity piece from page 6A in the back of this book. Give the students time to cut out the six strips.
● Who begins the chain of kindness in this story? (Ruth) Glue the strip in a ring which has Ruth pictured gleaning.
● Who notices Ruth's kindness and helps her? (Boaz) Glue the next link as shown.
● Who showed kindness to Ruth and Boaz when He saw their kindness? (God) God made the wedding dream come true. The wedding of Ruth and Boaz made someone else very happy. Who was that person? (Naomi)
● Who kindly gave Ruth and Boaz a son? (God) Now draw your face on the last link. You can keep the kindness chain going!
● Who can you help or make happy today?
● How can our class start a kindness chain in our church today?

EXPLORING WORSHIP

We can worship God in many ways. One of the ways is by our kindness to other children and adults. We have already thought of some ways to worship God through kindness. Another way to worship the Lord is by showing Him that we love Him at our group worship times. Let's look at some of the ways God's people used to worship Him. Each of the following verses has a worship activity in it. Let's decide whether our church worships God in that way and try to do this activity in our own worship service.

Have the children look up these verses one at a time as you call out the references. Choose a different child to read each one. Then discuss what the verse has to say about worship. See if the children can think of ways that your church worships in this way. All of the activities described in these verses are involved in today's In Worship. Let the students plan what they will do for each of these. For instance, let them choose a song which they have learned recently to sing as their new song at the beginning of the worship service. A reading is provided for praising God's names in the event that your students have difficulty writing their own. You may wish to fill in the In Worship outline as you go through this activity so that you will not forget what the children plan.
● Psalm 96:1—Decide which new song you will sing. Where will it be in the order of worship? Who will lead it?
● Psalm 106:1—Have two or three students prepare sentence prayers to use as the Invocation. "Thank You, Lord Jesus, for . . . ."
● Psalm 40:9, 10—The class may complete this sentence and elect someone to say it, "We know the Lord is righteous because He . . . ."

The teacher must both tell and model. The learner must both hear and see.
—Neal F. McBride

This could be the Call to Worship.

• **Psalm 47:1**—Make up a clapping rhythm to use as praise to the Lord. Choose a clapping leader. This could be done after reading the special Statement of Faith for today.

• **Psalm 46:10**—Decide how long to be silent before the Lord. A natural time for this to occur is after the prayer.

☐ **Psalm 51:10-12**—Write each verse on a separate slip of paper. Choose three students to read them, leading the children in David's humble prayer.

• **Psalm 66:13**—Choose someone to take the offering just before the Student Worship Talk.

• **Psalm 68:4**—Choose a person to praise God by reading His names: "You are Almighty God, Savior, our Father, and our Redeemer. You are Wonderful, Counselor, King of the Universe, Creator of All Things. You are Love, Truth, Light, The Bread of Life, The Living Water. We praise You in all of Your names. You are our God, the only Savior. Beside You there is no other." This could be done in place of Our Statement of Faith.

• **Psalm 73:28c**—Together list a few of God's great deeds in the Bible or in present days. Praise God by reading this list after the Invocation.

• **Psalm 119:15**—Choose a verse for the Scripture reading and have a volunteer read it. Worshipers will meditate on it as part of the service. Explain that meditation is quietly listening to what God is telling you about something.

This is an adventure in praise and worship. Enjoy it with your students. Use as many of the verses as your time schedule allows.

WORSHIPING TOGETHER

Worship practices are valuable in that they help people have a time of two-way communication with God. This is an important goal in children's worship. However, this goal will not be reached by merely staging a performance or by standing in front of the children and flipping through the pages of this guide. You can help the children have memorable experiences in God's presence by setting an example with your attitude. Enter into the songs, prayers, and clapping wholeheartedly, even though these things are geared for children. Give God your genuine praise, and the students will join you.

Today's In Worship is special. It will require more guidance from you because several different elements have been added to this particular service. You will need to help make the transitions between sections smooth so that the spirit of worship is not interrupted. If students have trouble selecting songs, you might want to suggest "We Give Thee but Thine Own" from your hymnal. Appropriate songs from *Worship Time Music Book* are "Give unto the Lord," page 30, and "Lend a Helping Hand," page 14.

For the applause worship section of today's order of worship, you might just clap a constant beat in unison, or your class may want to experiment with loud and soft clapping, cupping their hands, using flat hands, and making up a syncopated beat. This worship element can be introduced with the words, "Let's give the Lord an offering of praise by clapping!"

RESPONDING PERSONALLY

Effective teaching will be followed by decisions or action on the part of the students. Here is an activity to help the students apply the lesson to their lives.

The activity piece 6B in the back of this book, is a "Kindness Contract." Give each student a copy. Have them fill in the contract and color the border. They can act as witnesses to sign each other's contracts. It is best if students can think of something kind to do for someone within the next few hours to reinforce the lesson. The contract might include doing a kind deed every day. ■

IN WORSHIP
WE GIVE OURSELVES TO GOD

This is a special worship service plan. Fill in the outline with the worship activities selected during Exploring Worship.

1. Call to Worship
2. Invocation
3. Praise God—*Read a list of His great deeds.*
4. Hymn—*Sing a new song.*
5. Our Statement of Faith—*Read the list of names for God.*
6. Praise God—*Give God an offering of praise by clapping.*
7. Scripture Reading
8. Prayer—*Read David's prayer in Psalm 51:10-12*
9. A Time of Silence Before God
10. Hymn
11. Offering
12. Student Worship Talk—*Complete the following sentences in your own words.*

I. Read Ruth 1:16, 17.
  A. At a time when Naomi had many needs, Ruth gave herself to help Naomi. Naomi had special needs because _____.
  B. By helping Naomi, Ruth pleased God. Ruth helped Naomi by _____.
  C. I can please God by helping _____.
  D. Ruth gave herself to God by helping Naomi. One way I can show God I want to give myself to Him is by _____.

II. Read Ruth 4:13-16.
  A. God showed Ruth He was pleased that she gave herself to Him by serving Naomi. He showed His pleasure by _____.
  B. One time I served someone else by _____.
  C. I want God to help me give myself to Him more and more each day just as Ruth did to Naomi.

13. Benediction—May the Lord care for you in special ways as you give yourself to Him. ∎

SESSION 25
WORSHIP AIM:

GIVING IN FAITH

Journey into I Samuel 1—9: Samuel leads the Israelites to renew their faith in God (pp. 231-241).

Special Things You'll Need:
☐ Envelopes, one for each child
☐ Supplies for decorating the worship area
☐ Copies of "Giving in Faith," activity piece 6C from the back of this book
☐ Adult volunteer to explain church's use of offering
☐ "Offering Attitudes Cards," activity piece 6D from the back of this book
☐ Offering plate (or box)
☐ Paper plates
☐ Small inexpensive prizes or snacks

GETTING STARTED

As children arrive, involve them in one or more of the ideas below. These activities will help prepare them for the focus of this session.

☐ Provide envelopes for children to put their offerings in. They may decorate the envelopes as part of their offering, as a way of showing God that they love Him. The children will need to save these envelopes to use during the worship service. If they didn't bring money, that's okay. Have them write a note to God telling something else they will give Him. These other gifts could include obedience to parents, helping a younger brother or sister, baking cookies for a sick friend, etc.

☐ Those who arrive early can also decorate the worship area for today's service. The children could use streamers, bows, paper or real flower arrangements, posters, or even signs such as, "We worship You, God."

☐ Challenge students, working in small groups or pairs, to see how many examples they can find in the *Picture Bible* in stories they've already read of people giving something to God or to someone else. Allow students to share some examples they found. This activity helps introduce children to today's topic.

EXPLORING THE BIBLE

Today we want students to learn what it means to give in faith by looking at the life of Samuel.

The story is found on pages 231-241 in the *Picture Bible*. It covers Samuel's birth, dedication, prophecy, and dealings with Israel. And it goes on to the beginning of his search for a king for Israel. In the story, Hannah and Samuel give gifts and sacrifices to God. We want the children to learn about giving in faith as Hannah and Samuel did. We want them to give God gifts and trust God to use the gifts they give.

In advance, read the complete story in the *Picture Bible*. Reading the background passages in I Samuel would also be profitable. Tell the story as dramatically as possible.

Help students to understand the story by playing the following game. Divide students into two teams. Have each team work together as a group to see which team can answer the most questions. One team could be called the Shiloh Shepherds and the other might be the Mizpeh Marchers. Give one point for each correct answer, but subtract a point for a wrong answer. Award winning team members a small prize or treat.

Here are the questions:
● **What did Hannah ask God to give her?**
● **Why did Hannah take her son,**

Samuel, to live with Eli, the priest?
- How do you think Hannah felt when she took Samuel to the Tabernacle? (Probably sad, but also happy to keep her promise.)

Have a volunteer find Bethel and Shechem on the map. Point to the spot halfway between those two cities and explain to the children that that is where Shiloh was located. The Tabernacle where Samuel lived with Eli was located in Shiloh.
- Why did the Israelites take the ark into battle? (They were losing and they thought that if they had the ark, God would help them win.)
- Do you think God was pleased that they took the ark? Why or why not?
- What happened to the Philistines after they captured the ark? (They had plagues and many people got sick and died.)
- What did the Philistines do? (They gave the ark back to the Israelites.)
- What did Samuel ask the Israelites to do? (He asked them to stop worshiping idols and to offer a sacrifice to God.)
- What happened while the people were worshiping God? (The Philistines attacked them.)
- What did Samuel do when he found out about the attacking Philistines? (He prayed and asked God to save the people.)
- How did God defeat the Philistines? (He sent a bad thunderstorm.)
- When Samuel got old, what did the people ask him to do? (They asked him to find a king for them.)

Have another volunteer find Philistia, the territory where the Philistines lived, and Jerusalem on the map. Explain to them that the worship at Mizpeh and the battle

against the Philistines took place in the area between these two points.

There are two examples of giving in today's story. First, Hannah gave Samuel back to God. And second, Samuel gave a sacrifice to God. To help you discuss these examples with the children, distribute copies of the work sheet, "Giving in Faith." The children will also need crayons or colored markers.

Look at the first box. What is happening?

Hannah loved Samuel very much. It was probably hard for her to let him live in the Tabernacle with Eli. But Hannah also loved God and she knew that Samuel could serve God by helping Eli, the priest. Draw a picture of Hannah's face when she took Samuel to serve in the Tabernacle.

Give children time to draw. By letting Samuel help Eli, Hannah was giving God a gift. She knew God would use Samuel to serve Him.

Look at the next box. What is happening?

One of the ways God used Samuel was to convince the Israelites to stop worshiping idols and to start worshiping God again. How do you think Samuel felt when the people decided to worship God again? Draw a picture of his face when he was offering sacrifices to God.

Collect the "Giving in Faith" work sheets from the children and save them for the Responding Personally section of this session, when the children will fill in the third box.

EXPLORING WORSHIP

Last week we learned many ways we can give ourselves to God. Today we are going to learn about

something else that we can give to God. In our story, Samuel offered a sacrifice to God. Today, we don't offer sacrifices like Samuel did.
- What do we give instead? What do we call those gifts of money? When we give our offerings to God, we can give them in faith because we know that God will use that money by helping people in our church do His work.
- In what kinds of work do you think God uses the money? Make a list of the children's suggestions, or have a volunteer secretary do it.

Before the session, arrange for an adult who is familiar with how your church uses its offering to visit the children's church. Introduce the volunteer and have him or her discuss with the children what your church does with the money given to God in the offering.

Children also need to see that the attitude with which we give our offerings is even more important to God than the offerings we give. To help them discover this truth, have them do a roleplay game. Cut out the "Offering Attitude Cards," and give one to each volunteer. You will need an offering plate (or offering box) at the front of the room. One by one, have the volunteers pretend to put an offering in the plate and read their

Teaching is painful, continual, and difficult work to be done by kindness, by watching . . . and by praise, but above all by example.
—Ruskin

cards. After each card is read, have the rest of the children decide whether or not God would be pleased with that person's attitude.

After this activity, lead the children in a discussion of tithes.

● **Does anyone know what a tithe is?**

God's people in Israel used to give Him a part of the food that they grew on their farms, a part of the animals they raised, and a part of all that they had. Many of God's people today give one tenth of their paychecks to God. If they get paid $300 a week, they give away $30 to God. They might give it all to their church, or they might help a neighbor whose house burned down, or they might give it secretly to help a widow pay her heating bill.

The important thing about giving is not how much a person gives, but the attitude with which he or she gives. However, the Bible does speak about giving money regularly to God.

Point out to students that they can even tithe their allowances. Explain that many people give a tenth of their money because it is easy to figure out. Teach them how to figure out one tenth of their weekly allowance by dividing it by ten. Encourage the children to get their parents to help them figure out how much to give next week.

WORSHIPING TOGETHER

In today's worship service, the children will need the offering envelopes that they made during the Getting Started section of this session. If some of the children don't have money to put in their envelopes, have them take a slip of paper and a pencil and write down something that they can give to God.

The Call to Worship should be read loudly with enthusiasm. You will need two people to read the Bible in the Scripture Reading part of the worship service. Encourage the readers to practice their passages ahead of time.

When choosing hymns for today's worship, try to find hymns that talk about giving things to God like "Give unto the Lord," page 30, and "I Was Glad," page 3 from *Worship Time Music Book*. From the hymnal you might sing "Now Thank We All Our God."

RESPONDING PERSONALLY

Use the rest of the session for the children to respond to what they have learned by doing one of the following activities.

☐ Have the children complete last box of the "Giving in Faith" work sheet that they started in the Exploring Worship section of this session. They should draw two pictures. The first picture should show them giving some kind of gift to God. It could be anything from money, to helping their parents, to being a worship leader in children's church. In the second picture, they should draw how their faces look when they are giving their gifts to God.

While the children are working, discuss their pictures with them. If there is time when they finish drawing, encourage them to share their pictures with each other.

☐ Have children make a bank in which they can save money for next week's offering. Distribute one paper plate to each child. Have children fold their plates in half. Next, have the children staple or tape across the open part of the plates so that only a small opening remains. This opening should be large enough for coins to fit through.

Encourage the children to decorate their banks and also to take them home and use them during the week. ■

IN WORSHIP
WE GIVE IN FAITH

1. Call to Worship—Psalm 96:4-6

2. Invocation—Dear Lord, be with us as we worship You now. We love You very much. You are the best! Thank You for caring about us. Help us to worship You with our gifts. In Your name, we pray. Amen.

3. Hymn

4. Our Statement of Faith—*Repeat our church's creed with the leader.*

5. Scripture Reading—*Reader 1:* I Samuel 1:21-28
   Reader 2: I Samuel 7:3-6, 9, 10

6. Prayer—*Leader will allow a few moments for you to pray silently after each statement.*

Dear Lord Jesus, You take good care of us . . .

Forgive us for things that we do that displease You . . .

Thank You for all the ways You show that You love us . . .

Help us to give to You cheerfully and to believe that You will use our gifts. . .

Help us to learn what You are teaching us today. In Jesus' name. Amen.

7. Student Worship Talk—*Complete the following statements with your own ideas.*

   I. Read I Samuel 1:27, 28.
   A. Hannah gave her son, Samuel, to God to serve Him in the tabernacle.
   B. God used Hannah's gift of her son to do His work. Samuel became _____.
   C. Something I can give to God is _____.
   D. A way I would like to see God use my gift to Him is _____.

   II. Read I Samuel 7:3, 4, 9, 10.
   A. When Samuel became a man, he showed us that he gave himself to God by _____.
   B. A way I can give myself to God right now is _____.
   C. Two things that make me glad to give gifts to God are _____.

8. Offering—Usher's Prayer: Thank You, God, that You will use this offering for Your work.

9. Hymn—*Sing a jubilant song.*

10. Benediction—May God help us want to give more of ourselves to Him each day. May we also give ourselves to others because we love Him. ■

SESSION 26
WORSHIP AIM:

*G*IVING OUR TALENTS

Journey into I Samuel 9—16: Saul fails in using his talent of leadership for God (pp. 242-256).

Special Things You'll Need:
☐ Diamond-shaped slips of paper
☐ Poster with words "The Case of the Missing Crown Jewels"
☐ Jewelry box or envelope
☐ "Coat of Arms," page 113 in *THE Idea Book*
☐ Recorded music that fits worship aim
☐ Styrofoam meat trays and colored rubber bands
☐ Copies of "Channel 7 'I-WITNESS' News" script, page 24 in *THE Idea Book* with optional additional newsroom props
☐ Resource people to demonstrate their talents.
☐ Rhythm instruments
☐ One or two students, notified early in the week, prepared to share their talents

GETTING STARTED

In this session students will see that God is pleased not only when we offer Him our money but when we give Him our talents as well. The Bible story gives us the bad example of Saul, who failed to use his talent of leadership for God.

Here are some activities you can use to introduce today's session.
☐ As students enter today, have a mystery table set up near the door with a sign which reads "The Case of the Missing Crown Jewels." Every student should have a chance to solve the mystery before moving on to another activity. Label two index cards with the word "clue" on one side. On the other side, write these page numbers: (Card 1) pages 247,

248; (Card 2) pages 249-251. Students will refer to pages in the *Picture Bible* for clues to find out two things Saul did that made him lose the kingship. Lay diamond-shaped slips of paper next to the clue cards. The students should write their names and answers on one of the paper "jewels" and leave their answers in a jewelry box on the same table to be checked later. (An envelope will do if a jewelry box is not readily available.) You may want to draw answers from this box randomly later in the class time and give a small reward to two students whose correct answers you read first.
☐ Have students make a coat of arms. Do your own as a sample before the class time begins. Explain to the students that a coat of arms usually represents a family tree. The artwork shows something special or unique to that family's history. They should decorate their coat of arms by putting their name in the middle surrounded by pictures of things they like to do. It should show the things that make the students unique. For example, if a student is on the soccer team, he or she might draw a soccer ball or a pair of cleats as part of his or her coat of arms. While your students are working on this project, make it a point to talk to as many as possible about their individual interests and affirm them in any areas of talent that you may have noticed.
☐ If you have students who are good in drama, let them use this time to prepare the "Channel 7 'I-WITNESS' News" skit, page 24 in *THE Idea Book*, for use in Exploring the Bible section of today's lesson.
☐ Make a music center. Use the rhythm instruments made earlier this year. Let students practice playing these with a recorded song that you

have selected to be used in today's worship service. Some can make "harps" like the one David plays in today's lesson by stretching rubber bands around Styrofoam meat trays from the supermarket.

EXPLORING THE BIBLE

Bring the students together to check their answers from the "Crown Jewels" game and to show the projects they have made. Some have seen talents they have that God can use; some have worked on developing a talent at the music center. Others have seen how Saul misused his talents by disobeying God. The Bible lesson today will help them to see right and wrong uses of talents God gives us.

Discuss with the class how they feel about using their talents in front of people. You may wish to share a humorous instance from your own life of a time when you were nervous or embarrassed. If the children can laugh at your struggle, they will feel more free to share their own. Have two or three children share similar instances if they can think of them.

Today we are going to talk about a man who probably felt just like we do when he had a hard job to do.

Now read the story "Test for a King" on pages 242 and 243 in the *Picture Bible.*
● **How do you think Saul felt when he was hiding?** Saul's talent was being a leader. God had chosen him to be the king of the Israelites. Being a king was scary enough, but the worst part was that no one had ever been king of Israel before. He had to go first. This was not an easy assignment. **Let's look at some of the things Saul had to face as king.**

At this point, have the students who have prepared to present the "Channel 7 'I-WITNESS' News" skit take their places. Ask the rest of the class to think about the way that Saul used his talent while they listen to the news broadcast. How did Saul do? If you chose not to use the newscast, have two students who answered correctly in the Crown game earlier tell the class what they discovered about the ways Saul disobeyed God.

Saul was scared at first, but when God did make him a leader, he didn't depend on God anymore. He started to disobey. Today we would say that the whole thing went to his head. He thought that he was good enough to break God's laws and get away with it.
● **Have you ever known anyone like that?**

God does not want us to be too scared to use the talents He gives us. At the same time, He is not pleased when we brag about our talents and try to do them without Him. That is what happened to Saul. He broke God's rules. God had to pick a new king for His people because Saul blew it.

Because Saul failed as king, Israel had to have a new king. Samuel was sent to pick the new king from Jesse's sons. The sons lined up— kind of like the lineups we have to choose sports teams. Let's see what happened. Assign the parts of Samuel, Jesse, and the Narrator, and have the students read page 252 to the top of page 253.

God does not look at what people look like on the outside or at how many talents they have. He looks at the heart to see if we will let Him use our talents. If He thinks we will act like Saul, He is not pleased.

Assign new readers for David, his brothers, Samuel, and the Narrator and complete the reading through page 256.
● **How did David show that he was not afraid of using his talent for God?** (David was faithful and wanted to be the best shepherd he could be. He was also willing when he was asked to play his harp for the king.)
● **How do we know that David didn't think he was strong enough and smart enough to make it on his own?** Have a student read what David says in Psalm 27:1 or in the *Picture Bible* on page 255 at the bottom. (The Lord is my strength. What have I to fear?)

EXPLORING WORSHIP

Today have one to three teens or adults who have various abilities come and share with the class the way they use their talents in worship and what it means to them to participate in that way (hard work, as well as spiritual service and blessing). Interview these guests about the way they developed their talents. Were they ever nervous about using their talents? How did they get over it? If the church pianist or organist is not

The potential within a creative teacher is like a dare—a dare to think new thoughts and try new things . . .

113

involved in the adult service, he or she would be an ideal guest. If not, enlist a singer, a greeter, or even the person who decorates the sanctuary for special worship times. Try not to emphasize "performance" talents exclusively. Remind the students of the lesson from Ruth that worship is loving service.

Each of these resource people may help the students with a brief part of their own planning for worship today. For instance, the person who does flower arrangements for the front of the church might help the class make an arrangement for a table in the worship room. A choir director might teach several students to direct a simple 3/4 or 4/4 time. Students can then take turns leading the singing in their worship services. A greeter might talk to the children about the importance of friendly welcomes for visitors in children's church. Some of your more outgoing students could come to see this as their talent or ministry. If enough interesting resource people are available, you might even break into small interest groups for this sharing/training time with the guests. Let the students use as many of these ideas as possible in their worship service today.

. . . because he or she is following the Master Teacher who used interactive methods to prepare His small band of students to change history.
—Marlene LeFever

WORSHIPING TOGETHER

Today's worship service should be a chance for the students to present their talents to God. It is difficult to do this in a society which emphasizes performance and competition. Too often talents are used as a basis for proving superiority or inferiority. Many of your students have probably felt that they have no talents simply because they have never won the first-place ribbon in school talent shows or because they are not as athletic as their classmates. Be sensitive to the reactions of students in your class to today's lesson. Try to encourage those who complain that they have no talents.

Involve as many different students as possible in the worship service today. Let the students know that one talent is not superior to another by emphasizing many different kinds of talents. The children need to learn that what matters is their willingness and desire to let God use their talents. This worship experience should help each student to feel that he or she has something unique to offer to God in worship.

Let one or two students, who were notified ahead of time, share a vocal or instrumental solo, or some other talent that they have.

During In Worship, you might sing a hymn like "O for a Thousand Tongues to Sing" from the hymnal. "We've Got Work to Do," page 13, and "You Know, Lord," page 19, in *Worship Time Music Book*, would also be appropriate.

RESPONDING PERSONALLY

One way that David used his talents in worship was to write psalms to God. These were prayer poems in which David told God honestly how he felt, asked God to help him, and praised God for things. David's poems are written in the book of the Bible called Psalms. Distribute paper and markers to the students and encourage them to write their own brief psalms to God. These can be read to the group, displayed on a bulletin board, or saved for use in future worship services.

Some students may wish to write thank-you notes to the guests who visited your class today. If the students worked in small groups for that part of the lesson, let the groups work together to design a thank-you card for the speaker who worked with their group. They should tell the guests what they learned about talents from their talks. This activity will teach your students to be courteous while reinforcing what they have learned. ▪

IN WORSHIP
WE GIVE OUR TALENTS

1. Call to Worship—Psalm 150

2. Invocation—Dear God, today we want to give You our talents. We want the music that we make and the words that we say to bring glory to You. Amen.

3. Hymn

4. Our Statement of Faith—*Repeat this together.*

5. Scripture Reading—*Words of David in Psalm 27:1, 4-6.*

6. Prayer—*Offer sentence prayers to God thanking Him for talents He has given you.*

7. Hymn

8. Worship Talk—*Complete the sentences below with your own words and ideas.*

  I. Read I Samuel 13:13, 14.

    A. Samuel said this to Saul when Saul disobeyed God. Saul did not let God use his talent. Sometimes we do not want to use our talents because we feel _____.

    B. One time when I was nervous about using my talent, I _____.

    C. Sometimes people think that they can make it without God. One way that Saul tried to do this was _____.

    D. God gave us talents to use in worshiping Him. When we only use the talents God gave us for ourselves, God must feel _____.

  II. Read Psalm 27:1.

    A. David wrote this verse. He was not afraid to use his talents for God. Some of David's talents were _____.

    B. We have talents that God has given us to use for Him. Some talents that people in this room have are _____.

    C. We often think about what people can do or what they look like on the outside, but God cares more about _____.

    D. God chose David because He knew that in David's heart David was willing to let God use his talents. We can let God know that we are willing to let Him use our talents by _____.

9. Benediction—May God give us courage to use our talents for Him this week. Amen. ∎

SESSION 27
WORSHIP AIM:

GIVING OUR FRIENDSHIP

Journey into I Samuel 16—20: David and Jonathan show true friendship to God and to each other (pp. 257-268).

Special Things You'll Need:

☐ The book, *The Giving Tree* by Shel Silverstein, Harper and Rowe, 1964

☐ Props and costumes for the "Giving Pantomime," page 26 in *THE Idea Book*

☐ Copies of "Coupons," activity piece 6B in the back of this book

☐ Wrapping paper and bows

☐ "Giving Bulletin Board," *THE Idea Book*, page 124

☐ Polaroid camera and film

☐ Potted tree branch (Optional)

☐ Colored yarn (Optional)

GETTING STARTED

Choose one or more of the following activities to do as your children arrive and settle down.

☐ As students enter the room today, you may wish to take attendance by photographing each one with an instant camera. Lay the pictures on a table for the children to see. They will be used later in the lesson.

☐ Have students prepare the "Giving Pantomime." Today would be a good day to present the story to younger children as a culmination of your work in this unit on giving. When the group returns from its presentation, discuss the way that it feels to know that you have done something special for someone else. This pantomime can also be presented on a visit to the nursing home if you have planned to use the nursing home activity on page 12 of *THE Idea Book.*

☐ Today you may wish to read to

your students the book *The Giving Tree* by Shel Silverstein. It should be easy to find in public or elementary school libraries. The reading will only take a few minutes. This story is a memorable illustration of giving the best that we have to offer out of friendship for someone else. Be sure that you have read through the story several times so that you can read with expression. Children love to have someone read aloud to them if the reading is done creatively.

☐ If the book is not available, have the students draw pictures of something they could do for their friends. As the students work on these, discuss the joy that comes from doing things for our friends.

EXPLORING THE BIBLE

Today our emphasis in the Bible lesson is on friendship with others and with God. Divide the class into two groups. One group should read the story of David's risking his life for Israel on pages 260-263 in the *Picture Bible.* The other group should read pages 264, 267, and 268. This is the story of David and Jonathan. Both of these stories illustrate ways that people gave their very best because their friends needed help. Let the students read the stories silently or in small groups. Then pass out paper and crayons and have the students do doodle art. You may want to have a couple of examples of doodle art available to show them. Doodle art uses colors, lines, and shapes, rather than realistic pictures, to convey ideas or feelings.

The group who read about David and Goliath should doodle the way David felt when he went out to face Goliath. The second group should

draw the way that Jonathan felt about his friendship with David.

After both groups have had time to finish reading and drawing, bring the class together. Ask for volunteers from the first group to tell their story in their own words to group two. Students may help each other fill in the details. Then have several explain their drawings. Repeat this procedure with the second group telling its story to the first one.

● How did David show his love for Israel?

● How did Jonathan show his friendship for David? Most of us don't know any giants and we don't know any kings who are trying to kill our friends.

● What are some things that our friends might need?

● What are some ways that we can show our friendship to others?

David was probably not very excited about facing Goliath. It didn't sound like much fun. In fact, the whole idea was scary, but he did it anyway. He knew that his brothers and friends needed help. Sometimes there are things that we could do for our friends or family that are difficult, too. For instance, even though you hate doing dishes, you could wash the dishes for your sister when she has a lot of homework to do. You could tell a friend at school about Jesus even if you are nervous that your friend will laugh at you. Some things may seem as hard to you as it would be to face Goliath!

Think of one thing that you could do today to help someone. It could be something that scares you, or it could be a job that you don't especially like to do. Don't tell anyone else what you think of.

When all of the students have had

a chance to think of something, have them take turns pantomiming the activities for other students to guess.

EXPLORING WORSHIP

In this unit the students have learned how they can worship God by giving different kinds of offerings to Him. They have talked about participating in the worship service, giving tithes and offerings, and using their talents for God. Today's worship focus shows that God wants us to give Him our friendship.

When we love others, we want to show it in every way we can. Students have just seen beautiful examples of friendship in the lives of David and Jonathan. They have thought of ways to show their love for their friends. The concept of giving to friends should lead easily into an understanding of what it means to give offerings to show that we are true friends of Jesus. He is our best Friend.

Everyone close your eyes. Pretend that Jesus has just walked into our classroom. Hear the tapping of His shoes on the floor. Now He comes and sits down beside you. Think of something He would say to you. What would you say back? You want Jesus to know how much you love Him. Think of what you will do to let Him know. Allow a minute or two for the students to continue to think with their eyes closed.

Okay, open your eyes. Tell me what you thought of to do for Jesus. Get responses from several children. Help the students to see connections between their natural expressions of friendship and the ways we show God our friendship in a worship service. For example, when we love our

friends we want to tell them. In worship we tell God that we love Him, too.

At this point, you will want to explain the worship practices of your church which demonstrate friendship or loyalty to God. These may include kneeling at an altar, praying, speaking an affirmation of faith, or raising one's hand at a particular time in the service. Choose some of these expressions which are used by your church to incorporate in the worship time today.

WORSHIPING TOGETHER

Today In Worship focuses on giving our friendship to God. We show our friendship to God in worship by acts which declare our commitment. You are encouraged to include some worship practices which are unique to your church. However, one activity is described here for you to use if you wish.

During today's worship service, students can show God that they want to give themselves to be God's friends by walking to the front of the worship room and placing the Polaroid pictures of themselves in a basket, on a table, or on an altar if one is available. This should be a

Your character is a stream, a river, flowing down upon your children hour by hour.
—Horace Bushnell

117

serious time. You may wish to sing a song quietly or play music as the students do this. Make this activity optional. Let the students know that it is okay not to participate.

Explain this activity to the students and distribute the pictures before worship begins.

A good hymn of praise for students to sing after the invocation is "Praise Ye the Triune God" from your hymnal. Briefly explain the meaning of Triune, but it is not an essential concept for this session. We want students to praise God, their Father, for what He has done. Other songs you may want to use are "Working Together" and "Give unto the Lord" from *Worship Time Music Book*, pages 16 and 30.

RESPONDING PERSONALLY

If your students enjoyed the story of *The Giving Tree*, they may wish to make a giving tree at the close of class today. A tree branch can be potted in soil or in plaster of paris to make it steadier. If you wish, you may spray paint the branch white for a nice effect. Punch holes in the top of the instant pictures of the children and hang them from the branches with short lengths of colored yarn. This giving tree could become a permanent decoration in your classroom, reminding the students that true giving is always giving of ourselves.

If materials for the tree project are not available, let the children cut 6" by 6" squares out of a variety of wrapping papers. The students should mount their pictures on the wrapping-paper squares and put bows on their finished packages. Then they could hang their picture gifts on a

bulletin board in the classroom. The caption could read, "We Give Ourselves to God and to Others."

In the final moments of class, give each student some coupons. The coupons read "Good for one . . ." Students can fill in the blanks with things they will do for others this week. They can then distribute the coupons to parents or friends. This is a fun way to make sure that students follow through with what they have learned by doing things to show their love for others. ∎

WE GIVE OUR FRIENDSHIP

1. Call to Worship—Psalm 25:1, 2

2. Invocation—Dear Lord, be with us as we worship You today. We want You to know we love You. We want to give You our very best. We want to give You our friendship. Amen.

3. Hymn

4. Our Statement of Faith—*Recite this together.*

5. Scripture Reading—I Samuel 17:38-49

6. Prayer—Dear Heavenly Father, thank You that You gave us the example of David and Jonathan to show us what friendship is. Thank You that You want to be our Friend. Help us to do the things that let You know we want to be Your friend, too. We also need Your help to show our friendship to those around us. In Jesus' name, we pray. Amen.

7. Hymn

8. Student Worship Talk—*Complete these sentences with your own words.*

  I. Read I Samuel 17:49.

    A. David went out to face Goliath because he was a friend to God and to God's people, the Israelites. Since Goliath was over nine feet tall, David must have felt like
_____.

    B. Sometimes we face tough situations like David did. One tough thing that I faced this week was _____.

    C. When we face things like that, we need to remember what we learned in today's lesson. We need to remember that _____.

  II. Read I Samuel 18:1.

    A. David and Jonathan were best friends. This verse says that Jonathan loved David as much as he loved himself. One thing Jonathan did for his friend David was
_____.

    B. Today we thought of things we could do for our friends. Three of the ideas we thought of were _____

    C. By doing these things we can show our love not only for our friends but also for God and His Son, Jesus.

9. Benediction—May God help you to conquer any giants you may face this week as you show your love for Him and for others by your friendship. ■

SESSION 28
WORSHIP AIM:

SEEKING GOD'S DIRECTIONS

Children at this age are capable of prayer, but they often don't know much about it. Since they are ready to learn, we want to help them get started.

One of the best ways you can teach children about formal prayer is by example. Make prayer a natural part of each session. Children need to see that prayer fits into life, that it isn't just for Sundays or before meals. To help children see that they can pray at any time, pray at different points during the session. Look over each lesson and pick spots where it would be natural for you and the children to spend a few moments praying together.

In addition to the regular lessons, there are several optional ideas contained in *THE Idea Book*. These are designed so that if the children work on them for about 15 minutes at the beginning of every session, they will be able to complete them by the end of the unit. The play "The Shepherd King," page 27 in *THE Idea Book* gives children an opportunity to share David's story with another class or even their parents. Children might also make the "Prayer Bulletin Board," page 125 in *THE Idea Book*.

As you go through this unit, remember to pray for your students. ■

Journey into I Samuel 21—30: David needs God's help to escape from Saul (pp. 269-281).

Special Things You'll Need:
☐ Blankets and sheets
☐ Adult volunteer to tell the story
☐ Medium-sized safety pins
☐ Plastic beads
☐ "The Shepherd King" in *THE Idea Book*, page 29
☐ Materials for making a time line (optional)
☐ "Bible Spies," activity piece 7A from the back of this book (Optional)

GETTING STARTED

As children arrive, you will want to visit with them. The activities they do at the beginning of the session provide a good opportunity for you to introduce the children to today's session through an imaginative and fun activity. Choose from one of the following activities.

☐ To set the stage for today's story, have the children make a campsite resembling the kind of campsite that David and his men might have made when they were running away from Saul. You will need a supply of blankets and/or sheets for this activity. Explain to the children that today they will learn about a time when David and a lot of his friends were camping in the wilderness. Point out that sometimes they slept in tents and sometimes they slept in caves. Have the children use the blankets and chairs and tables to make tents and caves. They can pretend that they are setting up camp like David's men did.

Children will love a chance to hide under tables and crawl on the floor. Moving around at the beginning of the session will also help them sit still during the rest of it.

☐ If you decide to have the children do a dramatic reading of the story instead of using an adult volunteer, now is a good time for the volunteers to practice their parts.

☐ As an alternative to setting up camp, children can use this time to work on the unit-long project in *THE Idea Book*, "The Shepherd King."

EXPLORING THE BIBLE

David, the shepherd boy, is a good example of a person who sought God's help. Through this story and the worship focus, students will realize that prayer is a way of seeking God's help.

Reviewing the story from the previous week places the new story in context and helps children see how Bible events followed each other. Use the questions printed below.

● **How did David first meet Saul?**
● **What was Goliath doing when David arrived at the Israelite camp?**
● **How did Saul feel after David killed Goliath?**
● **Why did Saul try to kill David?**
● **What kinds of problems do you have where you need help?** Make a list on a chalkboard or newsprint.
● **Who do you turn to for help?** Have volunteers share their stories.

In today's story we'll find out about a time when David was in trouble and see what he did.

For today's session, you will need an adult volunteer to dress up like a Bible-times character and tell the story. (A bathrobe and sandals make a pretty good costume.)

Today's story tells about David

and his men camping in the wilderness. At night, they probably sat around a fire or in a cave and told stories. **Let's pretend that we are camping and let** (give storyteller's name) **tell us a story about David.**

The storyteller should follow the *Picture Bible* quite closely. This way the children will be able to follow along in their *Picture Bibles.* If your time is limited, have the storyteller concentrate on pages 269 to the middle of 277 and then summarize the rest of 277 to 281.

After the children hear the story, it is important to discuss it. This discussion helps them remember and understand the story better. One good way to review the story is by using the Old Testament picture time line which you may have been using since the first unit. If not, start a time line with this lesson. You can add to it during this unit. The time line helps kids see the order of events in David's life and provides a way to review previous weeks' material.

To make a time line for this unit, you could use computer paper, butcher paper, or shelf paper. Ideally, you should display the time line on a bulletin board, and keep it up for the entire unit. Place it so students will be able to add to it each week. To mark the events in David's life, children could put captions or simple symbols next to appropriate points along the line. For example, a caption might tell that David killed Goliath or became king. Students should illustrate these events.

Use the questions below to help the children discuss the story.
● **What happened to David in today's story?**
● **Why did Saul try to kill David?**
● **Who do you think David turned to for help?**

● **Who protected David from Saul?** Although the *Picture Bible* doesn't spell it out, the Book of I Samuel clearly demonstrates that God constantly took care of David.
● **Why didn't David kill Saul when he had the chance?**
● **Where did David go to get away from Saul?**

Have a volunteer find Philistia on the map.
● **Why wouldn't the Philistines let David go with them when they fought the Israelites?**
● **Who did Saul turn to when he needed help?**
● **Whose way of dealing with trouble was better, David's or Saul's? Why?**
● **What do you think David's experiences taught him about God?**

As an alternative to using an adult storyteller in today's lesson, make copies of the "Bible Spies" work sheet. Divide the group into pairs and assign each pair one or two pages of the story. Have children complete their work sheets and then share their spy reports with the rest of the group. You may want to display these reports on the bulletin board for parents and visitors to see.

EXPLORING WORSHIP

During the next five weeks, we will be learning about the different kinds of things we can pray about and how prayer fits into our worship. In today's story, we learned that when David needed help he prayed and asked God to help him. Asking God for help is an important part of prayer.

On a chalkboard or newsprint, write the following acrostic based on the word PRAY:

Praise
Repentance
Asking
Yourself
(From *What It Means to Be a Christian* by Stuart Briscoe and Jill Briscoe, David C. Cook, 1987)

Make sure the children understand what an acrostic is. Explain to them that this acrostic is a guide to help them when they pray. Each week they will use it to learn about another part of prayer. The acrostic reminds us of the kinds of things that we can pray about.

The ideal way to teach this acrostic is to start with "praise" and continue down the acrostic to "yourself." However, since the lessons are based on the chronology of the Old Testament, the children will learn the words of the acrostic out of order. By the end of the unit, though, they will have had a lesson about each word in the acrostic.

Explain that the acrostic word "yourself" means that one of the things the children can pray about is themselves. David did this when he asked God to help him escape from Saul. The children can ask God for help, just like David did.

When we worship God in church, we start our service by asking Him to help us worship.

I will instruct you and teach you in the way you should go;
I will counsel you and watch over you.
—Psalm 32:8

121

- **What is that kind of prayer called?**
- **Why do we have that kind of prayer?**

These questions review what students learned about the Invocation in the first unit.

As your time permits, try one or both of the prayer ideas below. Give special emphasis to the "palms down, palms up" prayer idea that follows. It will be used during prayer in the Worshiping Together section.

☐ Palms down, palms up prayers. This kind of praying helps children (and adults) visually represent releasing their problems, giving them into God's hands.

Encourage the children to think of several things with which they are struggling, things that require God's help. Have them hold their hands out in front of them with the palms turned down. Silently, they should pray for God's help with a problem. When they have prayed, they should say aloud, "Palms down." This action represents letting go of their problems so that God can take care of them. Next, the children should turn their palms upward and silently ask God to help them trust Him, to keep them from worrying about their problems. When they are finished, they should say aloud, "Palms up," which shows that they are open to God's help and blessing. Encourage your children to pray this way any time they face problems.

☐ Prayer notebook. Have each child take a sheet of paper and fold it in half so that it looks like a small book. This is the start of a notebook in which they can record things they want to pray about and also, in the future, write how God answered their prayers. Have them think of two or three problems with which they need

help. Once the children have written the problems in their "books," they can spend a few minutes praying silently for these requests. Encourage them to keep their books throughout the unit. Check back periodically and ask them to share answered prayers.

WORSHIPING TOGETHER

In today's worship service, the children will incorporate the "Palms up, palms down" style of prayer that they learned about in the Exploring Worship section of the session. The order of worship gives directions to the prayer leader but you will need to help facilitate this activity. Spend a few minutes before the worship service telling the children what to expect during the prayer time.

In your choosing hymns and songs for today's worship service, emphasize the idea of God as our Helper—God as our Friend. Children need to learn to have confidence in God, to realize that He loves and cares for them. You might start with "O God, Our Help in Ages Past" from your hymnal. "Lead On, Lord" and "Lord, I Am Calling" from *Worship Time Music Book* are also appropriate.

RESPONDING PERSONALLY

Children often make and exchange friendship pins. Have your children make friendship pins for God. Although they can't exchange these pins with God, they can wear them as a reminder that God is their Friend.

Give a medium-sized safety pin to each child. Make a quantity of small, plastic beads available to the

children. (These beads can be purchased at many craft stores.) Have the children put an assortment of the beads on their safety pins. Then they can loop their pins over their shoelaces. (If their shoes don't have laces, they could try attaching the pins to shoe buckles, purses, or buttonholes.) Explain to the children that, like the pins on their shoes, God goes with them everywhere they go. ■

IN WORSHIP
WE SEEK GOD'S DIRECTION

1. Call to Worship—Psalm 118:1

2. Invocation—Dear God, we praise You for Your goodness to us. Forgive us for doing wrong. We thank You that we can be together in church. Help us to worship You in a way that makes You happy. In Jesus' name, we pray. Amen.

3. Hymn

4. Our Statement of Faith—*Use your church's statement of faith. You should be familiar with it from Unit 2. Read it aloud or repeat it, phrase by phrase, after the leader.*

5. Scripture Reading—I Samuel 26:2-13

6. Prayer—Dear God, You take good care of us. Sometimes we try to do everything ourselves. Forgive us for not asking for Your help. Thank You for listening to us when we pray. Many times we have problems that are too big for us.

(Hold your hands out, palms down. Have the worshipers do the same. Give them some time to pray silently for God's help. After a few moments, have the group say in unison: "Palms down.")

Teach us to trust You to take care of us. Help us not to worry about our problems.

(Hold your hands out, palms up. Have worshipers do the same. Give them some time to pray silently for God to help them trust Him and not worry. After a few moments, have the group say in unison: "Palms up.")

We pray these things in Jesus' name. Amen.

7. Hymn

8. Student Worship Talk—Complete the following sentences.

I. Read I Samuel 26:3, 4.
  A. David had many troubles. One of them was _____.
  B. Two troubles I have are _____.

II. Read I Samuel 26:12
  A. God kept David safe in Saul's camp by _____.
  B. Two ways God has helped me are _____.

III. Read I Samuel 26:12, 13.
  A. We know from the Bible that God helped David and that David got out of Saul's camp alive.
  B. Two reasons I know that God will help me are

  _____.

9. Benediction—May each of us seek God's direction in all that we do this next week. Amen. ■

123

SESSION 29
WORSHIP AIM:

Praying for others

Journey into I Samuel 30; II Samuel 1—3: David prays for the kidnapped families of his men (pp. 282-291).

Special Things You'll Need:
☐ Newspapers and magazines
☐ "Crossword Puzzle" activity piece7B in the back of this guide
☐ Copies of "David's Song" on page 114 of THE Idea Book
☐ Volunteers from congregation to share prayer requests (Optional)
☐ Tape of readers and tape player (Optional)
☐ Materials for a bulletin board (Optional)

GETTING STARTED

If the children have just come from Sunday school, they are tired of sitting and listening. What they really need is recess, so try to make this period as active as possible without letting it become rowdy.

These activities should help you introduce this session while your students are arriving. Choose one or more to do with your group.

As these activities are going on, talk with your students about people they pray for. Is a relative sick? Is someone far away or having a problem? These conversations will help prepare students for today's theme.

☐ Bring a stack of current newspapers, both local and national, and magazines. Have kids look through them and cut out at least one story or picture about a problem or need. Have children save their stories and pictures to use later.

☐ Have children draw pictures showing a time when someone in their families needed help. Have volunteers explain their pictures.

☐ Sing an action song that the kids enjoy so they can use up some energy.

☐ Children can use this time to work on the unit-long project, *"The Shepherd King."*

EXPLORING THE BIBLE

Children at this age are beginning to gain a concept of history and chronology. They are ready to gain an understanding of the Bible not as a bunch of isolated stories about Moses, or Abraham, or David, but as a series of events, as history. It is important, therefore, to help them see the Bible in this light, to help them gain a sense for the chronology of the Bible. The Old Testament picture time line is an excellent tool to use for teaching chronology. You might assign one student to see that it is maintained throughout the year.

Begin this lesson by reviewing last week's story. If the children made a time line last week, you can use it to review. Otherwise, use the following questions.

● **What happened to Saul last week?** He went to war with the Philistines.

● **What happened to David last week?** He escaped from Saul twice and finally settled in the city of Ziklag in the country of Philistia.

Once students have discussed Ziklag, have someone find the country of Philistia on the map.

● **Have you ever had someone in your family or maybe your best friend need help and you couldn't help that person? What did you do?** Give children some time to respond. They may not say that they prayed. Suggest that even when we can't help others, we can ask God to help them.

Today we're going to find out

about a time when David asked God to help others.

Pass out copies of the "Crossword Puzzle." Make copies of the *Picture Bible* available so that the children can read pages 282 through 287 before completing the puzzle. Give them time to enjoy the puzzle. Then talk about the story.

● **How do you think David and his men felt when they found out the Amalekites had burned Ziklag and captured their families?**

● **Besides going to rescue their families, what else might David and his men have done?** They may have prayed to God that He would take care of their families and help them rescue them.

Next, either read or briefly summarize pages 288-291. Make sure students understand that David isn't king of the whole Israelite nation yet. Point out on the map the areas ruled by David and those ruled by Saul's son, Ish-Bosheth. (David ruled the dark pink portion of the map and Ish-Bosheth most of the red.)

If you have been making a time line, have the children add events from today's story to it.

Here are some other ideas for presenting the story. They may help get the children even more involved.

Divide the group into four or five smaller groups and assign each group a few pages in the *Picture Bible*. Have the groups read their section of the story and then draw a picture of how David (or perhaps another main character—Joab, Abner, Ish-Bosheth) felt during that part of the story. You will need to provide the children with poster board or large sheets of newsprint and colored markers. Have the small groups share their part of the story and explain their pictures. Make sure they present the story in the right order.

Before the session, have members of the junior- or senior-high class tape-record a dramatic reading of pages 282-291 in the *Picture Bible*. Play the tape while the children follow along in their *Picture Bibles*. Let one of the children, particularly one with a short attention span, run the tape player. Children love playing with machines!

EXPLORING WORSHIP

In this part of the session help children recognize that asking God to help others the way David did is a part of prayer. Help them also see how intercessory prayer fits into worship.

Last week we learned about praying for ourselves, asking God to help us. Today, we are learning about asking God to help others. As we learned in our story, David asked God to help his family and friends. Asking God to help other people is an important part of prayer.

Remind children of the PRAY acrostic learned last week:

Praise
Repent
Asking
Yourself

Help the children remember that "asking" means asking God to help other people.

We have been learning about how prayer is part of worship. When we worship God we pray about different kinds of things. One of the things we should pray about is other people.

Discuss with your children how your church incorporates prayers for other people into the worship service. Do you take prayer requests or have

people write them on the backs of the attendance cards? During the pastoral prayer, does the pastor pray for people in the congregation who are sick or traveling? (Be aware that many of your children may not have had enough experience with adult worship to know about these practices.)

● **What are some kinds of problems that people might have, that we can ask God to help them with?**

Point out to kids that in order to ask God to help people, we need to know what kind of help they need.

● **What are ways that we can find out about people who need help so that we can pray for them?** Kids will probably have different answers, things like taking prayer requests may come to their minds. Here are some other ways that you may want to discuss and try.

You might have one kind of prayer be called newspaper prayer. Point out that newspapers and magazines are one place where we can find out about people in our hometown, our country, and the world who need help, whom we can pray for. Have the children share the stories and pictures they cut out earlier.

You may want to use the pictures and articles to start a prayer bulletin board. Each week the children could

How one teaches and what one teaches are inseparable.
—Elliot Eisner

bring in a story or picture that tells about people who need help. You could spend a short time each session discussing the new additions and praying for them. The bulletin board helps to remind the children of people who need prayer.

This can be a fun activity for children and can help them learn to care about people around them. As an alternative, you could bring in the pictures and stories and share them with the children. Then together pray for the people on the bulletin board.

Arrange ahead of time to have a number of people in the congregation who have prayer requests and are willing to share them to come and talk to the kids about them. Have a volunteer write the people's names and their requests on a chalkboard or flip chart so that kids will be able to look at it and pray for the people during the worship service.

Children at this age need help learning how to pray. One way to teach them is through sentence completion prayers (you may be familiar with these from previous sessions). The prayers would take a form like this, "Dear God, thank You for . . ." The children would complete the sentence. They could do this silently or out loud. Or they could write them.

Another way of praying is to pray through pictures rather than words. Children could pray for other people by drawing pictures of how God could help them. For example, if a child has a sick friend, he or she could draw a prayer picture of the friend getting well, or perhaps a before-and-after picture. You could use this type of prayer in conjunction with some of the stories from the newspapers or with people from your congregation who may have shared prayer requests with the children.

WORSHIPING TOGETHER

In today's worship service, we want the children to put into practice what they have learned about prayer as a part of worship. Give special emphasis to prayer time. You can take several approaches here. If you began this session by clipping stories and pictures of people with needs, then children should spend part of the prayer time praying for these people. If you had several people from your congregation share some of their prayer needs, then the children should spend time praying for those people. They can refer to the list of needs that someone wrote down as the people shared.

During the prayer time, rather than having the prayer leader pray the entire prayer, he or she will mention a category and allow time for the children to pray quietly. The leader will say, "Help other people that we know about who need Your help." The children should then pray silently either for the people in the stories they clipped out or for the people from the congregation who shared prayer requests with them.

Choose hymns that focus on prayer and God's willingness to help people. If you have songs about David, these would also work well. Consider using "Joyful, Joyful, We Adore Thee" from your hymnal and, from *Worship Time Music Book*, "God Communication," page 22, or "And He Hears Me," page 24.

RESPONDING PERSONALLY

Conclude the session by allowing the children to personalize some of the things they have learned in worship. Pass out copies of "David's Song."

Read Psalm 145:1-12 to the children and allow them to doodle how David might have felt when he was writing this song. You may want to tell the children that in Hebrew, the language that David spoke, this Psalm is an acrostic poem based on the Hebrew alphabet. It is similar to the acrostic poems they have probably written. ■

IN WORSHIP
WE PRAY FOR OTHERS

1. Call to Worship—Psalm 95:1, 2

2. Invocation—Dear Lord, be with us as we are together today to worship You. Help us to think about You during this service. Help us to love You more. In Jesus' name we pray. Amen.

3. Hymn

4. Our Statement of Faith—*Say this together.*

5. Scripture Reading—I Samuel 30:3-8, 16-20

6. Prayer—*Complete the following sentences.*

Dear God, we praise You because . . .

Sometimes we do bad things like . . .

Please forgive us for these sins and for other sins.

We thank You that You love us and forgive us. We also thank You for . . .

Make us more like Jesus. Help us to . . .

Help other people that we know about who need Your help.
Take time to pray silently.

We know that You hear our prayers and that You answer them. We pray all these things in the name of Jesus our Savior. Amen.

7. Hymn

8. Student Worship Talk—*Complete the sentences below.*

I. Read I Samuel 30:7, 8.
  A. In this story when David prayed, he wore an ephod (EE-phodd). An ephod was a special kind of clothing worn by the priests. It was a little bit like a vest. David wore it to remind him that he was talking to God. One thing I do to remind me of God is _____.

  B. David prayed to God because his family was in trouble. He asked God to help them. I can ask God to help other people with many things. Two of them are _____.

II. Read I Samuel 30:17-19.
  A. David and his men were able to defeat the Amalekites because God helped them. God can help us with problems also. Two problems He can help me with are _____.

  B. One way we know that God answers prayers is that He answered David's prayer. Another way I know God answers prayer is _____.

9. Benediction—May the Lord bless you. May He give you hearts that love Him and hands that serve Him. Amen. ■

SESSION 30
WORSHIP AIM:

SEEKING GOD'S HELP

Journey into II Samuel 3—5: David becomes king and establishes his kingdom (pp. 292-300).

Special Things You'll Need:
☐ Copies of "Bible Spies" work sheet, activity piece 7A in the back of this book (Optional)

GETTING STARTED

Do one or more of the following activities as the children arrive and settle down.

☐ Have readers for the Exploring the Bible section of this session spend time looking over their parts.

☐ Play "What I Want to Be When I Grow Up" charades. Have kids think of something they want to be when they grow up and then pantomime it for the rest of the group to guess.

☐ If you have the space and if children are particularly restless, you might want to play a physical game to burn off some energy. Try a variation of the game "Duck, Duck, Goose." You could call it "Prince, Prince, King."

☐ Children can use this time to work on one of the unit-long projects in *THE Idea Book*, like "The Shepherd King."

EXPLORING THE BIBLE

Begin this lesson by reviewing last week's story. If you have been making a time line of David's life, this provides a good tool for review. Point out last week's events on the time line. Have volunteers retell portions of the story, or use these questions to guide the review:
● **What happened to the families of David and his men?** (They were

kidnapped by the Amalekites.)
● **What did David and his men do?** (Rescued them with God's help.)
● **What happened to Saul and Jonathan?** (They were killed while fighting the Philistines.)
● **Who is at war?** (David and his followers are fighting Ish-Bosheth, King Saul's son.)

Great people are people who have done great things, things that are difficult or important.
● **How many great people can you think of?** List the children's responses on a chalkboard or newsprint.
● **What great things did these people accomplish?** Again, record your students' responses.
● **Why were these accomplishments great?** Allow children to share for a few minutes.

Today, we are going to learn about some of the great things that David accomplished.

There are a number of ways that you can teach today's story. Pick the option your kids will enjoy most and fits with your time and resources.

Have the children make aluminum foil sculptures illustrating different parts of today's story. Divide the group into three teams and give each team a roll of aluminum foil. Assign each team three pages from the *Picture Bible*; logical divisions are pages 292-294, 295-297, and 298-300. Have each team mold something out of its aluminum foil that illustrates its part of the story. (If your teams are large, have them mold several different items.) When the teams are finished, have each one appoint a storyteller to explain its sculpture and tell its part of the story. Storytellers should take turns in such a way that the entire story is told chronologically.

Option two is doing a dramatic

---

*A*nd this is my prayer: that your love may abound more and more in knowledge and depth of insight, so that you may be able to discern what is best and may be pure and blameless until the day of Christ, filled with the fruit of righteousness that comes through Jesus Christ—to the glory and praise of God.
—Philippians 1:9-11

reading of the story using children from class. You will need 11 readers for the following parts: Narrator, Abner, Joab, David, Ishbosheth (ish-BOW-shith), two traitors, two tribal leaders, Israelite soldier, and Jerusalem defender. If your group is small, have kids double on some of the short parts. Also, have the whole group read the crowd's responses to David's coronation.

Choose readers at the beginning of the session. Give them time to look at their parts during the Getting Started section of the session.

Option three is to make copies of the "Bible Spies" work sheets. Divide the group into pairs and assign each pair one or two pages of the story. Have children complete the work sheets and then share their spy reports with the rest of the group. You may want to display these reports on the bulletin board.

After kids have completed one or more of the above options, review and discuss the story.
● **What happened to David in this story?** (He was crowned king over Israel as well as Judah.)
● **What countries did David rule now that he was king?** (He ruled all of Judah and Israel.) Have a volunteer find these on the map.
● **What was the first thing that David did as king?** (He captured Jerusalem to be his capitol.) Have a volunteer find Jerusalem on the map. It lies between Judah and Israel, the old and new parts of David's kingdom. Explain that it made sense for David to choose Jerusalem because it was in the middle, so both halves of the country would accept it as the capitol.
● **Who do you think helped David become king and conquer Jerusalem?** (God)

● **Do you think God helps us accomplish great things today? Why or why not?**

If you have been using the time line, review the story by having children add the events from this week's story to the time line. The children may want to draw pictures of each event. If some don't like to draw, they could write captions for the pictures. Kids that don't like either of those two activities may want to be in charge of taping (or stapling) the pictures to the time line.

EXPLORING WORSHIP

Last week we learned about asking God to help others. Today, we are learning about asking God to help us accomplish great things. As we learned in our story, God helped David become king and capture Jerusalem. But accomplishing great things does not mean becoming the president or prime minister, at least not until we're older. The greatest thing we can accomplish is to obey God. What are some ways that you can obey God? (Be kind to brothers and sisters even when they're not kind. Tell a friend about Jesus. Obey parents.)

Again, review the PRAY acrostic with the children.

Praise
Repent
Asking
Yourself

Make sure that the children understand the meaning of all those big words. Remind them that this is a guide to help us when we pray to God. Point out that asking God to help us be obedient is one way we can pray for ourselves.

During a worship service the people pray several different times. Today, we are going to learn about what is often called the "pastoral prayer."
● **Do we have a pastoral prayer in our church worship service?**
● **During which part of the worship service does it occur?**
● **Who do you think prays the pastoral prayer?**

The pastoral prayer is different from the prayers of Invocation and Benediction that we pray in church, because the pastor is praying for different things.
● **What do you think the pastoral prayer is about?** Make a list of the children's responses on a chalkboard or newsprint. Here are some possible answers: He admits to God his sins and those of the people in the church. He prays for people who are sick, or sad, or traveling. He asks God to help the church people love God more. He asks God to help the people obey the Bible.

Children at this age are ready to pray. But many of them don't know how to go about it. They need someone to teach them, to get them started, to show them that there are many ways to pray. Spend a little time, at least, with the Picture

Childhood is real life, not merely preparation for real life. . . . We must learn to look at children and see full human beings.
—Editors, Religious Education

Prayers idea that follows immediately since this will be used in the Worshiping Together section.

PICTURE PRAYERS. These kind of prayers help us pray with our imaginations. Suppose, for example, that the children are praying for God's help to obey their parents. As they pray, they should develop mental pictures in which they see themselves obeying. These pictures should include specific actions like cleaning their rooms, helping with the dishes, or doing their homework.

WORSHIPING TOGETHER

The worship service is the main section of this session. It allows children to worship God in a way that is understandable and meaningful to them. It also helps them learn about corporate worship and prepares them for worshiping with the entire congregation as they grow older.

The aim for today's session is to help students realize that praying for others is a way of worshiping God. Use the order of worship printed in this book as a guide. The choice of hymns has been left up to you. You might want to choose hymns that talk about prayer and accomplishing great things for God. If you have songs about David, these would also work well. Here are some suggestions: from your hymnal you might sing "Joyful, Joyful, We Adore Thee"; two songs about prayer are "God Communication," page 22, and "And He Hears Me," page 24, in *Worship Time Music Book*.

Incorporate student leaders in the worship service. Children love to take center stage and lead the group. You may want to identify worship

roles that are similar to those used in your church such as a song leader. Choose children with strong abilities in the various areas such as a good singer to lead the hymns.

To help the children learn different ways of praying, different types of prayer are included in this unit for use during the prayer time. In this session, the children will use picture prayers.

RESPONDING PERSONALLY

End this session by giving children an opportunity to personalize what they have learned in worship. Be sure to give kids enough time to complete this activity in class. Try one of the following activities.

Have the children make a triptych (three-paneled picture) illustrating three things they can accomplish for God.

Distribute crayons and a piece of light-colored construction paper to each child. Have the children fold the paper in thirds horizontally. Remind the children that when we obey God we are accomplishing great things in His eyes. Next, have them think of three ways they could obey God, three things they could do to make God happy. When they have thought of three things, have them draw a picture of themselves doing those things. They should draw one picture on each section of their papers. If some of the children are having trouble thinking of three things, give them some examples of obedience: telling a friend about Jesus, helping with the dishes, being kind on the playground at school, telling the truth, etc.

Children might want to stand these triptychs somewhere in their

rooms at home to remind them that God wants their obedience and that He will help them obey if they ask Him. ■

IN WORSHIP
WE SEEK GOD'S HELP

1. Call to Worship—Psalm 108:3-5

2. Invocation—Dear God, we want You to be with us today because we love You and You love us. Help us to think about You while we worship together. In Jesus' name we pray. Amen.

3. Hymn

4. Our Statement of Faith—*Read it aloud or repeat it, phrase by phrase, after the leader.*

5. Scripture Reading—Read II Samuel 5:1-12.

6. Prayer—Dear Lord, we praise You because You are always willing to help us. We know that every day we do things that make You unhappy. Thank You that You have said You will forgive us.

We want to make You happy by the way we live. We want Your help to accomplish great things in our lives, things like _____.

During these few moments of silence, pray "Picture Prayers" about great things you want to accomplish for God.

We know that You answer our prayers. We know that Your answers are what's best for us. In Jesus' name we pray. Amen.

7. Hymn

8. Worship Talk—*Complete the sentences below with your own words and ideas.*

I. Read II Samuel 5:4, 7.
   A. In these verses the two things that David did during his life are _____.
   B. Two things that I would like to do are _____.

II. Read II Samuel 5:12.
   A. David knew that God helped him become king. I know that God helps me because _____.
   B. Two things that God has helped me with are _____.
   C. Sometimes, before we can do great things for God we need to learn how to do little things.
   D. Here are some things I can do for God. (Example: Obey my parents.)

9. Benediction—"The Lord bless you and keep you; the Lord make his face shine upon you and be gracious to you; the Lord turn his face toward you and give you peace" (Numbers 6:24-26). ■

PRAISING GOD'S GREATNESS

Journey into II Samuel 6—11; I Chronicles 13—16: David and his people praise the Lord in their new capitol (pp. 301-306).

Special Things You'll Need:
☐ Rhythm musical instruments made in Unit 3
☐ Lump of modeling clay for each child (Optional)
☐ Index cards with examples of celebrations (Optional)
☐ "Private Eye Clue Sheet," activity piece 7C from the back of this book (Optional)

GETTING STARTED

Use one of the following activities to help introduce today's session and to fill the time it takes for all your students to arrive. Allow the children an opportunity to get some of the wiggles out, so they can concentrate during the Bible story and worship time.

☐ Give each child a medium-sized lump of modeling clay. Have the children form the clay into the shape of something that makes them happy (a pet, favorite toy, sport, parent, friend, church, etc.). Allow time for children to explain their sculptures.

☐ Have the children roleplay different kinds of celebrations. Before the session, print the names of different celebrations on index cards. Some celebrations you might include are birthdays, weddings, Christmas, Easter, Thanksgiving, Independence Day, Valentine Day, etc. During the session, have a volunteer pick a card and then act out whatever celebration is listed on the card. Think through some ways to roleplay each card beforehand. That way, if some children have difficulty acting

out their cards, you will be able to whisper some suggestions to them. To make a transition to the lesson, you may want to end the game by picking an outgoing child to act out Sunday worship. (After all, it is a celebration.)

☐ Children can use this time to work on the unit-long project in *THE Idea Book*, "The Shepherd King."

EXPLORING THE BIBLE

To help kids gain a sense of the Bible's chronology, start today's story by reviewing last week's. If you have been using the Old Testament picture time line, it will aid in this review. Point to each picture or caption that refers to something in last week's story. Have a volunteer retell that portion of the story. If you have not been making a time line, use the review questions printed below.

● **What happened to David last week?** (He became king over all of Judah and Israel.) Have a volunteer find these areas on the map.

● **What city did David capture?** (Jerusalem)

● **What did he do with it once he captured it?** (He made it the capitol.)

Today, we're going to talk about celebrations.

● **What kinds of things do we celebrate?** Make a list of these. **Now, let's learn about a celebration that King David and his people had.**

In today's story, concentrate on the part where David brings the Ark to Jerusalem (pp. 301 and 302). First, distribute rhythm instruments to the children. If your number of instruments is limited, distribute them to the rowdiest children. By

giving them an appropriate chance to be rowdy, you're showing positive acceptance of them as individuals. Before the story, arrange signals with the children so that they will know when to start playing their instruments and when to stop. You could use verbal commands such as "play" and "stop" or gestures. Practice these signals a few times.

Read the narrator's parts on pages 301 and 302, and have volunteers read the parts of the boy, father, and David. Have groups of students read the parts of the people. When you read about the musicians bursting into song, signal the children to play their instruments for a few moments. (The children will love this chance to make noise. Make sure they don't get too carried away, though.) Have the entire group read the lines that begin, "Give unto the Lord . . ."

Review what has just taken place.
● **Why were the people celebrating?**
● **Why did bringing the ark to Jerusalem make the people happy?**
● **Why didn't David build a temple to God?**

Summarize the rest of today's story (pages 303-306) or give children a few minutes to read it themselves. Then discuss it using the questions printed below.
● **Who did David invite to the palace?**
● **Why did David invite him?**
● **Why was Mephibosheth afraid of David?** The children may not understand the reason for Mephibosheth's fear. Explain that when one king took the throne away from another king, he often killed everyone in the other king's family so that they wouldn't be able to steal the throne back.
● **Why couldn't David marry Bath-sheba?**

If you have been adding to the time line each week, have the children work on pictures and captions for that rather than answer the questions above. Once they have completed this week's section of the time line, use it to discuss today's story.

An optional way to present and discuss the story is to use the "Private Eye Clue Sheet." Make copies and hand them out to the children. Encourage students to read pages 301-306 in the *Picture Bible* before trying to complete the Private Eye sheet. When the children are finished, go over the sheet and discuss the story with them.

EXPLORING WORSHIP

In today's story we learned how David and his people praised God. Praising God for His greatness and goodness to us is one of the most important parts of prayer.

Write the PRAY acrostic on the chalkboard. Review each term with the children.

Praise
Repent
Asking
Yourself

Explain that praise means to tell God how wonderful He is.

One of the first things we should tell God is that He is wonderful. The acrostic can help us remember that praising God should come first when we pray.
● **God is very great. What are some great things that He has done?** List these on a chalkboard or newsprint. **God is also good. He loves us the way kind parents love their children.**
● **What are some good things that God has done for you?** List these on the chalkboard, too. If children are hesitant to share, get them started by giving personal examples.

Save these lists. You will use them again during the prayer time in the worship service.

Encourage the children to pay attention to the portions of prayer and worship that are devoted to praise. Help them to see that praising God is an important part of worship.

Try one of the following prayers. All of us need to learn that we can pray to God in many different ways.

ALPHABET PRAYERS—This kind of prayer has different variations. First, choose a basic topic. Praise is a good topic for today. Next, assign each child a letter of the alphabet. Have the children think of something that begins with their letter, something for which they want to praise God. The children can praise God for who He is and for things that He has done. Here are a few examples: Apples, Bibles, Church, Dad, etc. The children could pray these prayers in several ways. They could act out their words, draw pictures of them, or write letters to God about them. Pick one response for the children to use in prayer.

WALKING PRAYER—Take the children for a walk. As they walk,

For everything that was written in the past was written to teach us.
—Roman 15:4

133

encourage them to pray silently, praising God for His creation that they see around them. Help the children maintain prayerful silence and an attitude of praise. After the walk, discuss with the children what they saw and why it made them want to praise God. If you have time, pray together as a group. Encourage the children to share their reasons for praise.

DOODLE-FEELINGS PRAYER— Distribute paper and crayons or colored markers. Have children think of something good God has done for them or an example of God's greatness. While they are thinking about this good and great act of God, the children should doodle how they feel. Encourage them to pick colors that reflect their feelings.

Doodle prayers are especially helpful for children that are oriented more toward the visual than the verbal. They also help children realize that God understands colors and pictures just as well as He understands words.

WORSHIPING TOGETHER

Today's worship focuses on praising God. During the prayer session, the prayer leader will complete statements praising God for His great deeds and for His acts of goodness. The worshipers will respond to each statement. Half will say "Amen," the other half will say, "Praise the Lord." Just like the Israelites did when the ark was brought to Jerusalem (I Chr. 16:36). The groups will take turns responding. To complete the praise statements, the prayer leader will refer to the two lists made during the Exploring Worship section of the session. This way of praying is fairly simple, but may seem confusing at first. If the prayer leader is a student, he or she will probably need some help explaining and organizing the prayer time. Make as smooth a transition to the prayer time as possible so the reverence and flow of the worship service is not broken.

Select music that praises God's greatness or speaks of prayer. From your hymnal you might sing "To God Be the Glory"; "God Is Great," page 6, and "Talking with God," page 21, from *Worship Time Music Book*, can also be used.

RESPONDING PERSONALLY

During the remainder of the session, allow the children to make a personal response to what they have learned today. From the activities printed below, choose one that fits with your resources and time.

☐ Have children write a short psalm of praise to God. Children this age often need help to get started writing. Explain the following model to them. Children will write a four-line psalm. The first line will be "Everybody, praise the Lord!" The last line will be "Praise the Lord!" In the second line, they should write a reason to praise God. In the third line, they should write the same reason using different words. Write the following example on a chalkboard or newsprint so that the children will have a model for their own psalms.
Everybody, praise the Lord!
God hears our prayers.
He listens when we talk to Him.
Praise the Lord!
Have volunteers read their praise psalms to the rest of the group. Children should put their psalms into their worship journey notebooks.

☐ Make praise buttons. Have the children draw a two-inch picture of something for which they want to praise God or something that helps them remember to praise God. Have the children cut out their pictures in the shape of a circle for a traditional button. They also could cut them in the shape of a square, a triangle, or a geometric shape of their own design. After they cut out their pictures, have them tape or pin the buttons to their blouses or shirts. ■

IN WORSHIP
WE PRAISE GOD'S GREATNESS

1. Call to Worship—Psalm 150:1, 2, 6

2. Invocation—Dear Lord, You are great and good. Please help us as we worship You. We are thankful that we can worship together today. Teach us how to praise You. In Jesus' name we pray. Amen.

3. Hymn

4. Our Statement of Faith—*Recite our church's statement of faith together.*

5. Scripture Reading—I Chronicles 15:27, 28; 16:7-13, 23-26

6. Prayer—Dear God, We praise You . . . *(Complete this statement with an item from one of the lists you made. If you have time, complete a statement using each item on the lists.)*
   In Jesus' name we pray. Amen.

7. Hymn

8. Student Worship Talk—*Complete the sentences below with your own words and ideas.*

I. Read I Chronicles 16:12.
   A. David tells his people to remember the wonderful things that God had done, things like saving the Ark from the Philistines.
   B. Two ways that God has been good to me are

      _____.

II. Read I Chronicles 16:23.
   A. David is telling us to sing praises to God. He wrote many songs to God. We call them psalms.
   B. One of my favorite songs of praise is _____.

III. Read I Chronicles 15:28.
   A. One way that David and his people praised God was

      _____.

   B. Two ways I can praise God are _____.

9. Benediction—May the Lord do many good and wonderful things in your life. May He help you to praise Him every day for His greatness. ■

**SESSION 32
WORSHIP AIM:**

SEEKING GOD'S FORGIVENESS

Journey into II Samuel 11—13: David arranges for Uriah's death and then confesses his sin (pp. 307-313).

Special Things You'll Need:
☐ Paper lunch bags
☐ Paper clips (regular size)
☐ Copies of the "Bible Spies" work sheet, activity piece 7A from the back of this book (Optional)
☐ Large manila envelope (Optional)
☐ Puppet stage, page 19 in *THE Idea Book* (Optional)

GETTING STARTED

☐ Start today's session by having the children make puppets that they can use to help tell today's story. See *THE Idea Book*, page 18 for instructions. The children will need to make at least five puppets for this session's story: David, Joab, Uriah, Nathan, a messenger. They could also make a Bathsheba for the wedding scene. The children should decorate the puppets according to who they are and what they do. Hats made from construction paper are one good way to decorate. For example, they could make a crown for David, or a helmet for General Joab.

You will need several volunteers to work the puppets and speak their parts. You may want to read the narrative parts (in the square boxes) yourself, or call on one or more good readers to read those parts. If your group is large, you may want to have the children make more puppets than you can actually use during today's story time. Children could use these puppets to tell the story to their parents or even start a neighborhood puppet show. If you have time, the children could play the story twice using a different set of puppets each time. You may also want to have several different children read David's parts. You could assign a few pages to each. Give these volunteer readers some time to look over their parts.

☐ Distribute paper and crayons or colored markers. Instruct the children to think of a time when they did something wrong and knew that it was wrong. Ask them how they felt at the time, but don't have them answer out loud. Have them draw pictures of themselves showing how they felt. If you have time, allow a few volunteers to share their pictures and feelings.

☐ Write a song about prayer using a well-known tune. Pick a tune that most of the children will know ("Jesus Loves Me," "London Bridge Is Falling Down," etc.). Have them think back over some of the things they have learned about prayer in this unit and then write lyrics about it. See if you can come up with at least one verse and maybe a chorus.

☐ Children can use this time to work on the unit-long project in *THE Idea Book*, "The Shepherd King."

EXPLORING THE BIBLE

In today's session we want students to see the importance of seeking God's forgiveness for wrong things they have done. The story of David helps do this. Introduce the story this way.

● **Have you ever done something wrong in order to get something you wanted but weren't supposed to have?** Children may not feel comfortable telling about such an event. Be prepared with a personal example, preferably from when you were the children's age. Remember that at this age such wrong actions might include taking something from a sibling without his or her permission, or going somewhere that was off limits.

Today, we're going to learn about a time when David did something wrong to get something that he wasn't supposed to have.

Have the volunteers read and act out the story using their puppets and a puppet stage (optional). You may want to have them kneel by a table and use the tabletop for a stage. After the story, review and discuss it with the children. You can review by adding to the time line, or you may want to use the questions that follow.

Today's story may raise many difficult questions. Be sensitive to any children in your group who come from broken homes. The story of David and Bathsheba may ring painfully true to their own situations. Even if none of your children are from broken homes, they probably know kids who are. Be honest with the children. They need to see that David's actions were wrong. They need to see that if their parents divorced, then some of their actions were probably wrong just as David's were. But do not dwell on the negative. The point of today's lesson is that God still loved David even though he sinned, and that God forgave David. (If questions about divorce do not come up, don't raise them.)

- What did David tell Joab to do?
- Why did David want Uriah killed?
- What did David do after Uriah was killed?

Nathan told David a story about a rich man and a poor man.
- Who was the rich man?

- Who was the poor man?
- What did David realize as Nathan told him the story?
- How do you think David felt when he realized that he'd sinned against God?
- What did David do when he realized his sin?
- Did God forgive David? How do you know?

When we sin against God, He doesn't send a prophet like Nathan to show us we've sinned.
- How does God help us realize when we've done something wrong? List responses on a chalkboard or newsprint. Help the children see that God uses the Bible and sometimes other people to show us our sins.
- When we sin, what can we do about it?

As an alternative to using puppets, you may want to use one of the story ideas which follow.

☐ Make copies of "Bible Spies" work sheet. Divide the group into pairs and assign each pair two or three pages of the story. Have children complete their work sheets and share their spy reports with the rest of the group. Discuss the story using the questions printed above. You may want to display the reports on the bulletin board.

☐ Read the story to the children while they follow along in the *Picture Bible*. Then have the children draw pictures of their favorite parts of the story. Discuss the story using the questions printed above. Give some time for volunteers to explain their pictures. Why not put the pictures on the bulletin board?

EXPLORING WORSHIP

In today's story, we learned how David asked God to forgive him for his sins. Asking for forgiveness is an important part of prayer.

Review the PRAY acrostic with the children.

Praise
Repent
Asking
Yourself

Let students explain the meaning of repent. We want them to know it involves admitting we have done something wrong. When we pray, we need to tell God about wrong things we have done—to confess. Then we need to ask God for help to not do those things.

Suppose you were going to a friend's house to play, but you and your friend had had a fight the day before.
- What's one of the first things you should do when you get there? (Apologize to the friend and ask for his or her forgiveness—make up.) That is what repentance is like. When we do bad things, it makes God sad. That's why when we pray we need to tell God we've done something wrong. It's like making up with God. And God does forgive us because He loves us.

Admitting to God that we have sinned is part of our prayer in worship.

*B*ring up a child with the information in ways he can grasp it at each stage of his development, and when he is grown he will not depart from the way.
—Franz Delitzsch

To help the children better understand repentance and forgiveness, have them make prayer chains. Distribute several strips of construction paper and crayons or colored markers. Instruct the children to try to think of several things for which they need forgiveness. Have them write these on the strips of paper, one item per strip. (If some of the children don't enjoy writing, they could draw stick figure pictures instead.) Make sure they keep what they create private. Next, the children should take the strips of paper and make a paper chain. They can use tape or glue to fasten the loops. Make sure that they keep the writing on the inside of the loop so no one can read it but themselves.

● **How are sins like a chain?** If the children are having trouble with this concept, help them see that when sin makes us feel bad or guilty it weighs us down like a heavy chain would.

● **How can we get rid of this heavy chain of bad things?** (We can ask God to forgive us and He will.)

The children should save these chains, since they will use them during the worship service.

If you have time, try one of these other ways of praying.

☐ Pray the Psalms. Explain to the children that in many ways the Psalms are like prayers as well as songs. Praying written prayers, such as the Psalms, can be a very good way of praying. Point out that a person wouldn't want to pray written prayers all the time. The prayers might lose their meaning if someone did that.

☐ Letter prayers. Have the children work together to write a letter to God. You can act as secretary or have a student volunteer do it. In addition to the letter from the whole group, have the children include their own private messages. Hand out sheets of paper, pencils, and crayons or colored markers. The children could write their own letters, poems, or stories, or draw pictures and give these to God. Collect all of these creative prayers and put them in a large manila envelope addressed to God. Children will feel free to express themselves honestly if you promise not to look at what they made. Point out that even though you can't actually mail the letter prayers to God, He knows what they wrote and drew. He hears their prayers.

WORSHIPING TOGETHER

Since this lesson is about asking God for forgiveness, make sure that this topic is emphasized in each part of In Worship.

The children will need the prayer chains they made in the Exploring Worship section. To make the prayer time meaningful for the children explain in advance how they will use the prayer chains.

You will want to be sure to select songs that relate to today's theme. You might begin with a hymn of praise, like "Praise Ye, the Triune God." Appropriate songs from *Worship Time Music Book* are "You Know, Lord," page 19, and "Lord, I'm Crying," page 32.

RESPONDING PERSONALLY

To help students personalize the aim of this session, give paper clips to each student. Have them make a wire sculpture that shows how a person feels when he or she has been forgiven. By using several paper clips they can shape an object that is meaningful to them, a person expressing happiness or gratitude, or a shape that is creatively free or joyful. They might even want to form a simple word by bending the wires.

Let students mount their wire sculpture, if they wish, on construction paper to put on the bulletin board. Or, sculptures may be taken home as a reminder to seek God's forgiveness when they do things that displease Him. ■

IN WORSHIP
WE SEEK GOD'S FORGIVENESS

1. Call to Worship—Isaiah 55:6, 7

2. Invocation—Dear God, we praise You because You are a forgiving God. We admit that we displease You many times. Please forgive us. Help us now to worship You. In Jesus' name, we pray. Amen.

3. Hymn

4. Our Statement of Faith—*Use our church's statement of faith.*

5. Scripture Reading—II Samuel 12:7-13

6. Prayer—Dear God, we praise You that You love us and care about us. We confess that we sin every day, that we do many things that make You unhappy. We believe that You forgive us for our sins.

(Silently ask God to forgive you for the sins that you wrote on your prayer chain.)

We thank You, God, that You forgive our sins, that You take away the guilt and bad feelings that weigh on us like a heavy chain.

(Break your chain as a way of showing how God takes away sin.)

Help us to be more obedient to You. In Jesus' name, we pray. Amen.

(Collect remains of chains and throw them away.)

7. Hymn

8. Student Worship Talk—*Complete the following sentences with your own words and ideas.*

I. Read II Samuel 12:9.
  A. The thing David did that was wrong was _____.
  B. Two wrongs things that I have done are _____.

II. Read II Samuel 12:1, 2.
  A. God showed David his sin by _____.
  B. One way God shows me my sin is _____.

III. Read II Samuel 12:13.
  A. When David admitted that he had sinned, God

    _____.
  B. When I sin, I can _____.
  C. I know that God forgives me because _____.

9. Benediction—May God help us to be seek His forgiveness for our sins. And may we know He will forgive us for them. ∎

SESSION 33
WORSHIP AIM:

DEALING WITH PROBLEMS

Your students are in the midst of a yearlong adventure that should help them grow in their appreciation of God's greatness and thus in their ability to worship Him. This journey moves straight through the Old Testament and at the same time through the various parts of your church's order of worship. But the purpose is more than sightseeing to learn about God and worship. We want your students to be excited participants, caught up in the drama of God's unfolding story and in the joy of worshiping Him.

Last month, Unit 7 focused on prayer. Through the stories of David, the students saw the need to pray to God for guidance, for help, and for forgiveness.

In Unit 8 our Old Testament journey continues with stories of David and his family. The students will see the ways that David learned from God. They will see how he dealt with problems, how he knew right from wrong, and how he got along with others.

In the worship time this month, there is a special emphasis on the sermon and the part it plays in helping us learn from God today. In order to help the students understand the purposes of the sermon, student activities in the Exploring Worship section will let the students actually prepare messages similar to a pastor's sermons. ■

Journey into II Samuel 12:26—15:12: David deals with the rebellion of his son (pp. 314-324).

Special Things You'll Need:
- [ ] Blindfolds
- [ ] Overhead projector
- [ ] Copies of "Tillie's Terrible Troubles," activity piece 8A in the back of this book
- [ ] Postcards
- [ ] Stickers

GETTING STARTED

These introductory activities should productively fill the time it takes for all of your students to arrive and settle down. Choose one or more to do with your group.

- [ ] Plan a faith walk for the students. In a faith walk, one person leads another blindfolded person through a course you've set up. The blindfolded person must trust the first person to lead them around the room, through a maze of chairs, or through some other activity which you have planned. Let each student have a chance to be blindfolded and to lead. This activity will help to reinforce for the children the idea that sometimes they need to be guided, and that ultimately they need to receive their guidance from God. If they don't listen to their friend in this activity, they will stumble or run into something.
- [ ] Have the students make a list of problems that they have today. This can be done on an overhead projector, newsprint, or on individual sheets of paper. The information you get about the students' problems will help you to apply the Bible lesson to real situations in their lives. It will also help to show the students their

own need for the lesson. We all need help in dealing with problems. This list may be used in the Responding Personally section of today's lesson.

EXPLORING THE BIBLE

The previous unit explored David's rise from a young man in Saul's court to king of Israel. Your students also learned of David's fall into sin and need for God's forgiveness. If time permits today, take time to review the stories of David's life. If your students have *Picture Bibles*, have them review pages 269-313. As a group, make a list of the problems David has faced so far.

David is about to face one of the worst problems yet. Have students read pages 314-324 of the *Picture Bible*.

In this passage, we see that David had a problem with one of his sons, Absalom. Family problems are not new. All families have times that are difficult.

Have the students relate some problems that families might face. (Do not ask them to tell problems that their families face. This could be embarrassing for some or cause some to break confidentialities.) Write their responses on newsprint or an overhead projector. Some problems that may be raised are: divorce, alcohol, lying, jealousy, greed, playing favorites by parents, etc.
- **How did David react when he had a problem?**
- **How do you think he felt when his son did wrong things to hurt him?**
- **What was his attitude towards Absalom?**
- **How would you have reacted if you were David? Would you have**

been able to forgive Absalom? Why or why not?

David knew that God would want him to love and forgive his son. **What do you think might have happened when David saw Absalom if David had not listened to what God said about forgiving?** If time permits, you may wish to have one group of students roleplay the angry way David could have reacted to Absalom. A second group of students could then roleplay what actually happened. Emphasize the difference that it makes when we listen to what God says.

EXPLORING WORSHIP

God's Word can help us to deal with problems, too, but it can't help us unless we know what it says. Sometimes we need to help each other by reminding one another what God's Word says about problems that we have.

Hand out copies of "Tillie's Terrible Troubles." This sheet describes some of Tillie's problems at home. Also listed on the sheet are Bible references which will help the students to suggest solutions for Tillie's problems. The students should write letters to Tillie, explaining how God's Word can help her with her problems. They will need to refer to regular Bibles in order to complete this activity. Encourage them to use Scripture and to be as specific as possible because sometimes Tillie has a hard time understanding. When the students have had time to finish their letters, have several students read their letters to the class. If you have students who are uncomfortable with writing, you may let them draw their advice for Tillie.

● **Do you think Tillie will be better off if she listens to our advice?**
● **What will happen if she doesn't listen?**

You have just done the same thing that a pastor does when he writes a sermon. He thinks about the problems that his congregation has, and he tells the people what God's Word has to say about them. If we listen, the sermon will help us to live like God wants us to live. It can help us with our problems.

Discuss with the children the importance of the sermon in the worship service. The children need to understand that God's Word is important in solving problems and that listening to the sermons that our pastors preach is one way that we can know what God says about those problems.

The children also need to realize that pastors are not the only people who are chosen by God to share what is in His Word. God uses a number of people within the church to share His message. These people may be elders, deacons, teachers, or lay people in the congregation.

WORSHIPING TOGETHER

In keeping with the worship aim—to receive God's guidance for problems that trouble us—you may want to choose hymns that focus on God being there when we face trials or on God's faithfulness. You might consider using "Great Is Thy Faithfulness" from your hymnal. From *Worship Time Music Book* you could have students sing "Lead On, Lord," page 10, and "The Lord Is My Shepherd," page 28.

RESPONDING PERSONALLY

To conclude this session, give the children an opportunity to personalize what they have gained from the worship experience.

☐ If your students made a list of their problems at the beginning of today's lesson, have them refer back to it now. If not, have them think for a minute of one problem that they are facing. Hand out blank postcards. Instruct the students to write a note addressed to themselves. Encourage them to think of what God would tell them about the problems they mentioned if He were to send them a

A creative teacher is willing to break out of the mold and risk failure because he or she believes that God can use a new idea.
—Marlene LeFever

141

postcard. You may help them find
Bible verses that speak to the issues
they are struggling with. Some
helpful verses for children are
Proverbs 3:5; I John 1:9; I Peter 5:7;
Jeremiah 33:3; and Philippians 4:13.

The finished postcard might read,
"Dear Janie, I am sorry that you are
so scared about taking spelling tests.
When you are scared, let Me take
care of it, because I care for you"
(I Peter 5: 7). When the students
have finished, let them choose
stickers to use in the place of stamps.
They can then take their postcards
home as a reminder that God's Word
speaks to them about their problems.
☐ Have your students make and
decorate cards for their parents. The
story of David and Absalom addresses
issues which students face in their
homes every day. Perhaps some of
your students will want to make cards
which say, "I'm sorry" for something
which they have done. While they
are making these cards for their
parents, let them discuss how things
might have been different if Absalom
had learned to say that he was
sorry. ■

WE RECEIVE GOD'S HELP WITH PROBLEMS

1. Call to Worship—Psalm 37:1, 7

2. Invocation—Dear Lord, thank You for allowing us to be here to worship You. We are grateful for this time to sing and speak our praise of You. Help us to remember the important things we hear today. In Jesus' name we pray. Amen.

3. Hymn

4. Our Statement of Faith—*Recite this together.*

5. Scripture Reading—Psalm 25:1-5

6. Prayer—*Complete the following sentences:*

Dear God, we praise You for _____.

We know, Father, that sometimes we have problems in our lives and that You help us by _____.

Help us to try to solve the problems we face. We also ask You to be with the people who are sick or in special need. Please help them, Father.

Thank You for hearing our prayers and for answering them. In Jesus' name we pray. Amen.

7. Hymn

8. Student Worship Talk—*Complete the following sentences.*
  Read II Samuel 13:28, 29.

  A. David had a problem with his son Absalom. Absalom killed his brother Amnon, and he even tried to take his father's kingdom away.

  B. David was sad because his son, Absalom, killed another son, Amnon. But David did not try to get back at Absalom because _____.

  C. David showed he was willing to let God solve his problems because David forgave his son, Absalom. One way that we can let God solve our problems is by _____.

  D. God does not want us to solve our problems by fighting and arguing, but by _____.

  E. We should be like David and ask God to help us with our problems.

  F. We should never be like Absalom. Absalom hated his brother and wanted his father's kingdom. Absalom's problems could have been solved if _____.

9. Benediction—Help us, Lord, when we have a problem in our lives. We want You to take charge of it and give us the answer to the problem. Thank You for Your Word that helps us to know Your will. In Jesus' name. Amen. ∎

**SESSION 34
WORSHIP AIM:**

Making Right Choices

**Journey into II Samuel 15—24;
I Kings 1:** Absalom's wrong choices cause many problems (pp. 325-336).

Special Things You'll Need:
☐ Magazines or newspapers
☐ Copies of true/false questions (found in the Exploring the Bible section of this lesson)
☐ Puppets
☐ Copies of script (found in the Exploring Worship section of this lesson)

GETTING STARTED

These introductory activities should productively fill the time it takes for all of your students to arrive and settle down. Choose one or more to do with your group. You also might ask several students, as you converse with them, what they enjoy most about children's church, what they have learned, or what they would like to do differently.

☐ Have the children form small teams and play a game called "20 Questions." Choose a Bible character from a previous week's session. The children must then guess who the character is by asking no more than 20 "yes" or "no" questions. The team that is first to name the Bible character wins. You should be prepared with a list of characters from previous lessons for the students to guess.

☐ Bring magazines and newspapers to the room and let the children make a collage of right choices and a collage of wrong choices. Discuss their choices. Explore any comments that will be covered in greater detail in this lesson.

EXPLORING THE BIBLE

Making right choices can be very difficult for each of us. Some choices are easy; others are very difficult.

Discuss making choices with students. By listening to their responses, we can learn what our students are thinking about and struggling with.

● **What are some easy choices you make everyday—choices when you know what is right?**
● **What choices are hard for kids your age to make?**
● **What makes some choices hard?**
Today we're looking at the story of a man who made wrong choices to see what we can learn. We are going to learn about David's son Absalom. Absalom is trying to steal the kingship away from his father. As we read the story, see if you can decide what choices of Absalom's are right or wrong. Today's worship centers around pages 325-336 in the *Picture Bible*. Read that passage to the children or let them read it to you.

Photocopy the questions below, pair the children, and let them answer the questions together.

TRUE or FALSE
1. David wanted to fight his son.
2. Absalom was about to attack Jerusalem.
3. David escaped from Jerusalem.
4. God's holy ark went with David.
5. As time went on, more and more people left David.
6. David sent Hushai to confuse Absalom.
7. David attacked Jerusalem.
8. David did not go with the army to fight Asbsalom.
9. David told General Joab to deal kindly with Absalom.

10. Joab returned Absalom to David unharmed.

When the students have finished this activity, give them a chance to share their answers.

Both David and Absalom had to make important choices in their lives. All of us do. They had to decide on choosing what was right or what was wrong. Their choices affected not only themselves, but also their families, friends, and the whole kingdom of Israel. The choices we make probably do not have an effect on our nation, but they may have an effect on our families and our friends.

Write David's name on one side of a chalkboard or newsprint and Absalom's name on the other. Have the children first tell of some right choices these men made and then some wrong choices they made. Then, for the wrong choices, ask the children what the right choice would have been.

Today we see that Absalom made wrong choices because he listened to bad advice.
● **Whose advice did he listen to? He listened to advice he wanted to hear. He did not realize that David had sent Hushai to give Absalom bad advice so that David and his followers could get away.**

EXPLORING WORSHIP

Absalom listened to bad advice, and he ended up making bad choices. Because David listened to good advice from God's messengers, he was able to make the right choices for himself and his family.
● **What are some ways God sends us good advice today?** If the children do not mention the advice that

comes in the pastor's sermon, ask them why the sermon might be considered good advice. **The sermon is an important part of our worship time. It is God's message coming to us by means of the pastor or other people who speak to us.**

Discuss with the children the importance of continually hearing God's Word proclaimed, and how it can make a real impact on the lives of the children and their friends. Then ask them for reasons why they feel that sermons are important (help for knowing right from wrong, making good choices, and dealing with problems).
● **What would you do in the following situation if you were Bill?** Use puppets or children to present this short drama.

Pete: Bill, what are you doing?
Bill: I'm listening to the sermon.
Pete: Will you hand me that pencil?
Bill: Please, be quiet.
Pete: Just hand me the pencil, okay!
Bill: Here, take it.
Pete: Hand me that paper.
Bill: Pay attention to the sermon.
Pete: Why should I do that? It's just for adults not for kids.
Bill: The sermon is for everyone . . . now listen.

Pete: Are you going to hand me that paper?
Bill: Pete, what am I going to do with you?
Pete: How about giving me that paper.
Bill: Oh, Pete!

● **What right choice was Bill making?**
● **What difference might this choice make in his life? In the life of his family?**
● **What would you do if you were Bill?**
● **How could you get Pete to be quiet?**
● **What would you say to him after the worship service?**
● **What are some of the choices you make when you are in the adult worship service?**

Sermons are for everyone. They help us to know God's Word in order that we can make right choices.

WORSHIPING TOGETHER

Today's worship emphasis is on the sermon. Your students have been learning that sermons are important because they help us to deal with

Children looking into our eyes do indeed want to know whether we are in there.
—John Holt

145

problems and to know the difference between right and wrong. Encourage them to listen carefully to the student worship talk leader today.

It is not as easy to select songs that fit this worship theme as other weeks. Consider using "A Wonderful World," page 7, and "Be Very Careful," page 29, from *Worship Time Music Book*. The familiar hymn, "Trust and Obey," also is appropriate.

RESPONDING PERSONALLY

To conclude this session, give the children an opportunity to personalize what they have gained from this worship experience. Choose one or both activities for this section of the lesson.

☐ Have some examples of "Dear Abby" letters clipped from a newspaper. Explain to the children that people write in asking Abby for advice. Encourage the children to write similar letters to the teacher or pastor. Give the children envelopes and let them deliver the letters. Answer those that are addressed to you and encourage other church leaders to do the same.

☐ Have the children write thank-you notes or draw pictures for the pastor or other teachers. These notes or drawings should tell how their advice has helped the children. Encourage the children to present these gifts of thanks today to the people who have given them advice from God's Word. ■

IN WORSHIP
WE MAKE RIGHT CHOICES

1. Call to Worship—Proverbs 2:6

2. Invocation—Dear God, we praise You today for all the things we have. We thank You for this church and that we can come here and worship You. Lord, today we ask for wisdom to know right from wrong. In Jesus' name. Amen.

3. Hymn

4. Our Statement of Faith—*Read our church's statement of faith aloud together.*

5. Scripture Reading—II Samuel 15:1-12

6. Prayer—*Complete the following sentences:*
Lord, We thank You for . . .
Today, we pray for the people who are ill in our congregation *(pray for specific people if you wish)*.
Help us, Father, to gain wisdom from You.
In Jesus' name. Amen.

7. Hymn

8. Student Worship Talk—*Complete the following sentences with your own words and ideas.*
   Read Psalm 119:9-11.
   A. These verses say that God's Word will help us make choices that will keep us pure. The Bible is God's good advice for us.
   B. It is important to listen to good advice. One time when I listened to bad advice _____.
   C. Some of the ways that we can know God's good advice are _____.
   D. Some of the people that tell us what God's Word says are _____.
   E. Two important things I have learned from the good advice in sermons are _____.
   F. Psalm 119:11 tells us the reason that we should hide God's Word in our hearts. God's good advice helps us not to _____.

9. Benediction—Lord, give us wisdom to make right choices. May we make choices that please You. ■

SESSION 35
WORSHIP AIM:

RECEIVING GOD'S WISDOM

*A*nd the Lord said: ". . . this people draw near with their mouth and honor me with their lips, while their hearts are far from me, and their fear of me is a commandment of men learned by rote. (Emphasis ours) —Isaiah 29:13 (RSV)

Journey into I Kings 1—2: God gives wisdom to Solomon to lead Israel as the new king (pp. 337-344).

Special Things You'll Need:
☐ Materials for "Wise Old Owl" puppet, page 75 of *THE Idea Book*
☐ "Wise Is Right" game show, page 93 in *THE Idea Book*
☐ Copies of antiphonal reading printed in this lesson
☐ Puppet, any kind
☐ Index card or report card
☐ "Sample Shape Prayer," activity piece 8B in the back of this book
☐ Supplies for "Wise Wooly Owl," page 76 in *THE Idea Book*
☐ Small prizes (Optional)

GETTING STARTED

These introductory activities should help you productively fill the time it takes for all of your children to arrive and settle down. Choose one or more to do with the group. As students involve themselves, talk to them about their hobbies. Are they in any clubs? Do they collect anything? Do they play on a team? Do they take lessons of any kind? You will also want to share with them special interests that you have.
☐ Create a wise old owl puppet. Students who arrive early may help with this project by cutting out eyes, ears, and feathers from construction paper. You may use the puppet to introduce today's story about the wisdom of Solomon.
☐ When most of the students have assembled, call them together for a mock game show, "The Wise Is Right."

EXPLORING THE BIBLE

● What is wisdom?
● Is there a difference between being smart and being wise? If so, what is it? See if children know the answer to these questions. Use the wise old owl puppet from the Getting Started activity to explain what wisdom is. Wisdom is more than just knowing a lot of facts; it is knowing how to do what is right. People who have wisdom often share it with other people. One gets wisdom by listening carefully to the advice of wise people. Use your creativity to explain this concept to the students with the puppet. You may wish to interview the puppet by asking him questions such as, "How did you get to be wise?" or "Do you have to be old to be wise?"

Have students name people that they think are wise and why they consider them wise. These could be people in history, current events, or people they know. **King David was a wise man. We have been learning about his life for several weeks now. In today's story, King David was growing weaker each day and was about to die. He had not announced who would be the new king. However, one of his sons, Adonijah (AD-oh-NY-juh), was plotting to be king even before David died. Let's see who got to be king.**

Tell the children the story on pages 337-341 in the *Picture Bible* or let them read it from their own copies.

David had lived a long time. He had learned God's wisdom. He knew it was best to live for God. God had taken care of his needs. David wrote about this in Psalm 23. Let's read it together. Hand out copies of the antiphonal reading printed below.

Divide the class into two groups and read the psalm together.

Group 1. The Lord is my Shepherd;
Group 2. I shall not want.
    1. He makes me to lie down in green pastures;
    2. He leads me beside the still waters.
    1. He restores my soul;
    2. He leads me in the paths of righteousness
  All For His name's sake.
    1. Yea, though I walk
    2. Through the valley of the shadow of death,
    1. I will fear no evil;
    2. For thou art with me;
    1. Thy rod
    2. And Thy staff
    1. They comfort me.
    2. Thou preparest a table before me in the presence of mine enemies
    1. Thou anointest my head with oil.
    2. My cup runneth over.
    1. Surely goodness and mercy
    2. Shall follow me all the days of my life;
  All: And I will dwell in the house of the Lord forever.

● **Was Adonijah wise like his father David?**

Have the students list the unwise things that Adonijah did (stealing the kingship, lying about being sorry, thinking he knew best).

● **Was Solomon wise? What made him wise?**

Read the rest of today's story through page 344. Have students list things that made Solomon wise (listening to David's advice, obeying God, asking God for wisdom). Discuss good things that happened because he had God's wisdom.

The wisdom that God gave Solomon helped him a great deal in making his treaties with neighboring countries and in dealing with his own people. God helped Solomon by giving him the wisdom to know what to do, and God can do that for us, too. We must ask for wisdom.

EXPLORING WORSHIP

Today our lesson focuses on the sermon. We want the students to understand that one purpose of the sermon is to pass on God's wisdom. To help students understand how the pastor does this, they will share their own wisdom or advice with a puppet.

Unless you have a helper who is able to do impromptu puppet skits, you may wish to practice a basic outline for this skit early in the week. Only one puppet is needed. If you do not have puppets, a simple paper bag or sock puppet can be made easily for this skit. The puppet, name her Jackie (or name him Jack), in this skit is beginning school for the first time. She is afraid to ask questions, but she doesn't understand what the teacher is talking about, so she keeps daydreaming or getting in trouble for talking. Now she is getting bad grades. She is in the process of trying to hide her report card from her mother when your students meet her, and she is embarrassed and startled at being caught in the act. Begin a conversation with the puppet and let the children share wisdom to help in her situation. Spend ten to fifteen minutes on this activity. Let as many students as possible share some wise advice with the puppet.

You were able to give the puppet wise advice because you have already started school. You have learned that it is okay to ask questions and that it is important to listen well. You just shared your wisdom about starting school with the puppet.

● Do you think she will listen to what you had to say?
● What will happen if she does?
● What will happen if she doesn't?

In the sermon, the pastor gives us advice like you just gave the puppet. He tells us what he has learned about how to live for Jesus. It is just as important for us to listen well to the sermon as it was for the puppet to listen to your advice. Through the sermon we learn God's wisdom. If we daydream or talk during the sermon, we will miss the advice that we need to hear.

The younger a child, the more his learning involves touching, seeing, feeling, playing in the physical environment.
—Jean Piaget

WORSHIPING TOGETHER

Today as you come to the worship time, encourage the students to listen well to the sermon. Tell them ahead of time that you will discuss it afterwards. You may wish to give them a specific question, so that they can listen for the answer. For example:

● **In James 1:5, what are we told to do if we want to have God's wisdom?**

You will want to select hymns and songs to sing during In Worship that keep with the theme of receiving God's wisdom. A hymn of praise you might want to start with could be "Praise to the Lord, the Almighty." Songs from *Worship Time Music Book* that would be appropriate and "Psalm 100," page 5, and "Lord, I Am Calling," page 23.

RESPONDING PERSONALLY

Before moving into one of the final activities suggested here, take time to review with the children today's worship talk. What did they learn? Do they have any questions?

Give your students a chance to respond to today's lesson on God's wisdom by making one of the following crafts.

☐ Have your students ask God for wisdom by writing shape poetry. This poem could be a prayer written in the shape of something for which the students need wisdom. The children may wish to copy the money shape or to think of their own shape idea. Encourage them to write their own prayer poem instead of copying the sample.

☐ If you have more time for a craft project, your students may wish to

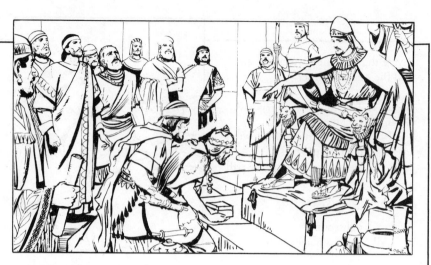

make Wise Wooly Owls. Have students select a Proverb written by King Solomon and write it on the bottom of the craft. ■

150

IN WORSHIP
WE RECEIVE GOD'S WISDOM

1. Call to Worship—Come, Christians! Come together and hear the wisdom of our great God.

2. Invocation—Father, You have given us many things. We have food, clothes, and many other blessings. We thank You, Father, for those things. But, Father, we also thank You for gifts we cannot see like Your Holy Spirit and the wisdom that You give us. In Jesus' name. Amen.

3. Hymn

4. Our Statement of Faith—*Read this aloud together.*

5. Scripture Reading—I Kings 2:1-4; 4:29

6. Prayer—*Complete the following sentences.*

Dear Lord, today we thank You for _____.

We also thank You for helping the sick people of our church. Some people today who need Your help are _____.

Lord, help us to look to You for wisdom. In Jesus' name. Amen.

7. Hymn

8. Student Worship Talk—*Complete the sentences below with your own words and ideas.*

   I. Read I Kings 2:1-4.

     A. David is about to die. He has learned that his son, Adonijah, is trying to become king. David had promised the kingdom to Solomon, the son of his wife, Bathsheba.

     B. Adonijah was not wise. He was disobedient. One unwise thing that he did was _____.

     C. David knew that Solomon would be a better king. He called Solomon to his side and told him _____.

  II. Read I Kings 4:29 and James 1:5.

     A. Solomon became a wise man. One reason he became wise was _____.

     B. The verse in James says that God will give us wisdom if we _____.

     C. Let's pray. Lord, please give us Your wisdom so that we will know how to live for You. Amen.

9. Benediction—Thank You, Lord, for giving us Your wisdom. Keep us safe this week and let us return to this place next week to worship You. In Jesus' name. Amen. ∎

SESSION 36
WORSHIP AIM:

REMEMBERING TO WORSHIP

Journey into I Kings 8—12: Solomon's selfishness and idol worship begin to weaken his great kingdom (pp. 345-353).

Special Things You'll Need:
☐ Questions from "Bible Tic-Tac-Toe," activity piece 8C in the back of this book
☐ Cassette recorder and blank tape
☐ Record player and Christian albums
☐ Colored felt

GETTING STARTED

Today's worship theme has to do with remembering—remembering to worship. We want this theme to be present in everything that is done today.

These introductory activities should help you to productively fill the time it takes for all of your students to arrive and settle down. Choose one or more to do with your group. As they do these activities, why not talk with them about things that are hard to remember. Things they tend to forget, like picking up their clothes, brushing their teeth, or saying "thank you." You may want to share things that are hard for you to remember. These kinds of conversations help you know your students better, and help them to know you.

☐ As the students enter today, tie a piece of string around each person's finger. Today's lesson is on remembering to worship and obey God. Tell the students to remember each time they see the string that they are in children's church to worship God.

☐ Have the children draw pictures of times when they forgot something—permission slips, lunch money, a friend's party, their homework. On the back of the same paper, have them draw what they felt like when they realized they had forgotten or what happened as a result. These drawings can be used in today's Exploring Worship time.

EXPLORING THE BIBLE

Today's session deals with Solomon—his accomplishments and his downfall. One of Solomon's greatest accomplishments was the building of the Temple of God in Jerusalem. It was a tremendously ornate building. Gold was everywhere. But late in his life, Solomon forgot about God and relied on his own power. He built big buildings and ships for himself while life was miserable for the people he ruled. The Israelites went hungry. Their taxes were very high. But Solomon's many wives had temples built for the worship of their pagan gods. Solomon even prayed to these gods. When Solomon forgot to worship and obey God, he got into serious trouble.

We also find trouble in our lives when we do not remember to worship and obey God.

The children may wonder why a wise man like Solomon would not continue to do the will of God. You might want to tell them that sometimes greed and power can overcome a good heart. So many people were telling Solomon how wonderful he was that he probably began to believe it. When pride comes into a man's heart, there is no room for God.

Have the children read pages 345-353 in the *Picture Bible*. For a more dramatic effect, assign different characters in the text to some of the children and have a readers' theater. The characters in this session are: Solomon, Israelite 1, Israelite 2, Israelite 3, Israelite 4, Queen of Sheba, Jeroboam, Ahijah, Egyptian, Wife of Solomon, Messenger to Jeroboam, Solomon's servant. If your group is small, some children could read more than one part.

● **What was wrong with the things Solomon did?**
● **What happened as a result?**
● **What are some ways that people are selfish today?**
● **What are some ways that people worship other gods today?**

Help the children understand that gods are not necessarily statues of stone. They are anything in our lives that makes us forget God.

If you have a lengthy class time today, you may wish to review the story with "Bible Tic-Tac-Toe." However, if time is short, you will want to move quickly into the Exploring Worship time. The activities in that section will take a lot of class time to complete.

EXPLORING WORSHIP

Have students think back to Getting Started. They recalled times when they had forgotten things. Have them share the pictures they drew if they wish.

● **How did you feel when you forgot?**
● **Did you wish someone had reminded you?**
● **Or did someone remind you and you just didn't listen?**

Reminders are very important. They keep us from making serious mistakes.

Today we need to create a reminder for some friends of mine. These people live in Walkman Way, and they are always listening to their radios. At first, when the governor gave them all radios, they only listened a little. Now they listen all the time. You can see them every day walking down the street with their headphones on. The problem is that with the radio on they cannot hear God's voice anymore. They never turn their radios off to pray, and they never take time to read their Bibles. Who could read in all that noise? The people of Walkman Way have forgotten about God just like Solomon did. They need to be reminded to worship God. Let's make a radio program for them that will remind them.

Let the students work together to plan and record a radio show for the people of Walkman Way. The main emphasis of the show should be to remind the people to worship and obey God. Tape the show on a cassette player using students as disc jockeys. If no tape player is available, you may wish to present the radio show live. Let some of the students pick out songs to play from Christian albums. Let others choose appropriate Bible verses. Some may wish to

create commercials about worshiping God or listening to the sermon. When the whole show is recorded listen to it as a group.
● **Do you think that this show will help the people remember to worship God?**
● **What would happen if we did not remind them?**
● **What will happen if they listen to our show?**
● **What if our show plays, but nobody listens?**
● **How will that make you feel?**

When the pastor plans his sermons, he wants us to be reminded to obey and worship God. He takes a lot of time to think about what he will say in his reminder—just like it took a long time to make our radio show. He knows that we need to hear what he has to say.
● **How do you think the pastor feels when no one listens to his sermons?**
● **What can we do during the pastor's sermons to make sure that we do not miss the reminders that he gives us?**

It is important to listen to reminders about worshiping and obeying God. We do not want to be like Solomon and forget about God.

The only true method here is the method of faith: to be more perfectly and wholly trusted to God, more singly, simply Christian.
—Horace Bushnell

153

WORSHIPING TOGETHER

Once again the emphasis in worship is the sermon. Today your students have learned that the sermon is a reminder not to forget God like Solomon did. Before today's worship begins, challenge the students to listen to the student worship talk and see what it reminds us to do. Tell them to listen carefully so that you can ask them about it afterwards.

For today's hymns, choose songs in keeping with the aim of remembering to worship and obey God. Have the first hymn be a way of praising God. You may want to consider singing "O for a Thousand Tongues to Sing." Students may also enjoy singing "I Was Glad," page 3, and "Psalm 100," page 5, from *Worship Time Music Book*.

RESPONDING PERSONALLY

To conclude this session give the children an opportunity to respond personally to what they have gained from this worship experience.

☐ Spend a few minutes discussing today's worship talk.

● **Was it hard to pay attention?**
● **What things kept you from listening?**
● **What things reminded you to listen?**
● **What did the worship talk leader say was one way that we could remember God this week?**

☐ Have the students make Bible bookmarks that will remind them to worship God and read their Bibles. These bookmarks can be made from strips of colored felt. Make the bookmarks long enough to extend four inches out of the students'

Bibles. The bottom of the bookmarks can be cut into fringe. Print the words from Ecclesiastes 12:1a on the bookmarks. If possible, use fabric or permanent markers to do this. ■

IN WORSHIP

WE PRAISE GOD BY REMEMBERING TO WORSHIP

1. Call to Worship—Psalm 27:11

2. Invocation—Dear Lord, meet with us today and help us remember to worship and obey You. Help us to follow Your will instead of trying to do things our way. In Jesus' name. Amen.

3. Hymn

4. Our Statement of Faith—*Read this aloud together.*

5. Scripture Reading—I Kings 11:9-13

6. Prayer—*Complete the following sentences:*

Dear Lord, thank You for Jesus Christ who saves us from our sin. Father, we also thank You for _____.

Thank You for helping the sick people in our church. Please continue to help _____.

Help us to put Your Word into practice. In Jesus' name. Amen.

7. Hymn

8. Student Worship Talk—*Complete the sentences below with your own words and ideas.*

  I. Read I Kings 11:9.

    A. God became angry with Solomon because _____.

    B. God becomes disappointed with us because we

    _____.

    C. Solomon worshiped other gods and was selfish with his riches. Because of that _____.

  II. Read Ecclesiastes 12:1a.

    A. This verse says to remember God. We can do this by

    _____.

    B. When we forget to worship God, He must feel

    _____.

    C. One way that I will try to remember God this week is

    _____.

9. Benediction—Dear God, thank You for this day and for Your Word, the Bible, that reminds us of You. Help us to read it each day this week so that we will not forget You. Amen. ∎

UNIT 9
WORSHIP
SERVICE
FOCUS:
WORSHIP
LEADERS

Many children of this age are attracted to people based only on their appearance and personalities. We want to help students learn how to evaluate a leader's values before following along.

This unit will help them discriminate between leaders who guide people toward or away from God. They will also identify the qualities they want to imitate in God's leaders and will learn how they can help God's leaders in worshiping and in caring for needy people.

Our journey through the Old Testament centers on the lives of two powerful leaders, Elijah and Elisha. Students will evaluate the actions of these godly leaders as well as those of other leaders living at the time.

Before the sessions in this unit begin, you may wish to invite a panel of church leaders to visit children's church and answer questions about church leadership. If that is not possible, you might interview your pastor or different lay leaders on tape (or video tape, if you can). Specific instructions are given in *THE Idea Book*.

We hope that, through this year's journey into the worship service, your students will feel comfortable participating in various responsibilities of the church. Students are already leading worship in various capacities. We also want to help them reach out to others. You also might repeat the "Befriend the Elderly" experience from Unit 6 (*THE Idea Book*, page 12). ■

SESSION 37
WORSHIP AIM:

Meeting God's Leaders

Journey into I Kings 12—17: Prophets give God's messages to kings of Israel and Judah (pp. 354-362).

Special Things You'll Need:
☐ Pictures of celebrities cut from newspapers and magazines
☐ "Divided Kingdom" map
☐ Copies of "Problems! Problems!" activity piece 9A in the back of this book

GETTING STARTED

As the children arrive, involve them in an activity designed to help them think about leaders they might be attracted to and want to follow.
☐ On the chalkboard, write the following questions:
● **Have you ever followed someone's advice and later been sorry that you did?**
● **If so, why did you do what this person said?**
● **How did you discover your mistake?**

Provide children with paper and pencil, and have them jot down their answers. When all children have arrived, have volunteers share their experiences.
☐ Show pictures of a variety of celebrities, some of whom are famous Christian leaders. You might include athletes, singers, and TV stars. Have children identify celebrities and pick out several that attract kids their age.
● **Why do kids admire this celebrity?**
● **If you had a problem, would you ask this person to give you some advice? Why or why not?**
● **What might be the results of following this person's advice?**
● **Is this person a leader you want to follow?**

This activity should help children begin to think about why they are attracted to certain leaders and the consequences of following them.

EXPLORING THE BIBLE

To help the children remember some of the things leading up to the events in today's Bible story, rip a cloth into several pieces. Ask children to team up and discuss why the prophet Ahijah tore a robe into 12 strips. If children cannot recall, have them look for clues in *Picture Bibles*, pages 351-52.

Explain that Ahijah's prophecy came true soon after Solomon's death. Using "Divided Kingdom" map provided in this curriculum box, point to the line that divides the kingdom and to the capital cities of Jerusalem and Samaria. You might explain that although the Israelites would now be living in two separate kingdoms, they knew that God had commanded them to celebrate feast days in Jerusalem three times a year.
● **What problems might erupt when the two separate kingdoms worshiped together in Jerusalem?**

Explain that the Bible story today will show how the kings solved these and other problems. **The kings of the Northern and Southern Kingdoms were powerful leaders. Their decisions affected thousands of people. But even the kings followed leaders. When the kings had tough problems, they would call in their friends or a prophet to help them decide what to do. Because these friends and prophets advised the king, they were powerful leaders, too.**

Have volunteers read aloud page 354.

- **What was the first tough problem King Rehoboam had to solve?**
- **What two groups did he turn to for advice?**
- **Do you think King Rehoboam followed the right group of advisers? Why or why not?**

Explain that Rehoboam's decision was very important, for it would affect everyone in the kingdom of Israel. But Rehoboam made his decision without praying for God's help.

- **Why do you suppose King Rehoboam neglected to pray?**

On the chalkboard, list Bible kings and other advisers that will appear in the story. Help children with pronunciation:

King Rehoboam (ree-uh-BOH-um)
Ahijah (uh-HI-juh)
King Jeroboam (jer-uh-BOH-um)
King Ahab
Queen Jezebel
Elijah

Have the children read aloud pages 355-362 in the *Picture Bible.* You may want to read with them or have them read the story in sections. Ask them to think about whether each person listed on the chalkboard tried to lead people to God or away from God.

Afterwards, ask the following questions about each person listed:
- **Was this person leading people to God or away from God?**
- **What did this leader do or say that shows you whether he or she loved God?**
- **What might people get from following this leader?**
- **How might it be dangerous to follow this leader?**
- **If you had only one of these leaders to follow, which would it be? Why?**

If your group enjoys drama, they might enjoy acting out events in the Bible story in which a king had to make an important decision. Instead of reenacting what actually happened, have kids decide how they would act if they could take the leader's place. What leader would they turn to for advice? Select one or more of the following situations. If drama is not appropriate, have students tell what they might do.

Group 1: King Rehoboam has just come to the throne. He must decide whether to make the people pay heavy taxes, pages 355-56. What should he do?

Group 2: King Jeroboam knows that his people are traveling to Jerusalem for worship, and he is afraid that King Rehoboam will turn them against him, page 357. What should he do?

Group 3: King Ahab wants to get married, so he must choose a wife, page 358-59. How should he select the right woman?

Like the kings in this Bible story, each of us has decisions to make. God provides us with spiritual leaders. They give us advice from God's Word in Sunday school lessons, in sermons, and in devotional talks. If we learn what they teach us, then we will have help in solving difficult problems. But if our problem is really tough, we still may want to talk about the problem and ask a leader for some advice.

Hand out copies of "Problems! Problems!" Have children read aloud the problems and suggest an answer to each one. If a problem is too tough, have them write the name of a person they might approach for advice. This might be a parent, an older brother or sister, Sunday school teacher, coach, the pastor, good friend, etc.

- **What makes the people you'd ask for help good advisers?** (Answers will vary: they are good listeners; they love us; they know us well; they help other people with problems; they have had similar problems; they love God; etc.)
- **What might we gain from praying before we make a decision?**

EXPLORING WORSHIP

Today your students have learned the importance of carefully evaluating leaders before following their advice. When the Old Testament kings turned away from God and God's spiritual leaders, they brought trouble on themselves and their people.

The children have learned that God continues to provide us with spiritual leaders who advise us from God's Word. When we have problems, we can turn to godly leaders who can advise us.

During the next few weeks, your students will continue to explore church leadership. Children will realize that they can help their church leaders carry out the mission of the church and, at the same time, develop their own leadership skills.

If you interviewed your pastor or a

I desire to do your will, O my God; your law is within my heart.
—Psalm 40:8

lay leader, play the tape at this time to help students understand how he views his position.

WORSHIPING TOGETHER

In today's lesson we have helped students see the influence leaders can have on us. By looking at a period in the history of God's people, we contrasted the influence of God's leaders with that of leaders who don't follow God. Now we want to prepare students for a worship time when we will praise God for His leaders. Explain that worship leaders usually plan the service around one idea, called the worship theme. The songs, prayers, and worship talk are expressions of this theme. Some churches print the worship theme in the bulletin.

● **What is the theme of this morning's worship?**
● **Who are our worship leaders this morning?**
● **At what points in the worship service might our leaders offer advice from God's Word?**
● **How can we best use this advice?**

To help carry out this theme during In Worship, select songs that praise God and encourage students how to live. Your first hymn might be "Joyful, Joyful, We Adore Thee." Songs from *Worship Time Music Book* that you could use are "Give unto the Lord," page 30, and "God's Way, the Best Way," page 20.

RESPONDING PERSONALLY

To conclude this session, give the children an opportunity to personalize what they have learned. On the chalkboard, list names of

church leaders whom the children know and respect, such as the pastor, choir director, Sunday school teacher, youth leader, coach, or custodian.

Give the children paper and crayons to make thank-you notes. Have them fold the sheet in half and on the outside have them draw the outside of your building or a certain part of the interior of the building. On the inside, they can write something like this:

Dear Pastor _____
(or Mr./Mrs./Miss _____),
    Thank you for _____. I'm really glad that you help us to know God better and to worship God each week. From you I have learned to
_____.
Sincerely,
_____ (Your Name)

Choose two or three of the children to distribute the thank-you notes to the pastor and other leaders. ■

IN WORSHIP
WE PRAISE GOD FOR OUR LEADERS

1. Call to Worship—Proverbs 3:5

2. Invocation—Dear God, thank You for letting us come here today to worship You. Be with us as we read and study Your Word. We want You to enjoy our praise. In Jesus' name. Amen.

3. Hymn

4. Our Statement of Faith—*Read this aloud together or repeat it phrase by phrase after the leader.*

5. Scripture Reading—I Kings 12:21-24

6. Prayer—*Complete the following sentences:*
Dear Lord, we thank You for letting us make choices, such as

_____.

We do not want to follow leaders who might lead us to

_____.

Help us to follow leaders who lead us to _____.
Thank You for providing us with worship leaders such as

_____.

Help us to follow them by _____. In Jesus' name. Amen.

7. Hymn

8. Worship Talk—*Complete the sentences below with your own words and ideas.*

  I. Read I Kings 12:21, 22.

    A. When Rehoboam became King of Israel, he and his people planned to _____.

    B. Sometimes we are like Rehoboam and make plans, like

      _____.

    C. But God sent Rehoboam a message through a man of God named Shemaiah.

    D. Sometimes we hear God's Word through different worship leaders like _____.

  II. Read verse 24.

    A. Rehoboam and his people listened to the Word of God and they decided to _____.

    B. When our worship leaders tell us how to please God, we should follow their advice.

    C. Rehoboam obeyed God's Word. Some of the things I have done to obey God's Word are _____.

    D. We must be careful to listen to our worship leaders, and do as God wants.

9. Benediction—Dear Lord, thank You for our worship leaders. Help them to guide us through the right path. Thank You for Your love. In Jesus' name. Amen. ■

UNIT 9
WORSHIP SERVICE
FOCUS: WORSHIP LEADERS

Session 38
WORSHIP AIM:

Being LIKE OUR LEADERS

Journey into I Kings 18—19: Elijah warns against idol worship on Mount Carmel (pp. 363-373).

Special Things You'll Need:
☐ Empty water glass
☐ Slips of paper
☐ Cardboard circles, glitter, ribbon, hole punch

GETTING STARTED

Today's lesson is designed to help your students realize that imitating other people is a normal part of life, but that they must be careful to select good people and actions to follow. As the children arrive, choose one or more of the following activities.

☐ Provide children with paper and crayons/markers, and have them fold the paper in half. On one half they should draw a picture of something they would like to do. On the other, they will draw something they want to avoid. Have children display their pictures as they tell about a time when they saw someone doing one of those things.

● **Did you admire the person who acted in this way?**

● **If you acted in this way, what effect might it have on you? On other people?**

Explain that we get ideas for what we would like to do or avoid from seeing how other people act. Watching people is one way to learn.

☐ Have children draw or write a description of a real person they wish they could be like when they are older.

● **How did you get to know about this person?**

● **What effect does this person have on you? On other people?**

EXPLORING THE BIBLE

Last week, the children were introduced to Elijah, one of the greatest Old Testament prophets. In today's story, the children will read about Elijah's contest with 450 prophets of Baal. Through this showdown, Elijah proved to the Hebrews that he and the God he served were far more powerful than their opponents. Yet in spite of Elijah's strength of character in confronting the false prophets, the next day he revealed his weak side. The children will be helped to realize that godly leaders like Elijah have both strengths and weaknesses. God wants us to imitate their strengths.

Review events leading up to the Bible story by holding up an empty glass. Ask the children to team up and help each other recall the events in last week's Bible story that led to empty glasses in Israel. (Children may refer to pages 361 and 362 in the *Picture Bible.*)

● **How might the Hebrew people fill their glasses again?**

Mark off two columns on the chalkboard. One column should be labeled: "Things I'd Like to Do." The other should read: "Things I'd Like to Avoid." Have children read pages 363-370 in *Picture Bible* and decide what things Elijah did that they would like to do or avoid doing. After students have completed the reading, have volunteers help you fill up the columns. Accept all answers, including such responses as "stop the rain from falling" or "outrace a chariot."

If children need help in answering the following questions, guide them to specific pages in *Picture Bibles*.

● **Why did God give Elijah power to**

160

keep the rain from falling? (pages 361 and 363)

• Why did God answer Elijah's prayer by sending down fire on Mount Carmel? (pages 364 and 366)

• Why might God have given Elijah power to outrun King Ahab's chariot? (Answers will vary since the *Picture Bible* does not give reasons.)

• Do you think God would give us power to do these kinds of miracles? Why or why not?

• What effect did Elijah have on people?

• In what ways might God want us to be like Elijah? (Children may mention Elijah's courage to point out sins; his willingness to challenge people to choose between God and an idol; his willingness to face death, if necessary; his great faith in God.)

After the 450 prophets of Baal were killed, Queen Jezebel was furious with Elijah.

• If you were Elijah, would you be scared of Queen Jezebel? Why or why not?

• When Elijah hears that the queen is out to kill him, what might he have done? Why? The answer to this question is not as important as the reasons for the answers.

Have teams read pages 371-373 and finish the lists on the chalkboard.

• Do you think Elijah needed to hide from Queen Jezebel? Why or why not?

• How did Elijah show that he was so discouraged he wanted to quit living? (pages 371-373)

• Who did Elijah turn to for encouragement? (page 372)

• What are ways God encouraged Elijah? (pages 372 and 373)

• How might we be like Elijah when we are discouraged?

On the chalkboard, begin a list of character traits, both good and bad. You might include friendliness, courage, faithfulness to God, self-pity, easily discouraged, dishonesty, etc. Have children help you by calling out traits they see in their friends and themselves.

• Which of the traits listed on the chalkboard did Elijah have?

• What traits did Elijah have that are not listed?

Elijah was a powerful man, but he also had a weak side. Even though he felt sorry for himself and wanted to give up on life, Elijah was still a great leader.

Take a vote to see which of Elijah's strengths the group would most like to have. Erase all character traits except this one.

Have children brainstorm to think of everyday situations in which they might need to have Elijah's strong character trait. To get them started, tell about a time when you needed that character trait.

EXPLORING WORSHIP

Children of this age idolize certain children and imitate their actions and attitudes. If the admired children in the group have successfully played musical instruments or given rousing worship talks, the other children will be eager to be like them.

However, if the admired children have made fun of worship activities or complained about having to take part, the other children may feel reluctant to take leadership roles in worship.

The following activity can help children realize that they can choose to imitate the good and avoid the bad actions of student worship leaders.

Spiritual leaders like Elijah set a

good example for us to follow. For many weeks, we have had different students lead us in worshiping God. These kids have also set a good example. Let's think about the things they do that have helped make our worship time meaningful.

On a large piece of newsprint, write: "Good Acts to Follow in Worship." Underneath, list one thing student worship leaders do that you appreciate. Next, ask a helper to add something to the list. Then have children contribute. To stimulate thinking, refer to specific parts of the worship program (call to worship, invocation, singing, Scripture reading, etc.). Leave room for drawings to illustrate each item on the list. (See Responding Personally.)

On another piece of newsprint, write: "Actions That Hurt Worship." Point out an action that hinders meaningful worship, such as making fun of worship leaders who make mistakes or trying to make kids laugh. Then have the rest of the group add to the list.

Like Elijah, our student worship leaders have both strengths and weaknesses. Let's pick one of their strengths to imitate.

Hand out slips of paper, and have each student copy the helpful act he

The Christian Church comes into being as we come to know our own gifts and help others to know theirs.
—Elizabeth O'Connor

or she wants to do. Explain that volunteers will read these slips of paper during the worship time.

WORSHIPING TOGETHER

Now as your students worship together, we want them to realize the importance of being like leaders who please God.

Today's lesson has shown students that they can decide to follow the good examples set by their leaders. They have recognized both strengths and weaknesses of the prophet, Elijah. They have also listed the helpful and harmful actions of their worship leaders.

During prayer time, volunteers will offer sentence prayers, asking God to help them imitate the good actions of worship leaders. If students feel nervous about praying aloud, they can read the slips of paper they prepared during Exploring the Bible.

During In Worship, you might sing "Holy, Holy, Holy" from your hymnal. "Be Very Careful" and "Talking with God," from *Worship Time Music Book*, are other suggestions.

RESPONDING PERSONALLY

Choose one of the following activities to help your students personalize what they have learned.

☐ Have students draw and color illustrations on the "Good Acts to Follow in Worship" chart. You might assign each student a specific item to illustrate. Encourage children to picture themselves in the clothing they are wearing today. After the chart is illustrated, hang it in a prominent place.

☐ Several students may wish to decorate medals for people in your church who are faithful servants of God. These may be made easily by covering one side of a cardboard circle with glue and then with gold glitter. On the other side you can write the words "God's Hero." Punch a hole in the circle and place it on a ribbon long enough to hang around an adult's neck. The students may present these to the adults they have chosen after church today or in an adult service. ■

IN WORSHIP
WE ACT LIKE OUR LEADERS

1. Call to Worship—Joshua 24:15

2. Invocation—Father, thank You that You have brought us here today. Help us to think about You so that we worship You. Help each worship leader to please You. Bless us, we pray. In Jesus' name. Amen.

3. Hymn

4. Our Statement of Faith—*Read this aloud together.*

5. Scripture Reading—Remember your leaders, who spoke the word of God to you. Consider the outcome of their way of life and imitate their faith (Hebrews 13:7).

6. Prayer—Dear Lord, we thank You today for our student worship leaders. We want to follow their good example. Help us to _____.
In Jesus' name. Amen.

7. Hymn

8. Student Worship Talk—*Complete the sentences below with your own thoughts and ideas.*

  I. Read Hebrews 13:7a.
    A. Elijah was a prophet sent from God to tell the Word of God to the people Israel. Elijah told them to _____.
    B. Our worship leaders also tell us what is in God's Word. Two things they have told us are _____.

  II. Read Hebrews 13:7b.
    A. Elijah set a good example for us to follow because he had great faith in God. He showed his faith when he _____.
    B. I can follow Elijah's example when I _____.
    C. Our worship leaders set a good example when they _____.
    D. I follow their example when I _____.
    E. Let's all please God by following the good examples of our leaders.

9. Benediction—May the Lord help us as we try to be like His leaders this week. May each of us have Elijah's great faith in our God. ■

UNIT 9
WORSHIP
SERVICE
FOCUS:
WORSHIP
LEADERS

Do not merely listen to the word, and so deceive yourselves. Do what it says. Anyone who listens to the word but does not do what it says is like a man who looks at his face in a mirror and, after looking at himself, goes away and immediately forgets what he looks like. But the man who looks intently into the perfect law that gives freedom, and continues to do this, not forgetting what he has heard, but doing it—he will be blessed in what he does.
James 1:22-25

SESSION 39
WORSHIP AIM:

HELPING IN WORSHIP

Journey into I Kings 19—22; II Kings 2: Elijah picks Elisha to help him (pp. 374-383).

Special Things You'll Need:
☐ Bowl, spoons, recipe, flour container, milk carton (Optional)
☐ "Blow Your Own Horn," page 115 in *THE Idea Book*
☐ Large container of water, piece of bread
☐ Two teen/adult helpers who like to write (Optional)
☐ Tape recorder (Optional)

GETTING STARTED

This morning children will explore benefits of helping in worship. As children arrive, have them do one or more of these activities.
☐ Ask a group of girls to prepare the following skit. A girl and her three friends are having a sleep over. The girl decides to bake cookies, so she gets out a recipe and starts to mix ingredients. But she gets confused, so she asks her friends for help. The first friend says she's too sleepy to help. The second friend says okay, but she starts complaining and finally quits. The third friend helps but does everything in slow motion. You may want to provide props: a bowl, spoons, milk carton, recipe, etc.

When all children have arrived, ask the girls to perform the skit, and then discuss it using the following questions.
● What are some ways the friends showed they didn't want to help make cookies?
● How do you think the cookie maker felt when her friends refused to help?
● If she finishes baking the cookies, how will they probably taste?

☐ Distribute copies of "Blow Your Own Horn," and have children who are not in the skit complete it. They might write or draw their answers.
☐ Have students recall a time when an adult asked for their help and they enjoyed helping.
● **Did you have to give up anything to help this person?**
● **How did you feel about being asked?**
● **What might have happened if you hadn't helped?**

EXPLORING THE BIBLE

Review the story from the previous week so that students have background for the new story. You might hold up a big container of water and a slice of bread. Have children team up and help each other recall what part the two objects played in last week's story. (Refer children to pages 363-367; 371-372.)
● **How did water help make Elijah's miracle really spectacular?**
● **How did God encourage Elijah when he was feeling tired and discouraged?**

In today's Bible story, we find that the prophet Elijah needed someone to take his place, so he asked a young man named Elisha to give him some help.
● **Would being a prophet like Elijah be an easy job? Why or why not?**

On the chalkboard, write "Possible Gains, Possible Losses," and leave space under each title for answers. Have the group read pages 374 and the top of 375 in the *Picture Bible* and look for clues as to the things Elisha might lose and gain when he became a prophet.
● **What was Elisha's reason for accepting the job?**

• Why was it a good reason?

Elijah was getting old, and soon he would go to Heaven. The next events in the Bible story show why the people in Israel still needed a powerful prophet sent from God. Elisha would have to learn how to be that prophet. As Elijah's student, Elisha probably heard the older prophet talking about how King Ahab and Queen Jezebel killed a man to get his vineyard.

To understand the story of Naboth's vineyard, children need to know that the Hebrews believed that God had given each Hebrew family their land as a special gift. They lived on their property all their lives, and when they were old they gave the land to their children. Hebrew families did not believe they should sell their property. The only reason a family would sell their land was because they were so poor that they had to sell it to stay alive.

You may need two teen or adult leaders to assist you in the next activity. If you do not have them, help each group get started on the following activity. Divide students into three groups, and assign them a leader. Have each group prepare a report based on the story beginning on the bottom of page 375 and continuing through page 382. Each leader will help the group think about their report.

Group 1—Pretend that you are Naboth. You have died and must give a report before God. Tell what happened to you and your vineyard. At the end of your report, ask God to do something.

Group 2—Pretend that you are King Ahab. You have died and must give a report before God. Explain your part in the story of Naboth's vineyard. At the end of your report,

ask God to do something.

Group 3—Pretend that you are the elders of the city where Naboth lived. God has called you to Heaven to find out why you acted toward Naboth as you did. At the end of your report, ask God to do something.

Have a good reader from each group present the report.

• **How do you think God would respond to Naboth? King Ahab? The elders?**

• **Why did the Hebrews need prophets like Elijah and Elisha?**

Read aloud the bottom of page 382 to the end of page 383.

• **How do you think Elisha felt when he realized Elijah was going to Heaven?**

• **What might happen to the people in Israel if Elisha said he didn't feel like being a prophet?**

EXPLORING WORSHIP

We want students to be aware that someday people who now hold leadership positions in the church will be gone.

Today's Bible story has shown that Elijah would not always be alive to serve as prophet. Thus, he prepared Elisha to take his place. This training process allows God's work to be carried out by each generation.

The following activities will help the children understand that helping in worship has many benefits to themselves and to others.

• **How did Elisha know that God wanted him to be a prophet?**

Customs are different today than they were in Old Testament days. People do not usually throw cloaks over young people's shoulders and tell them God is calling them to

serve in the church.

Explain that many pastors believe that they have received a special call from God just as Elisha did. You might play the tape of the interview with your pastor or lay leader at this time. The tape should help children understand how someone is called to be a pastor.

If you do not have such a tape, tell how you became involved in church work. Explain that most people begin serving God because someone needs their help. They pray and ask God to help them decide whether to do it. Then they simply trust that God is helping them to make a wise decision.

• **How have you been asked to serve God in this church?**

Some of you have been leading in worship for a long time. Think about the ways you have helped.

• **How did you feel the first time you led this group in worship?**

• **How do you feel when you lead the group now?**

• **How can you use this experience in the future?**

Sometimes pastors have a hard time getting adults to help them lead worship. Some adults are frightened of standing in front of the congregation. Their hands shake, and they feel jittery inside. They

One mark of a great educator is the ability to lead students out . . . to new places where even the educator has never been.
—Thomas Groome

165

have never had to speak to a group before, and they are really scared.

● What advice can you give these frightened adults?

WORSHIPING TOGETHER

In advance, ask a child and an adult helper to lead in a new way during the worship time. They might sing, give a testimony, show the group pictures of Christians leading worship, etc.

In your choice of hymns and songs for today's worship service, emphasize service to God. You might begin by singing a hymn of praise to God, "To God Be the Glory." Other songs from *Worship Time Music Book* which fit this theme are "Praise the Lord," page 4, and "Give unto the Lord," page 30.

RESPONDING PERSONALLY

To conclude this session, give children an opportunity to personalize what they have learned.

☐ Have students think of adult worship services they have attended.

● What things took place that helped you to worship God?

● How did they help you worship?

Following the discussion, hand out construction paper, pencils, and crayons or felt-tipped markers. Have kids fold the paper in half and then in half again. When they open up the paper, they should have four squares in which to work. Have children make leadergrams that show in two cartoon frames a worship leader in action. For example, they might show the choir director talking to the organist and leading the choir in singing. The other two frames

should show the kids helping this person. They might picture themselves singing in the choir, handing out the music, playing the organ, or praying for the leader. Send leadergrams to adult worship leaders, or display them on a bulletin board.

☐ Hand out pieces of construction paper, pencils, and scissors. Have children and adult helpers draw around their left and right hands on construction paper and cut them out. Ask everyone to write the ways they have helped in worship on the left hand.

● Why should we try new ways of helping in worship?

Have students write one new way to help in worship on the right hand. Beginning with the adults who are present, have the group tell when they will try this new activity.

After everyone has contributed to the discussion, tack hands to a bulletin board or wall. ■

IN WORSHIP
WE HELP OUR WORSHIP LEADERS

1. Call to Worship—Psalm 134:1, 2

2. Invocation—Dear God, we are glad we can help lead in worship today. Please be with all our worship leaders as they guide us. In Jesus' name. Amen.

3. Hymn

4. Our Statement of Faith—*Read this aloud together.*

5. Scripture Reading—I Kings 19:19-21

6. Prayer—*Complete the following sentences:*
Today, God, we thank You for prophets like _____.
We also thank You for our church leaders like _____.
Help us as we learn to _____ so that we will be prepared to serve You. In Jesus' name. Amen.

7. Hymn

8. Student Worship Talk—*Complete the sentences below with your own thoughts and ideas.*

  I. Read I Kings 19:19.
    A. Elijah was getting old and needed to find someone to take his place. He let Elisha know that he was the man God wanted by _____.
    B. God wants people to serve. God uses people to _____.
    C. Some of the ways people are asked to serve God are by _____.

  II. Read I Kings 19:20, 21.
    A. Elisha had to live with Elijah to receive his training. He had to learn to _____.
    B. We are receiving our training, too, for we are learning to _____.
    C. We need to thank God for wanting our help and for giving us opportunities to learn how to serve.

9. Benediction—We thank You, Lord, for the worship leaders in this church. May they continue to please You and to prepare us to serve You in the future. In Jesus' name. Amen. ■

UNIT 9
WORSHIP
SERVICE
FOCUS:
WORSHIP
LEADERS

SESSION 40
WORSHIP AIM:

HELPING THOSE IN NEED

Journey into II Kings 2—4: Elisha helps a poor widow (pp. 384-389).

Special Things You'll Need:
- [ ] Play money
- [ ] Christian magazines
- [ ] Play dough (recipe provided on page 67 of *THE Idea Book*)

GETTING STARTED

Today's lesson deals with the power of the Christian community to overcome evil and suffering in the world. Your students will learn how Elisha helped prevent injustice against a poor Hebrew widow. Students will also have opportunity to examine their own power as Christians to help others. They will explore the needs of people in their community and will think of ways they can help overcome them.

[ ] In advance, clip ads from Christian magazines or a local newspaper reporting rural and city ministries as well as foreign missions. Try to find a range of ministries designed to combat injustice, poverty, crime, ignorance, abuse, etc. Display these on a table.

Divide children into groups. Have them pretend to be the church's missions committee. Explain that every month people in the church give money to help people here and around the world. Give each group $500 play dollars to represent the monthly missions budget. Have groups decide which organizations to support and how much to give each one. Have them present their budgets and reasons for spending the money the way they did.

● How did you feel pretending to have the power to divide up $500 to help needy people?

● How did you decide which groups to support?

● Do you suppose God approves of this way to use our money? Why or why not?

[ ] To help students think of different types of help that can be given, share with the children a time when you were teased, bullied, or snubbed. How did you cope with the situation? What was the result? Have the children think about a time when they were victims of injustice like that.

● How did you feel when you were being unfairly treated?

● Did you turn to anyone for help? If so, what special ability or power did this person have?

● If the person helped you, did your helper expect you to help yourself in some way? If so, how?

[ ] Ask a group of students to take part in a panel discussion later in this session. Explain that they will recall a situation in which they helped someone who was in trouble. You might photocopy the following questions for them to think about.

● Why did you decide to help the person who was in trouble?

● What danger or inconvenience did you face by getting involved in the situation?

● What might have happened if you hadn't tried to help?

● How did you feel about what you did?

EXPLORING THE BIBLE

To put today's Bible story in context, help students recall that at the end of last week's Bible story, Elijah said that soon he would be going to Heaven. God had given the prophet Elijah great spiritual power

to combat evil and injustice. When King Ahab and Queen Jezebel did wrong, Elijah stood firm against them and proved that God would bring justice to the situation.
● After Elijah went to Heaven, how do you think Queen Jezebel would act toward the people?
● What special gift would Elijah's student, Elisha, need to carry on God's work in Israel? (Have students refer to page 383 if they cannot recall.)

The Bible story today shows how God answered Elisha's request. Immediately Elisha used the power God had given him to help a poor widow.

Assign one page of the story, found on pages 384-389, to a child or small group. You may want to hand out the remaining play dough, and have each child or group make a representation of the main event on that page. Children should explain what their creation is and how it relates to the story on that page.
● Why did the moneylender think he could get away with selling the widow's sons into slavery?

Elisha could have prayed and asked God to send an angel with the money that the widow needed. Instead, Elisha asked the widow to take part in the miracle.
● What did the widow and her son need to do in order to complete the miracle?
● How would you have felt following Elisha's instructions if you were the widow?
● What might the widow's neighbors have felt about lending their pots?
● What might have happened if the neighbors had not loaned their pots?

The story of Elisha and the poor widow happened long ago. But injustice continues to go on in our world.
● Name some people in the news who are being treated badly.
● When have you seen kids or adults being treated unfairly in our community?

God wants us to help those people. Churches collect money each week to send to missionaries throughout the world. Sometimes our church leaders write letters, telling our government to put a stop to injustice. Some of you can also recall a time when you helped a person who was treated badly.

Ask a panel of students to discuss experiences they have had helping a needy person. (See Getting Started for details.)
● What attributes or qualities do I need to help people? List responses on the chalkboard. If students have trouble thinking of attributes, guide them. (See II Peter 1:3-7.)

None of us has all these qualities. God wants us to ask for them and to use them.
● Which of these spiritual qualities has the panel used to help needy people?

Have students think about the spiritual qualities that God has begun to develop in them. Discuss ways they have used them to help needy people. Then have kids think about the qualities they don't have.
● Which one of these spiritual qualities do you want God to help you develop so that you can be more help to needy people?

Help kids understand that we help God develop our spiritual qualities when we put them into action.
● Why might it be easier for us to work as a group to help needy people?

EXPLORING WORSHIP

Children of this age are beginning to be able to feel the hurts of other people. When asked to share prayer requests, they are quick to mention people's illnesses and injuries. You can increase their motivation to help others by showing them God is pleased with worship that includes helping others. Meeting people's needs is not restricted to the worship service but should continue throughout the week.

The Bible teaches that one good way to worship God is to help needy people.
● Why do you suppose God is pleased by this kind of worship? When we meet to worship God, often we tell the entire group about needs of our neighbors.
● At what points in the worship service do we usually talk about our neighbors' needs?
● Do we help our neighbors during the worship service? If so, how? (We pray for specific people; we give an offering of money that may go to help those in need; we begin to think about helping in other ways.)
● What are some things each of you students can do during the week to help people in need?

Students are wonderful people. We sometimes forget that in the busyness and frustrations of being a teacher.
—Marlene LeFever

169

Play the tape of the interview with your pastor or lay leader. This will help the children to understand how the church works together to meet community and world needs. (See page 32 in *THE Idea Book* for complete instructions.)

WORSHIPING TOGETHER

Now it is time for students to worship together. Today your students have learned that God uses people to help those who are victims of injustice. Students have seen how God protected a woman from injustice through the prophet Elisha. He used his spiritual power for her good. Students have focused on their own spiritual qualities and have seen how they can help people.

Today's worship service focuses on worshiping God by helping those in need. To prepare for group prayer, have students think of people they know who are being treated unfairly. Help volunteers prepare to offer sentence prayers for these people during the time of prayer.

Ask other students to take part in the worship talk. Explain that volunteers are needed to stand and share specific needs of people they know. (Let them know they do not need to share the person's name.) Later during the worship talk, the same students will stand and explain how they plan to continue helping this person during the week.

Songs you might use during In Worship are "O God, Our Help in Ages Past," from your hymnal, and "Working Together" and "Lend a Helping Hand" from *Worship Time Music Book.*

RESPONDING PERSONALLY

The following activity should help students make specific plans for helping a neighbor. Hand out paper, and have children make a chart of the week. Draw a pattern on the chalkboard and title it "How I Can Help . . ." Have students fill in the name of a person they want to help. If some students cannot think of a needy person, they can help another student meet someone's needs.

We have been thinking about needy people in our community. We have prayed for these people, and we have thought of ways we might help them. Now let's plan what we will do this week. First, we must decide whether to work alone or together. Have students decide whether they will work together as one group, in small groups, or as individuals. **Next, we need to get an idea of when we can help and how much time we can give to the needy person.**

Have students fill in the chart showing the time they spend in church, school, clubs, sports, household chores, etc.

● **What is your best day for helping the person?**

Have students star that day. Mention some ways students have already said they might help needy people. Then have them brainstorm to think of other things they can do. Explain that helping people can take a small or big amount of time. Students must decide what they can give and which acts would be most beneficial.

After students have agreed on a strategy, explain that next week they will give a report of what they did during the week. ■

IN WORSHIP
WE HELP THOSE IN NEED

1. Call to Worship—Psalm 33:1-5

2. Invocation—Dear Lord, thank You for allowing us to be here to worship You. We want You to be happy with our praise. Be with us as we sing, praise You, and help needy people. In Jesus' name we pray. Amen.

3. Hymn

4. Our Statement of Faith—*Read this aloud together.*

5. Scripture Reading—II Kings 4:1-7

6. Prayer—*Complete the following sentences:*

Dear Lord, we praise You for times when You have helped us, such as _____.

Father, there are people who need our help, like _____.

We ask, Father, that You would help us think of good ways to help these people. Thank you for hearing our prayers. In Jesus' name we pray. Amen.

7. Hymn

8. Student Worship Talk—*Complete the sentences below with your own thoughts and ideas.*

I. Read II Kings 4:1, 2.
   A. Long ago in Israel, a poor widow was in trouble because _____.
   B. Today there are people in our community with problems such as _____.
   C. We know that God cares about these people, and God wants us to _____.

II. Read II Kings 4:6, 7.
   A. The Hebrew widow's needs were supplied by God through _____.
   B. Today when people come to the church with needs, God helps them through us.
   C. Some ways that we can help people in need are by _____.

9. Benediction—May God give each of us love so that we see when people need our help. May God give us good ideas to help these people. And may God help us work together as we reach out to them. ■

SESSION 41
WORSHIP AIM:

BELIEVING GOD MEETS US

In the last unit, the children learned about the role of pastors and lay leaders in worship. In this unit, the children will discover their own roles in worship. Worship is not merely an active time for pastors and leaders. Children need to learn to be eager, active participants in worship. This unit begins with the story of an Israelite girl whose faith changed the lives of the adults around her. As your students learn about the characters in this unit—Elisha, Jehu, and Hezekiah—they will come to see practical ways that they can contribute to worship. Elisha and his servant realize that God's team is always the winning team. Children can join God's team by choosing to worship God.

Jehu wants to worship God so much that he bravely destroys all of the enemies that stand in the way. People who chose to worship God today will also have enemies to defeat. Your children will look at some of these, especially the hurry and hassle of Sunday morning routines that can put them in negative moods for worship. They will devise strategies for conquering these enemies.

Hezekiah does not give in to the advice of others to worship idols. The decision he makes is unpopular with some people, but it pleases God. The children will learn from Hezekiah that sometimes we must stand apart from our friends if we are to truly worship God during our children's church times. ■

Journey into II Kings 5—6: A servant girl's belief in God saves Naaman's life (pp. 390-394).

Special Things You'll Need:

☐ Play dough, recipe provided on page 67, and instructions for making a mortar and pestle, page 61, of *THE Idea Book*

☐ Materials for baking bread, recipe on page 61 of *THE Idea Book*

☐ "Kidnapped!" sign for writing table

☐ Story starter, printed in Getting Started section of lesson, copied on 3″ by 5″ cards

☐ Actors prepared for a skit

☐ Copies of "Sunday Search," page 116 of *THE Idea Book*

☐ Copies of "Faith-sharing Letter," activity piece 10A in the back of this book

☐ "Parchment Messages," page 62 in *THE Idea Book.*

GETTING STARTED

As your students enter today, let them choose one of the following activities to get them involved in today's story.

☐ At a writing center, have a big sign which reads "Kidnapped!" Have the following story starter available for the children to read, "You have been kidnapped by officials in the Syrian army. They have taken you far away from your family and friends to be a servant for a general in the army. You cannot contact your family to let them know you are okay. You know there is no chance of escaping. How do you feel? What kind of servant will you be? Do you believe that God is still with you? How will He take care of you away from your parents?"

The students should draw cartoon-strip stories that show how they would feel in these circumstances. This activity will help the children understand the plight of the servant girl in today's story. You will want to let the students share their stories at the beginning of the Exploring the Bible time.

☐ At a clay modeling table, have the students make a mortar and pestle from play dough and explain that these were used in Old Testament times to grind wheat to make flour for bread. Discuss what it must have been like to be a slave girl and have to make bread that way. This activity will help the students to understand the hard work of the Israelite slave girl in today's story.

☐ If time permits, let the children bake bread to eat at the end of your class session. You may wish to mix the ingredients and let the dough rise before class begins. Then the children can knead it and oversee the baking. As you do this activity, you may wish to pretend that you are actually kidnapped slaves conversing in the kitchen. Talk about whether or not you still believe that God can help you.

EXPLORING THE BIBLE

Today's story deals with the healing of Naaman, a general in the Syrian army. Naaman was healed because he obeyed the instructions of God's prophet, Elisha. However, Naaman would never have heard of Elisha if his servant girl had not cared enough and been brave enough to speak up. The servant girl is the real heroine we wish to introduce to the students today. Even in her difficult circumstances, she believed that God could do mighty things. Your children need to see the difference that one little girl made by her faith.

Because today's story is brief, it provides an excellent opportunity to involve some other members of your congregation. You might enlist some teens or adults to help with the story. Give them photocopies of pages 390-394 in the *Picture Bible* and ask them to prepare a skit. You will need a talkative girl to act as the servant girl. Other characters you will need are: Naaman, Naaman's wife, the King of Syria, the King of Israel, Elisha, Elisha's servant, and Naaman's servant.

Before the skit begins, have a few students share their "Kidnapped" stories.
● **Would you try to help your masters if they had kidnapped you? Why or why not?**
Watch in this story to see what the kidnapped servant girl does. Then have the actors present the skit.

When the skit is over, interview the servant girl. (She should be coached ahead of time to stay in character.) **That was a brave thing you did.**
● **How did it make you feel?**
● **Did you really think that God could help Naaman? Why?**

Encourage the students to think of all of the people that the message had to go through before Elisha could tell Naaman how to be healed. The servant girl told Naaman's wife, who told Naaman, who told the King of Syria, who told the King of Israel. Elisha heard because everyone was talking about the king's problem. As the students recall this progression, you might write the names on the board with arrows showing the flow of communication. When the chain

is complete, talk about the importance of the servant girl. What if she had been too scared to speak up? Erase her name from the beginning of the chain.
● **What would have happened if the servant girl had not believed in God?**
● **Would Naaman ever have been healed?**

EXPLORING WORSHIP

Your students have heard the story of the faith of Naaman's servant girl. She believed that God was real.
● **Is God real?**
● **How do you know?**
● **What difference does it make if we believe that God is real?**
● **What difference did it make for the servant girl?**
● **What difference will it make for us as we come to children's church?**
● **How can we show that we believe that God is real like Naaman's servant girl did?**

Hand out copies of the "Sunday Search." You may wish to read through this with the children and make plans with them for their participation in the Sunday Search each Sunday throughout this unit. If the children have been keeping

worship notebooks, they may add these pages to their notebooks at this time.

WORSHIPING TOGETHER

As you move into the worship service, encourage the children to close their eyes and picture that God is there with them. Let them pray silently for a minute or two.

In keeping with today's worship aim—believing that God will meet with us in worship—choose songs that deal with God's presence in our lives or in our place of worship. From *Worship Time Music Book* you might select "The Lord Is My Shepherd," page 28, and "Talking with God," page 21. "Praise Ye the Triune God," found in your hymnal, is good to sing at the beginning of In Worship.

RESPONDING PERSONALLY

Today your students have learned that it is important for children to believe that God is real. It is especially important to come to worship believing that God is real and that we can worship Him. In the last few moments of your class session, let the children choose one

A good way to be more creative is to look for the second right answer. . . .

of the following projects to respond personally to what they have learned.

☐ In today's story, the servant girl helped others because of her faith in God. Have your students follow her example by writing letters to their friends who do not attend church. They can tell their friends that God meets with them when they come to see Him at church. Hand out copies of "Faith-sharing Letter." The students may use this as an example to write their own letter to a friend or they may actually use this one, coloring in the pictures and writing the names in the appropriate blanks.

☐ The message from the King of Syria to the King of Israel in today's story was probably written on parchment and sealed with the king's seal. If you have about fifteen minutes after the worship today, have the students make parchment according to the instructions. They can then write or draw something for their parents telling them what they learned today in today's Sunday Search. Roll the parchments and seal them with wax from a melted candle before the children take them home. ■

. . . There are many ways to pursue these answers, but the important thing is to do it. Often the really creative idea is just around the corner.
—Roger von Oech

IN WORSHIP
WE BELIEVE GOD MEETS US

1. Call to Worship—Psalm 122:1

2. Invocation—Dear Lord, today we are coming to meet with You. We want to please You by spending time with You. Meet with us in our worship time. Amen.

3. Hymn

4. Statement of Faith—*Repeat our church's creed together.*

5. Scripture Reading—Read II Kings 5:1-14.

6. Prayer—Dear Heavenly Father, thank You that You meet with us as we worship You. Thank You for the wonderful example that the servant girl gives us of someone who believes in You. We're glad that You love us even when we need to believe in You more. Help us to realize how much You want us to believe in You. In Jesus' name, we pray. Amen.

7. Hymn

8. Student Worship Talk—*Complete the following sentences with your own words.*

Read II Kings 5:2, 3.

A. An Israelite girl was kidnapped to be a servant to Naaman's wife. She must have felt _____.

B. When Naaman got sick with leprosy, the Israelite girl knew who could help. She said _____.

C. Naaman was healed because his servant girl believed that _____.

D. I believe that God is real, too. One way that I know this is _____.

E. We can show that we believe God is real by coming to church to worship Him.

F. When we come to church to do other things instead of to worship God, God must feel _____.

G. We can show God that we have come to meet Him by _____.

9. Benediction—Lord, help us today to believe that You have met with us here in children's church. We believe that You are real. Help us to tell others. Amen. ■

SESSION 42
WORSHIP AIM:

JOINING GOD'S TEAM

Journey into II Kings 6—9: By saving Israel from the Syrians, God shows Elisha that His team is always the winning team (pp. 394-406).

Special Things You'll Need:
☐ Several issues of sports and news-magazines
☐ Three large sheets of poster board
☐ 4″ x 5″ cards, one for each student
☐ "God's Team Membership Requirements," activity piece 10B in the back of this book
☐ "God's Team Headbands," page 77 in *THE Idea Book*

GETTING STARTED

As the children arrive, help them to focus on team membership by doing one or both of the following activities.

☐ Ask each student what kind of teams they have been on. Make a list on the chalkboard of all their responses. Informally discuss these experiences with them.

☐ Place a variety of sports and newsmagazines and scissors on a large table. Instruct the children to cut out pictures of various types of teams. You might need to guide them to see that teams can be found in business, government, and clubs, as well as in sports. As they cut out pictures of teams, have them sort them into two piles, teams on which they would like to be members and those which they would not care to join. They should think of reasons why they would or would not want to be on each team.

List all the reasons that the children give—one column for positive reasons, one for negative. Individuals might have feelings about a specific team like the Pittsburgh

Steelers or a more general type of team like an emergency paramedic team. Encourage each of them to share personal preferences. Save the lists for later use.

☐ Give the students a piece of poster board labeled "Popular Teams" and let them make a collage of the team pictures they have found. This poster will be used for comparison in the Exploring the Bible section of the lesson.

EXPLORING THE BIBLE

Incidents from the life of Elisha, a man who chose to be on God's team, are the focus of the Bible lesson today. We want to help the children to see that being on God's team is different than being on any other kind of team. Most teams are made up of members selected by the captain or some other person in authority, based on the skill or ability of the individual. Not so with God's team. God wants everyone to be on His team. No one is to be excluded. Sometimes other teams lose, but God's team is always the winning team. One way that we can participate on God's team is to faithfully worship God.

Today's Bible lesson addresses the way God worked through one of His team members, Elisha, to help the children of Israel in some crisis situations.

To start the lesson time for today help the children to think about how they feel when teams are chosen that they will be on.

● **How are teams selected at your school? in gym class? during a game after school?**
● **How do you think the person feels who is chosen first?**

- What about the one who is chosen last?
- If a person is always selected first, what might that individual think about himself or herself?
- What if a person is always chosen last?
- If you were the person that got to select the team members, what would you look for in the individuals that you pick? Make a list of these characteristics.
- If God was selecting people to be on His team, what kind of people would He look for? Make another list of these qualities.

Today we are going to look at Elisha. He was on God's team. We need to find out what kind of a person he was. We want the students to think about what it is like to be on God's team.

Read or tell the story on pages 394-398. This is the story where God blinded the soldiers in the Syrian army so that they were defeated by the Israelites without a battle. Elisha's servant was afraid that the Israelites would be defeated, but Elisha prayed, and God showed the servant that His team is always the winning team, no matter how many are on the enemy's side.

- What special things did God do for Elisha?
- What did Elisha do that showed he was on God's team?
- What did Elisha's servant learn about God's team?

Read or tell the story on pages 398-406 of how God delivered starving Samaria from a long siege by the Syrians.

- How did God help His team?
- In this incident how did Elisha show that he was on God's team?
- From this story what things do you see in Elisha that God would

want to find in people who are on His team?
- Are there any other qualities that God might want His team members to have?

Make a list of all these qualities. Have children compare this list with the lists they made at the beginning of the lesson. Those lists contain what the children would look for in people if they selected a team and things they initially thought God would look for.

- What differences do you see in the types of things found in the three lists?
- What do you think it is like to be on God's team?
- Would anyone be left out? If so, why?
- What did we see God do for Elisha in this Bible story?
- If I am on God's team, will He do those same things for me? Why or why not?
- What are some things that God might do for each of us who are on His team?

These kinds of things may seem less spectacular than what God did for Elisha, but they are no less important.

Have the students draw self-portraits on 4″ x 5″ cards and label them with their names. Have them paste these on a poster entitled "God's Team." This poster can be displayed next to the "Popular Teams" poster made earlier in the Getting Started section of the lesson.

EXPLORING WORSHIP

The aim of this unit is to determine the role of the individual in worship. We want the student to realize that by choosing to worship

God we are showing Him that we are on His team.

To help prepare the children to make the transition from the Old Testament story of Elisha to the present worship experience, it is helpful for students to see the relevance of being on God's team today. During the week ask three or four people who are active in their faith and in the church (maybe some parents of students) to come into the class at a designated time and share with the students.

Interview the visitors in the format of a sports broadcast. Find out about their position on God's worship team. Ask them how they came to join God's team and how being on His team in worship has helped them. Encourage them to share the place that worship has in their lives. Allow the children to ask them questions.

WORSHIPING TOGETHER

Now that the students have seen what God can do today for people on His team, help them to explore what they can do for God as an act of worship that would help them to show Him that they have chosen to be on His team. Prepare for the worship time by selecting student

Because pupils are full of surprises, we should always be ready to shift gears, moving flexibly toward our goals. . . .

participants. Distribute verses, such as the following, for students to rehearse: Isaiah 55:1-7; Joel 2:32; Matthew 11:28-30; John 3:16, 17; John 6:35; Titus 2:11; II Peter 3:9.

This lesson is an appropriate place to discuss salvation with your students if you feel that they are ready. For guidelines on how to lead a child to Christ, see the section in the front of this book. You may wish to incorporate an invitation to salvation as part of today's worship service.

Select music that is fitting for the week's In Worship theme. After singing an opening hymn of praise, like "Praise to the Lord, the Almighty," you might want to include "Who Is on the Lord's Side," which may be found your hymnal. "I Can Join" and "My Deliverer," from *Worship Time Music Book*, also fit this theme. An appropriate way to close the worship time would be to sing "I Have Decided to Follow Jesus," but change the words to "I Have Decided to Be on God's Team."

RESPONDING PERSONALLY

Today the class has learned about being on God's team. They have seen how God's team is different from any other team. Use one or more of the following activities to help the students personalize what they have learned.

☐ Use the last sheet of poster board to make a chart of requirements for membership in God's team, characteristics of team members, rules for behavior, uniform, exercise needed to stay in shape. Guide the direction of the children's thinking, but the responses should be their own. This poster could be mounted beside the one containing the roster "God's Team."

☐ Hand out copies of "God's Team Membership Requirements" and let the students complete the activities prescribed there. This can be taken home to be put in a special place in their bedrooms as a reminder that they have chosen to be on God's team.

☐ Your students may wish to make "God's Team Headbands" as a take-home reminder that they have chosen to be on God's team by worshiping Him. ■

. . . If several possibilities are pondered, the teacher is freer to follow the lead of the pupils.
—Lois E. LeBar

IN WORSHIP
WE ARE ON GOD'S TEAM

1. Call to Worship—Psalm 146:1, 2

2. Invocation—Dear God, today we have thought about what it means to be on Your team. Help us to worship You now so that we can show You that we are choosing to be on Your team. Amen.

3. Hymn

4. Our Statement of Faith—*Recite this together.*

5. Scripture Readings—*Read selected passages given out earlier.*

6. Prayer—*Pray that you will always want to be on God's team and that you will be willing to do what God wants His team members to do.*

7. Hymn

8. Student Worship Talk—*Complete these sentences with your own words.*

    Read II Kings 6:15-17.

    A. Elisha was on God's team. He showed that he was on God's team by _____.

    B. Because Elisha was on God's team, God did special things for him and his people like the time when _____.

    C. Being on God's team meant that Elisha sometimes did some things that seem to us very difficult to do. He showed kindness to his enemies by _____.

    D. In this lesson, the reason that we know that Elisha was on God's team was because _____.

    E. Being on God's team does not mean that God always does spectacular things like making the sound of a mighty army. Today, if we are on His team, He helps us by _____.

    F. We know that God's team is the best team because _____.

9. Closing Song

10. Benediction—May God help each of us want to be on His team. May God also help those of us who have chosen to be on His team to worship Him daily this week. ■

179

SESSION 43
WORSHIP AIM:

DEFEATING WORSHIP ENEMIES

Journey into II Kings 9—11: Jehu defeats the worshipers of Baal (pp. 407-418).

Special Things You'll Need:
☐ Adult volunteer or helper to purposefully arrive late (see lesson for necessary props)
☐ Copies of "Worship Monsters," activity piece 10C in this book
☐ Yarn or fabric scraps

GETTING STARTED

Today's lesson deals with conquering things that keep us from worshiping God. Your students will study the life of Jehu, the king who destroyed the practice of idol worship in Israel. They will also have opportunity to examine their own lives to see those areas where bad habits keep them from really worshiping God. They will look specifically at things that happen in the home on Sunday morning that keep Sunday from being the special day of worship that God intended it to be.

It seems that chaotic Sunday mornings are a common plague in Christian homes. Students who come from non-Christian homes may have even more difficulty in getting to church on Sunday. Frustrations carried over from the home or the ride to church can have a negative effect on our attitudes and concentration in worship. In today's lesson, we will look at practical ways to counteract these "enemies."

In the opening moments of class today, choose one or more of the following activities to involve your students in today's lesson.

☐ As students arrive, place them in groups of four or five. Encourage them to plan skits which show what it is like to get ready for church on Sunday morning. Students can pretend that one child is the mother, one the father, and the rest their children. Be sensitive to children who don't come from traditional homes. Children could prepare skits showing what it's like on Sunday in a single-parent home or in a home where parents don't go to church. When all students have arrived, let them present their skits to the class. Discuss these presentations.

● **Is this the way it is at your house?**
● **How is your Sunday morning like this or not like this?**
● **How do you feel when you get to church?**

☐ If your church has a video library, plan to show the opening skit from *What Makes a Christian Family Christian* featuring David and Karen Mains of Chapel of the Air and their four children. In this three-minute skit, this family shows what getting ready for Sunday can sometimes be like. (The entire video is intended for teen and adult use, but your students will love the opening slapstick skit.)

☐ As a class, write a poem about Sunday morning. Begin by talking about frustrating things that happen at home or on the way to church. Then talk about what happens in worship. Help the students to see that the way they feel when they get to church often influences the way they participate in worship. Then fill in the following free verse poem:

Sunday morning at home is (color)
It tastes like . . .
It sounds like . . .
By the time I get to worship, I feel like . . .

I think God meant Sunday to be (different color)

Then worship would be more like . . .

If time permits, let the students write poems individually using this guide. They can share them with the group or they can illustrate them and display them on a church bulletin board for the adults to see.

☐ While the children are getting settled, have a worker or another member of the congregation rush in as if he or she is late for church. This person may cause quite a scene— panting for breath and apologizing profusely for being late. Plan ahead of time to have at least ten things wrong with the person's appearance: rollers in hair, carrying an encyclopedia instead of a Bible, two different shoes, juice marks around mouth, etc. Let the person tell the class how horrible his or her Sunday morning has been so far. Then have the actor rush off to the rest room to finish getting ready for worship.

When the person has left the room, encourage students to draw pictures of the character. They should try to remember how many ways the person was not ready for worship and include these in their drawings. When the students have had a few minutes to draw, review the list of ten things. How many remembered all of them? Discuss the reasons why this person was unprepared for worship.

- **What could the person have done differently?**
- **How will the person feel in the worship service?**
- **Will the person be able to concentrate on worshiping God? Why or why not?**

EXPLORING THE BIBLE

We aren't the only people who face problems when we try to worship God. Today's Bible story is about a man who faced big problems because he wanted to worship God. His name is King Jehu.

Tell the story of Jehu found on pages 407-411 of the *Picture Bible.* This story covers the anointing of Jehu as king of Israel and his destruction of the worshipers of Baal. The story should emphasize Jehu's determination to get rid of anything that would keep Israel from worshiping God. There are three events which should be highlighted: the death of King Jehoram, the death of wicked Jezebel, and the destruction of the idols and heathen temple. These are the three enemies which Jehu had to defeat in order to worship God. The students will need to remember these to do the activity piece.

Hand out copies of "Worship Monsters." The top row of this sheet contains three monsters. The students should label these monsters with the names of the enemies that Jehu had to defeat in today's story. If they cannot remember, they may refer back to the *Picture Bible* for the answers.

The second half of the activity piece contains three additional monsters. The children should label these monsters with names of three problems that keep them from worshiping God. These may be problems which were discussed in Getting Started or they may be the students' own ideas. If there is time, the students may color in the monster figures or glue on yarn or fabric to make them hairy.

EXPLORING WORSHIP

- **What differences are there between the kind of worship monsters Jehu faced and the kind of worship monsters we face?**
- **Why can't we get rid of our monsters like he got rid of his?**
- **What can we do about the things that keep us from being ready to worship when we come to church?**

Discuss practical ways to alleviate the problems the students have mentioned. Specifically focus on things that the students can do to make Sunday morning less of a hassle. Help them think of things they can do to put them in a more worshipful mind-set when they come to children's church.

After a few minutes of brainstorming together, plan a schedule for getting ready for church on Saturday night and Sunday morning. Incorporate the students' suggestions for getting ready for church. Help them to nail down specific goals. For instance, "I will take my bath on Saturday night. I will lay out my clothes on Saturday night. I will go to bed by 9:00 on Saturday night so that I will not be sleepy in worship. I will set my alarm for 7:00 on Sunday morning so that I

From the very beginning of his education, the child should experience the joy of discovery.
—Alfred North Whitehead

can have breakfast and still have time to get ready. I will take time before I leave for church to pray that God will help me to worship Him."

WORSHIPING TOGETHER

Today your students have learned that a hurried, hassled schedule can make them inattentive in worship. They have planned ways to conquer some of these "worship monsters" in the future. Before you move into worship time today, give the students a few minutes to prepare themselves for worship. Put on some quiet worship music and let the students sit and rest. Encourage them to say silent prayers that God will help them to worship Him in the worship time today. Students who are participating in today's worship time may also use this time to read through their parts.

Consider using the following songs for worshipers to sing: "A Mighty Fortress Is Our God" from your hymnal; "Sing for Joy," page 18, and "My Deliverer," page 9, from *Worship Time Music Book.*

RESPONDING PERSONALLY

Today your students have looked at practical ways to break habits that keep them from worshiping God in your worship times. Before they leave today, let them make one of the following reminders to help them apply what they have learned.

☐ Have the students make charts on which they can print the schedule or goals the class made earlier for preparing for worship. They can take these home and try to follow them next week.

☐ As a class, prepare a letter for the adults in your church about what you have learned today. You may wish to write the letter on a chalkboard or newsprint as the children share their ideas. Include some of the students' poetry about Sunday mornings or some of their practical ideas for how to make Sundays more worshipful. This letter can be typed and distributed to parents or it can be included in your church's weekly newsletter. ■

IN WORSHIP
WE NEED TO BE PREPARED

1. Call to Worship—Read Deuteronomy 6:13-15, 18, 19 in a modern translation.

2. Invocation—Dear Lord, we want to worship You today. Help us to defeat any enemy that would keep us from doing that. Amen.

3. Hymn

4. Our Statement of Faith—*Recite our church's statement of faith in unison here.*

5. Scripture Reading—II Kings 9:6, 7; 10:28, 30.

6. Prayer—*Pray that God will help you to concentrate on worshiping Him through the rest of the service.*

7. Hymn

8. Student Worship Talk—*Complete the following sentences with your own words and ideas.*

  I. Read II Kings 9:6, 7.

    A. God appointed Jehu to be the King of Israel and to defeat the worshipers of Baal. The names of some of the worshipers of Baal were _____.

    B. Jehu needed to destroy the worship of Baal because _____.

    C. Some of the things that keep us from worshiping God are _____.

  II. Read II Kings 10:28, 30.

    A. Jehu obeyed God and destroyed the people who were not worshiping Him. He also destroyed the idols of Baal and the temple of Baal.

    B. Some of the ways that we can defeat things which keep us from worshiping God are _____.

9. Benediction—May God help you to live for Him every day this week and to return again next Sunday prepared to worship Him. ■

183

SESSION 44
WORSHIP AIM:

*P*AYING
ATTENTION TO GOD

Journey into II Kings 11—21; II Chronicles 24—33: Friends of Joash and Manasseh influence them not to worship God, but Hezekiah remains faithful (pp. 419-428).

Special Things You'll Need:
☐ Two different colors of paper
☐ Straight pins
☐ Report folder for collecting student drawings
☐ Teens or workers prepared to do a skit
☐ Copies of "Hezekiah Club Membership Kit," activity piece 10D in the back of this book
☐ Instructions and supplies for "Shadow Drama," page 38 in *THE Idea Book*

GETTING STARTED

☐ During the Getting Started activities today, divide the students into two teams. The teams may pin on construction paper badges of different colors. The blue team will try to get the red team to talk to them. If a red team member gives in and talks to a blue team member even accidentally, the red team member will lose his or her badge. This game will show the students that they can resist the urge to talk if they really concentrate on it. It will also provide a good discussion starter for your Exploring Worship time today.

☐ As a class, make a booklet entitled "101 Things to Do During a Church Service." Let students illustrate the pages with crazy things that children might do to avoid listening to the sermon. This will be a fun activity for the children, but it will also make them more aware of the distracting things which they do

during worship. You may allow some silliness during the drawing time, but you will want to eventually bring the conversation around to things that the students actually do during worship times that prevent them from really worshiping God.

☐ If you have two or three workers or teens who can come in to help today, have them prepare a skit in which they act like children playing during the worship service. The skit should be exaggerated and very humorous, showing how the children make airplanes out of offering envelopes, crawling under pews, and whispering about people in the congregation. Have a good time with this activity. You may complete this activity by discussing the ways that children might misbehave during worship. Do not direct the lesson to certain kids within your group. The object of this activity is to make them aware of such behavior, not to embarrass your problem students.

EXPLORING THE BIBLE

Joash promised the high priest that he would obey God's law and rule the people according to God's Word. However, he did not keep his promise. Tell the rest of the story, emphasizing the fact that Joash and Manasseh were both influenced by their friends to turn away from God. Make it clear that Hezekiah stayed true to God.

A more exciting way to present today's story is through shadow drama. Follow instructions for presenting a shadow drama. Scenes for today's story include: Joash talking to his friends, people worshiping idols, Zechariah predicting disaster, Joash's men presenting gifts to the

enemy, Joash's servants plotting to kill him while he sleeps, Hezekiah making a speech to the people, the people rejoicing at their victory over the enemy, Manasseh worshiping an idol, Manasseh in the Babylonian prison.

When the shadow drama is finished, discuss the story with your students.

• Who were the characters who worshiped God?
• Who were the characters who turned away from worshiping God?
• What made them turn away?
• Who did they listen to?
• Who should they have listened to?
• If you had been Joash, what could you have said to your friends when they tried to keep you from worshiping God?
• What happened to these men who did not worship God?

EXPLORING WORSHIP

Children often feel pressure from others to misbehave during the worship time. Today's lesson has attempted to show them that it is okay to stand alone like Hezekiah did. The Exploring Worship activities today will turn peer pressure in a new direction. They are designed so that the students who choose to behave in worship will feel like a part of the group.

Talk about the activities your group did in Getting Started.

• Was it difficult for the red team to keep from talking to the blue team?
• How did the red team members keep their lips buttoned?

Read through the book you created or talk about the skit by the workers.

• What things do we do in worship that keep other kids and ourselves from worshiping God?
• Are those children more like Hezekiah or like Manasseh and Joash?
• Why do kids misbehave in worship?
• What do other children do that makes you feel like talking or acting silly during the service?
• What are some reasons that we should worship God?
• Why is it important to pay attention in worship?

Help the children to see that behaving during worship shows respect for God and helps us to concentrate on Him. It also helps others to concentrate.

Today you are going to have a chance to join a very special club called the "Hezekiah Club." This club is only for people like Hezekiah who want to worship God enough to refuse to listen to others who try to keep them from doing this.

• How many of you would like to be members of this club?

Good! You can all be a part. Before I hand out the membership kits, let's make some rules for members of the club to follow during worship times. These rules

will remind us not to turn away from worshiping God to talk to our friends or to do other things.

Let the students suggest rules for members of the Hezekiah Club to follow during worship time. List these on a chalkboard or newsprint. It is important that the children make their own rules for behavior in worship. They will be more likely to keep them and enforce them if they had a hand in creating them. Don't be surprised if the rules they make for themselves are much more strict than any you would have made for them!

WORSHIPING TOGETHER

Today your students have been learning how to resist distractions from peers during worship time. They have looked at the example of Hezekiah, and they have formed rules to follow so that they can be like Hezekiah in their worship time today.

Hand out the "Hezekiah Club Membership Kits." Let the children sign the membership certificates and cut out their "Hezekiah Club" buttons. Let them pin on their buttons before moving into the worship area today.

If anyone tries to keep you from listening today, point to your button

Tell me, I forget. Show me, I remember. Involve me, I understand.
—Ancient Chinese Proverb

to remind that person and keep listening!

Select appropriate music to sing during In Worship. A song of praise from your hymnal that you might want to use is "O for a Thousand Tongues to Sing." From *Worship Time Music Book* you could use "You Know, Lord," page 19, and "Joshua and Caleb," page 12.

RESPONDING PERSONALLY

Today your students have learned ways to resist distractions during worship. After today's worship service, talk to the students about their behavior.
● **Was it difficult to listen when everyone was trying?**
● **What could you have done better?**
● **Were the rules helpful?**
● **What changes would you like to make in the rules in order to make them better?**

Let the students plan how they will respond to temptations to talk and disrupt the services in the future. After your discussion, give the children opportunity to respond to today's lesson by making one of the following reminders.

☐ Let the students make construction paper or cardboard frames for their "Hezekiah Club" certificates. Display the framed certificates on a bulletin board for a few weeks. Then let the children take them home.

☐ Make an illustrated chart of the children's worship rules to display in the worship area. You may wish to do the printing so that it is consistent, but let the children illustrate each rule with colored markers. ■

IN WORSHIP
WE PAY ATTENTION TO GOD

1. Call to Worship—Psalm 66:1

2. Invocation—Dear Lord, be with us today as we worship You. Help us to be like Hezekiah. We want to worship You. Help us to listen, to sing, and to praise You today. Amen.

3. Hymn

4. Statement of Faith

5. Scripture Reading—II Kings 18:1-7

6. Prayer—*Pray that you will have courage to be true worshipers of God even when those around you are not worshiping.*

7. Hymn

8. Student Worship Talk—*Complete the following sentences in your own words:*

I. Read II Kings 18:5, 6.
   A. Hezekiah did not stop worshiping God even when
   _____.
   B. Hezekiah told the people _____.
   C. God is pleased when we worship Him like Hezekiah did. One way that we can do that is _____.

II. Read II Kings 21:1-4.
   A. Manasseh was not like his father Hezekiah. He disobeyed God by _____.
   B. God was not pleased with Manasseh because
   _____.
   C. Sometimes we let other people talk us into misbehaving during worship. When that happens, we turn away from worshiping God like Manasseh did. One way that we can stop that from happening is _____.
   D. Let's pray. Lord, help us to be like Hezekiah today. Help us to listen carefully and to worship You. Amen.

9. Benediction—May God help you to be faithful like Hezekiah in living for Him, even when the people around you are not following God. ■

SESSION 45
WORSHIP AIM:

SENSING GOD'S PRESENCE

Your students are almost to the end of our yearlong journey through the Old Testament, an adventure which has shown God's love and care for His people time and time again. This journey has also focused on God's people growing in their ability and desire to worship Him, repenting of their unfaithfulness, and praising Him for His faithfulness to them.

In Unit 11, we see the people of God taken into captivity because of their disobedience, and we see the city of Jerusalem and the Temple destroyed. Through story telling and drama, the students will participate in the devastation of losing God's special presence when they are no longer able to gather and worship in God's house. They will also share in the adventure of returning and rebuilding the Temple once more. God's presence will also be realized in His care and protection for His people in a strange land through the story of Esther, a queen whose courage saves her people from destruction.

The three sessions in this unit will help give children a new appreciation for the sanctuary or church auditorium—a special place which enables us to gather with God's people, a place which helps remind us of God's majesty, a place which allows us to be together in common worship and celebration.

A final note, Session 46 requires an adult volunteer to dress as a Bible-time character and tell the story. Be sure to give the volunteer as much advance warning as possible. ■

Journey into II Kings 22—25; II Chronicles 33—36: Josiah has the Temple repaired and finds the lost Book of Law (pp. 429-437).

Special Things You'll Need:
☐ "Bible Time Scroll," page 78 of THE Idea Book.
☐ About 12 cardboard boxes, grocery size
☐ Copies of "I Have Hidden," activity piece 11A in the back of this book (Optional)
☐ Supplies for worship decorations, poster board, streamers, balloons, etc.

GETTING STARTED

Before the students arrive, hide a scroll which you have prepared ahead of time and on which you have written the Ten Commandments. It must be hidden well enough so that no one accidentally finds it before you wish it to be found. The children will hunt for it during the story about workers finding the lost book as they repaired the Temple.

As you are waiting for all your students to arrive, help the early ones to fill the time productively and prepare for the exploration and worship ahead through one or more of the following activities.

☐ Ask two or three students to help set up the cardboard boxes you brought. Stack the boxes in a back corner of the room to make a three-walled "fort." They could stack them four across and three high. This structure represents the city of Jerusalem. Students will use it during the story to act out the destruction of Jerusalem by the Babylonians. Students may imaginatively decorate the "walls of Jerusalem."

☐ Distribute paper and pencils and have the children imagine that all the Bibles in the churches and homes have been burned. The only parts of the Bible left will be the parts that people can remember by heart. Have the children write down all the Bible verses and parts of Bible verses that they can remember. This activity should help students realize how important it is to have copies of the whole Bible. It will also help them to understand the Israelites' joy at finding the Book of the Law, which they will learn about in today's story.

☐ Have students make scrolls. They should write several favorite Bible verses on the scrolls. You might make a list of references for verses that are important for students this age. Let them illustrate the verses on the scrolls. These may be placed in the worship journey notebooks at the end of this session.

EXPLORING THE BIBLE

Introduce today's Bible adventure having the kids imagine that our country has been taken over by another country that forbids any kind of religion—no churches, no Bibles, no Christian holidays, etc.
● How easy do you think it would be to meet together and follow God with only the small portions of the Bible that we can remember? Why?
● What do you think would happen to most people?
● How do you think people might change?
● How would people teach the Bible?
This is what it was like to live in Judah at the time of our story.

Now read the story of "The Lost Book" on page 429 in a lively way.

Or if you have several good, strong readers, one could read the narration, and two or three others the speaking parts.

At the end of the story (page 431), stop suddenly.

● **There is a scroll in our room today, just like the lost scroll in the temple. Can anyone find it?** Be prepared for a bit of pandemonium as all the children look for the scroll. When it is found, ask the finder to sit in front of the group and read from the scroll when you request it.

Now read the second Bible story, "The Prophetess Speaks" (page 432), in the same manner as above. Stop at the point where Josiah calls a meeting of all the people and reads God's Law. Ask the scroll finder to stand and read God's Laws (the Ten Commandments) to the rest of the group in a loud, clear voice. Then continue with the Bible story.

Before you read the third story, "The Fall of Jerusalem" (page 435), ask all the children to get up and go sit on the floor behind the wall of boxes. Select two children to sit on the outside of the wall. **This is the city of Jerusalem and you are the people. The two outside the wall are the Babylonian soldiers. Those of you behind the wall are scared and waiting to see what is going to happen.**

Now read the story. When you come to the end of the story, instruct the two soldiers to knock the wall of boxes down and make the people follow them to Babylon. The group follows the soldiers around the room until they end up back in their seats.

The people of Israel are now captives in a strange land. They are still God's people, but since they disobeyed Him, He allowed their city to be ruined. We don't know
what it would feel like to be captives, but the captives probably felt like some of us have felt who have moved and had to leave behind good friends or our old school.

● **Has anyone ever moved from one town or one state to another?** Interview several kids who have moved. Ask them about places they miss and how they felt about moving.

● **Do you want to go back?**

● **What things do you see or have which remind you of where you used to live and of your old friends? Pictures? Letters?**

Point out that the Jews missed Jerusalem very much. They also missed the Temple. They probably had things which reminded them of Jerusalem and the Temple and their lives there.

● **What kinds of things might they have had to remind them of the Temple?**

EXPLORING WORSHIP

Discuss with the children what our own place of worship means to us, using questions like the following.

● **The Israelites called their place of worship the Temple. What words do we use for our place of worship?** (Church, sanctuary, meetinghouse, Sunday school, God's house)

● **Why do we have a special place to worship God?** (So we can be together with other people who want to worship God; it makes Sunday special to have a special place for learning about God and worshiping Him; a church is built especially to help people learn about God and worship Him.)

● **What are some of the important objects in the sanctuary?** You may want to list these on a chalkboard or
newsprint. Point out to the children that many objects in the sanctuary, like crosses and Communion tables, remind us of things that God has done. These symbols are like the pictures that reminded some of the children of old friends.

● **What are some of the important things that happen in our special place of worship?**

● **What is something you especially like about our sanctuary?** Encourage the children to freely express their opinions; accept each idea and make sure no one laughs at someone else's idea.

● **Where else can we worship God?** Make sure the children know that we can worship God anywhere. Remind them that the Israelites still worshiped God in Babylon, even without the Temple. **Name some other places you can worship God and what you do there.** (At mealtimes—pray before we eat; in the car—sing Gospel songs; at home with family—read the Bible and pray together; in my bedroom—pray before bedtime; at school—pray quietly to myself; on vacation—praise God for all the beauty of the world.)

● **What would we do if something happened to our sanctuary—if it burned down or got destroyed? Where would we worship?**

I know something you should know and I'm going to make you learn it—is above all else what prevents learning.
—John Holt

After the children answer this question, hand out paper and crayons. Instruct the children to draw a picture of something in your sanctuary that reminds them of God. If you have time, encourage some of the children to share their pictures.

One thing that helps us remember God is the Bible. The Bible tells what God is like. It also tells how God takes care of His people. The Bible gives God's words to us, which we can read anytime, not just on Sunday. We need to hide God's Word in our hearts. Hiding God's Word in our hearts means to study it, to memorize it, to learn what it says, and obey it. Remember how hard it was for the Israelites to obey God when they had lost the scroll that contained the Law? If we will hide God's Word in our hearts, then we'll have it with us even if we lose our Bibles.

WORSHIPING TOGETHER

You have explored the Bible story of Josiah, who found the lost scroll of the Scriptures and tried to encourage the people of Judah to obey God's laws. The children have participated in the story, imagining what it would be like to have God's Word and their worship place taken away from them.

You have also explored some of what it means to have a special place—a sanctuary, a house of worship—where we go to worship God and learn His Word and how to obey Him. This exploration has included the importance of knowing that God is everywhere and that we can worship Him anywhere. When we study, learn, and memorize the Bible, we are writing God's Law in our hearts where it can never be lost.

Today's worship service focuses on praising God for being with us in our place of worship. In keeping with this week's worship aim—to sense that God is with us in our place of worship—choose hymns or choruses that focus on God's house and God's presence. Consider singing "Holy, Holy, Holy." From *Worship Time Music Book* you might select "I Was Glad" and "Talking with God."

It is important that the children participate, making the worship their own as much as possible. Distribute leadership responsibilities for the various parts of the worship time. (Try not to choose the same students each week!)

RESPONDING PERSONALLY

We want the children to respond in a personal way to what they have learned today—that God is everywhere so He is with them where they worship Him.

Let students make signs and other decorations that will remind them that God is in their worship area. Provide necessary materials. Balloons are not usually used in sanctuaries, but make them available for the kids to use to help create an atmosphere of praise and celebration.

After the decorating is finished, encourage children to straighten up the worship area. This way they will have a neat, pleasant place in which to worship God next week. You might want to take an instant photograph of the decorated room to place in the class worship journey notebook. ■

> **B**e still, and know that I am God;
>   I will be exalted among the nations,
>   I will be exalted in the earth.
> —Psalm 46:10

IN WORSHIP
WE SENSE GOD'S PRESENCE

1. Call to Worship—Psalm 150:1, 6

2. Invocation—Be with us in Your house today. Help us to sense Your presence. Help us learn to respect and appreciate our place of worship. In Jesus' name. Amen.

3. Hymn

4. Our Statement of Faith—*In unison, read our church's doctrinal creed which you studied in Unit 2.*

5. Scripture Reading—II Kings 23:1-3

6. Prayer—*After each sentence, respond with, "We praise You, O God."*

Dear God, for being with us here in this place today . . .
We thank You that You are not only here, but everywhere.
We praise You that we can worship You here, and anywhere.
Forgive us, dear Lord, for sometimes not being thankful for Your house and Your Word. Help us learn to respect and appreciate them in a new way.
In Jesus' name we pray. Amen.

7. Hymn

8. Student Worship Talk—*Complete the sentences below with your own words and ideas.*

  I. Read II Kings 23:1, 2.
   A. In this verse, King Josiah called everyone in Jerusalem to come together at the Temple because _____.
   B. We come together in a sanctuary because _____.
   C. Some of the people who read and teach God's Word to us are _____.
   D. God is disappointed when sometimes we don't want to hear from the Bible. We would rather _____.

 II. Read II Kings 23:3.
   A. The people in Jerusalem made a promise to worship God once again and to obey His Word.
   B. God wants us to obey His Word. Two ways we can obey it are _____.

III. God is everywhere.
   A. It is good to worship Him at church because _____.
   B. I know that God is with us when we worship Him because _____.

9. Benediction—May you sense God's presence with you everywhere you go. May we come together gladly next week to worship and praise Him with all God's people. ■

SESSION 46
WORSHIP AIM:

ENJOYING GOD'S HOUSE

Journey into Ezra and Nehemiah: The Jews rebuild Jerusalem and its Temple (pp. 438-446).

Special Things You'll Need:
☐ Candles (10-15) of different sizes and colors
☐ Adult volunteer to tell the story
☐ Poem, "I Was Glad," activity piece 11B in the back of this book
☐ "Captivity Quiz Game," activity piece 11C in the back of this book (Optional)
☐ Supplies for "Make a Stained-glass Window," page 80 of *THE Idea Book* (Optional)
☐ Supplies for "Banners That Praise God," see page 79 of *THE Idea Book* (Optional)

GETTING STARTED

Welcome the children as they come to children's church. As you are waiting for all students to arrive, choose one or more of the following activities to help them prepare for your time together. Encourage each child to participate.

☐ Select two or three children to help you decorate your worship area. The children can set up candles all around the room to give it a festive air. You can light the candles now or wait and light them at the beginning of the worship service. Use candles of all sizes and colors. They can be used (but make sure they are more than stubs, as you will want them to last throughout the service). Encourage the children to be careful around the lit candles. You will probably need to ask the head of the property committee, or other appropriate official, for permission to light candles in the classroom.

☐ Later in the lesson, the children

will have an opportunity to make stained-glass windows or banners. Ask several students to help you set out the supplies for the stained-glass project, or the banner project. If you have enough time and a large enough staff, you may want to set up both projects and let each child choose which one he or she wants to do.

☐ This activity is designed to help the children gain a better understanding of how the Jews might have felt their first few nights in Babylon. Distribute paper and crayons or colored markers.

● **Have you ever spent the night in a strange place? How did you feel?**

Instruct the children to draw a picture of themselves spending the night in a strange place. The pictures should show how they felt about it. Spend some time showing the pictures to each other. Discuss with the children the similarities between how they felt that night and how the Jews probably felt when they first arrived in Babylon.

☐ Make final preparations for In Worship. Do you have volunteers to take part in the worship service? Besides the song leader, Scripture reader(s), worship talk and prayer givers, you will need three readers to practice the poem, "I Was Glad!" Give the readers copies of the poem found in the Worshiping Together section; also give a copy of the Order of Worship to each participant to help him or her prepare.

EXPLORING THE BIBLE

In this session we want students to realize that they can enjoy worshiping in God's house as much as the Jews did back in Bible days. While we know that the Church is God's people, the church building is the place today where we get together to worship God.

Review where we left our Bible adventure last session with a summary like this:

Remember what happened to the Jews in our last story? King Josiah (who had found the Book of Law and read it to the people) died, and the people once again began to disobey God's laws. After many years, God allowed the Babylonian army to conquer the city of Jerusalem, and they took most of the Jews back to their own country as captives. But before the soldiers left, they burned the Temple and the city to the ground.

Now, let's talk to one of the captives and find out what happened to the people in Babylon.

Have an adult volunteer enter the room, dressed like a person from Bible times, and tell today's story. (Be sure to contact your volunteer early in the week.) The storyteller may want to pick a Bible name like Aaron or Hannah. Encourage the storyteller to be creative in telling the story. The *Picture Bible* should serve as a rough guide for the story. The volunteer may want to work some of the dialogue into the story by saying things like, "I heard someone in the crowd say . . ." and so on.

After the storyteller is finished, discuss the story with the children. If you have time, you may want the children to play the "Captivity Quiz Game." You will need to make sure that the storyteller covers all the points in the quiz when he or she tells the story.

This game provides a fun and factual review of today's story. Don't limit your review to this quiz, however. The children need to learn the facts of the story, but even more important, they need to understand the flow of the story and discover what the story means in terms of their lives today. The following questions should help you achieve the latter goal.

● Why do you think Cyrus, the Persian king, let the Jews go back to Jerusalem?

● What did the Jews start rebuilding first? (the Temple)

● Why do you think they decided to work on it first?

● What did the people do after they laid the foundation of the Temple? Why?

● Why did the Samaritans get the king to stop the Israelites from building the Temple?

● Why did the priest, Ezra, come to Jerusalem?

● What did Nehemiah tell the Jewish leaders?

● How did the workers protect themselves from their enemies?

EXPLORING WORSHIP

Lead into an exploration of how our sanctuary helps us worship today with the following comments:

The Temple was very important to the Jews. It was a sign of God's presence among them. When Solomon built the Temple, he included important aspects of the Tabernacle like the Holy of Holies. He also insisted on the finest materials and workmanship. His workers made the Temple very beautiful. When the Jews returned from the Babylonian Captivity, they made the new Temple even more splendid with many reminders of God's greatness, His faithfulness, and holiness.

● Why do you think the Jews wanted the Temple to be so beautiful?

● How do beautiful things remind us of God?

Ask your students to list the many special things used in your own sanctuary (church building) as reminders of God. Ask one of the students to record the suggestions given by the class on the chalkboard or a piece of newsprint. The list might include: A steeple or spire which points to God; the shape of a cross inside the sanctuary; beautiful stained-glass windows (some might depict a Biblical scene); banners or posters which praise God; candles which remind us of the "Light of the World"; a special pulpit Bible which stays in the sanctuary; etc.

Encourage students to think about why your church building is built and decorated the way it is, and the ways these things help you worship God and think about Him.

● What are some ways that we could make our special worship place beautiful?

After discussing this question with the children. Give them the experience of making a beautiful reminder of God. Use either the project "Make a Stained-glass Window," or "Banners That Praise

Where did we get the idea that God loves sh-h-h and drab and anything will do? I think it's blasphemy not to bring our joy into His Church.
—Ann Weems

193

God." (If you have the time, staff, and materials, you could do both projects and let the children choose one or the other.)

As the children work, encourage them to use their own creativity to give their projects individuality. The windows of the stained-glass project can be cut out in different designs. The banners, of course, can be decorated in a variety of ways and colors; each child can also choose his or her own saying instead of the ones suggested.

Use these reminders to decorate your children's church room for several weeks. Then have the children take them home.

WORSHIPING TOGETHER

You have helped students journey with God's people out of captivity in Babylon back to their own land where they rebuilt their Temple, their city, and their lives. Students have begun to understand the beauty of God's house, and how things can be reminders of God.

Now it is time to move your students into a time of worship when you praise God together and enjoy beautiful reminders of Him in your worship place. Adapt the following plan to complement your church's order of worship. In keeping with this week's worship aim—to praise God as we enjoy beautiful reminders of Him in our worship place—choose hymns or choruses that remind us of God's house and praising Him. How about singing "To God Be the Glory" as a hymn of praise. Other songs for today's theme from *Worship Time Music Book* are "Give unto the Lord" and "I Was Glad."

You will need three students to

read the poem, "I Was Glad," that follows the reading of the Statement of Faith.

RESPONDING PERSONALLY

Choose one of the following ideas to help kids respond to what they have learned.

☐ Encourage the children to think of all the things in the church building that remind them of God. Have them pick the one that is their favorite and draw a picture of it or write a description of it. (You will need to make paper, pencils, and crayons available.) If there is time at the end, allow the children to tell what they drew or wrote about. Help the children see that their pictures and descriptions can remind them of God throughout the week.

☐ To help the children express their thanks to God for His presence in worship, have them write a song based on a well-known hymn tune. ("Amazing Grace," "Jesus Loves Me," or "Trust and Obey" would all work well.) The children could include verses that praise God for the beautiful objects at church which remind them of Him. You could have the entire group work on the song

together, or divide it into smaller groups and have each group take a verse. Spend a few minutes singing the verses that you have written.

☐ When it is time to close, let individual children blow out a candle (lit at the beginning of this session) and give thanks for one thing they appreciate or that reminds them of God in our sanctuary. After the candles are blown out, close with a prayer of thanksgiving. ∎

IN WORSHIP
WE ENJOY GOD'S HOUSE

1. Call to Worship—Psalm 122:1

2. Invocation—Almighty God, be with us today as we enjoy Your house together. We are glad to be here. Help us respect and care for this place of worship. In Jesus' name we pray. Amen.

3. Hymn

4. Our Statement of Faith—*Recite our church's doctrinal creed here.*

5. Scripture Reading—Read Ezra 3:10-13.

6. Poem—"I Was Glad!"

7. Hymn

8. Student Worship Talk—*Complete the sentences below with your own words and ideas.*

I. Read Ezra 6:16.
  A. The people were very happy when the Temple was rebuilt. A time when I felt happy about our church was

  _____.

  B. The people not only worked hard to build the Temple again, but they gave their own jewels and fine cloth to make it beautiful. Some of the things which make our place of worship beautiful are _____.

  C. We can help keep our sanctuary beautiful by

  _____.

II. Read Ezra 6:18.
  A. Different groups of people served God in the Temple in different ways. We can serve God in our church by

  _____.

  B. God was happy because the people were obeying Him once more. Two things we can do to make God happy are _____.

  C. This week I will obey God by _____.

9. Benediction—May God help us to enjoy meeting in His house more and more. May we also enjoy Him during the week by reading His Word and praying. ■

**SESSION 47
WORSHIP AIM:**

CELEBRATING TOGETHER

Journey into Esther: Haman tries to destroy the Jews but Esther saves them (pp. 447-460).

Special Things You'll Need:
- [ ] Copies of "Who's Who?" work sheet, activity piece 11D in the back of this book
- [ ] "Crown and Mustache Props," page 23 in THE Idea Book
- [ ] Copies of "The Story of Queen Esther" mini-drama, pages 34-37 of THE Idea Book; also props and cue cards
- [ ] Items for a celebration (see lesson plan)
- [ ] Sample invitation for students to copy
- [ ] Poem, "I Was Glad," activity piece 11B in the back of this book
- [ ] Supplies for "The Feast of Purim," see page 63 of THE Idea Book (Optional)

GETTING STARTED

As your children arrive, use one or more of the following introductory activities to prepare them for today's session. Some activities use all the children; others can be done by smaller groups.

- [ ] Pass out copies of the work sheet "Who's Who?" This is an icebreaker to encourage the children to get to know each other better and enjoy each other more. This activity should help the children better enjoy their opportunities to celebrate together later in the lesson.
- [ ] Enjoy a Feast of Purim together. Note that the mini-dramas about Queen Esther fit right in with celebrating the Feast of Purim.
- [ ] Choose participants for the Esther mini-dramas. They will need some time to read over their scripts.

Choose three artistic students to make props for the Esther play: a construction paper crown for the King, another for Queen Esther, and a villain's moustache for Haman. You will need construction paper, scissors, and tape or glue.

EXPLORING THE BIBLE

The story of Esther is an exciting one. Your students will enjoy acting it out. There are three scenes, each takes one page. Don't have the students attempt to memorize the play; let them read right from their scripts.

To use the most students possible in the mini-dramas about Esther, choose different groups to act out each scene. This arrangement means there will be three Queen Esthers, three Kings, etc. Each group can rehearse its scene briefly, then present it to the rest of the children. You will need only one set of props; props can be passed from one group to the next when it is its turn to perform. Or, if you prefer, you can use one group of children to act out all three scenes of the mini-drama. In this case, the group of players will need a little longer to read through the play together.

(Alternative: Make paper bag puppets as described on page 18 of THE Idea Book, one for each character in the Esther mini-drama; use the puppets to act out the play.)

Notice that there is a "crowd cue card person" in each scene. This person holds up cue cards that tell the audience what to do at different points, involving all the children in the drama.

Lead into today's mini-drama in the following way.

In our last session, we saw what happened when some of the Jews returned to their own land from captivity in Babylon to rebuild the Temple. But some of the Jews were settled in Babylon and Persia and decided to stay. Today's Bible story tells us what happened to some of the Jews who stayed.

Now enjoy the mini-drama about Esther.

After the children finish the play, explain that they still haven't heard the whole story. Then read pages 459 and 460 in the *Picture Bible*.

It is important that you make sure the children understand what happened in the story and why it happened. You also want to help them see what this story can teach them about celebrating. Use the following questions to help you in your review and discussion.

- **Who were the Jews in the story?**
- **Why was Haman mad at Mordecai?**
- **Why wouldn't Mordecai bow to Haman?**
- **What did Haman decide to do to get back at Mordecai?**
- **Why was Esther afraid to go before the king?**
- **How did the King save the Jews?**
- **Why did Mordecai decide to start the Feast of Purim?**
- **What were they celebrating?**
- **How do you think they felt toward God?**

EXPLORING WORSHIP

Call the children's attention to the time when Mordecai, the new Prime Minister of Persia, instituted a yearly celebration to commemorate how the Jews were saved from their enemy. This celebration is called the Feast of Purim and is still celebrated by the Jews to this day. If you have not already done so earlier in this session, review for your students what happens on the Feast of Purim.

During the Feast of Purim, the Jews celebrate the time when God saved them from being killed by the Persians. When we worship with other Christians in the church sanctuary, we are also celebrating. We are celebrating that God saves us from our sins. We celebrate other things at church, too.

Ask your students to review some of the holidays and events that you celebrate regularly in your church: Christmas, Good Friday, Easter, Pentecost, the Lord's Supper (Communion), baptism, etc.
- **What is being celebrated on each of these occasions? What are some of the different ways to celebrate?** (Many of these were studied in Unit 10.)

Now explore with your students new things you have to celebrate:
- **Is there a special way God is taking care of us?**
- **What is God doing for us and for others?**
- **What are some recent good things that are happening at our church or among the people of the church?**
- **Is there someone we especially appreciate in our church?** Use a chalkboard or newsprint to list all the things mentioned.

Move into a discussion about what makes a good celebration. Invite the children's ideas and contributions, and list them on another part of the chalkboard, or another sheet of newsprint. Some of the areas to consider:
- Being together with other people who also want to celebrate this event;

- Doing something that helps recall the thing being celebrated (e.g. a story or play, reenacting the event, using symbols that remind us of the event);
- Doing things that express joy: singing, laughing, playing games, etc.;
- Decorations that are symbolic of the event, or that give a festive air;
- Special foods to share that become traditional with this celebration;
- Showing appreciation to others: giving gifts, saying thanks, etc.;
- Showing appreciation to God: giving gifts to God, prayers of thanksgiving, songs of worship.

Now ask your students to choose one event on their list that they would like to celebrate. Guide them in their choice to consider something that relates closely to their own experience together in your church, something that means a lot to them. This could be a person, an event, a continuing blessing. Use the general ideas they listed above to make a good celebration.
- **What specific things could we do to celebrate this event (or person or blessing, etc.)?**

Indicate that you want to celebrate this event as you move into your worship time together and also at the end of the session.

It is easier and more pleasant for us to carry out ideas we have discovered for ourselves.
—Lois E. LeBar

WORSHIPING TOGETHER

Now it is time to move your students into a time of worship, when you can praise God together and celebrate the event you have chosen. Adapt the following plan to complement your church's order of worship. In keeping with this week's worship aim—to celebrate with God's people in our worship place—choose hymns or choruses that focus on celebrating salvation and life together as the church. "Joyful, Joyful, We Adore Thee" is a good opening hymn. *Worship Time Music Book* has songs that fit this theme for you to consider: "The Church Is God's People," page 24, and "I Need You and You Need Me," page 15.

It is important that the children participate, making the worship time their own as much as possible. Distribute leadership responsibilities for the various parts of the worship time: song leader, Scripture reader(s), three readers for the poem "I Was Glad!" worship talk leader, prayer leader, etc. (Try not to choose the same students each week!) You may photocopy the suggestions below, or write a similar order of worship, adapting it to your particular group and situation. Give copies to each one who will participate in the service.

Notice that the poem "I Was Glad!" is used in this worship service as well as the last session. Ask three different students to volunteer to be readers. A second reading will emphasize the importance of being **together** in God's house in a new way.

RESPONDING PERSONALLY

Continue the spirit of celebration by moving into a time of festivity, with the event (person/blessing/etc.) chosen earlier as the focus of your joy. Some ingredients for spontaneous celebration might be:
- Balloons, streamers;
- Treats: cookies, punch;
- Allowing time for different children to say why they are thankful for the focused event (person/blessing/etc.);
- If a person is being honored and can be present, allow time for different children to say why they appreciate this person;
- Any other elements of celebration mentioned by the children earlier in the session which can be done simply at this time.

An alternative might be to plan a more elaborate celebration at another time if the event is a major one or if you would like to honor a person who isn't present today. If so, incorporate the children's suggestions for celebrating this event in a more deliberate way. Make use of symbols as reminders—storytelling, festive food, decorations, a time for sharing thanksgivings. You may wish to make this an annual event.

The children are feeling joyful about being together in God's house, celebrating His goodness through people and events. This would be a good time to encourage them to share this joy of being together by inviting a friend to come with them next Sunday. If you have time, write the following invitation on the chalkboard and let the children copy it, using nice paper and colorful markers:

Dear _____,
I would like to invite you to come with me to (*your church*) next Sunday. I enjoy meeting together at church to learn about God. I think you would enjoy it, too.
Your friend,
_____ ■

IN WORSHIP
WE CELEBRATE TOGETHER

1. Call to Worship—Psalm 27:4

2. Invocation—Dear Lord, we are truly thankful that we can be together to celebrate Your love for us. We praise You for Your care for us each day, especially for . . . . *(insert chosen event to celebrate)*. In Jesus' name, we pray. Amen.

3. Hymn

4. Our Statement of Faith—*Recite together our church's doctrinal creed which we learned in Unit 2.*

5. Scripture Reading—Esther 9:20-23, 26-28

6. Prayer—*Thank God that together we can celebrate special things about Him. Ask Him to help us be aware of the joy of celebrating.*

7. Poem—"I Was Glad"

8. Hymn

9. Student Worship Talk—*Complete the sentences below with your own words and ideas:*

 I. Read Esther 9:22a.
 A. The Jews celebrated being saved from their enemies. One thing that God has saved us from is _____.
 B. The Jews celebrated that their sorrow had been turned into joy. Today we are feeling joyful about _____.
 C. The Jews had been afraid, but instead of being killed they had a day of celebration. Some of the reasons we would like to celebrate are _____.

 II. Read Esther 9:22b.
 A. The Jews celebrated by feasting and joy. Today we have suggested many ways to celebrate. Two ways are

 _____.
 B. Another way of celebrating at the Feast of Purim is giving presents of food to one another and gifts to the poor. Some of the ways we can share our blessings with others are _____.
 C. It's easy to take God's care for us for granted. This week I want to help remind myself of God's love and care for me by _____.

10. Benediction—May God grant us eyes to see, ears to hear, and hearts to understand all the ways that He loves and cares for us. Let us go from here in a spirit of celebration. ■

SESSION 48
WORSHIP AIM:

Telling Others

We have come to the final unit of our yearlong journey through the Old Testament and the study of the worship service. Appropriately, this unit is about conclusions. But it is also about beginnings.

Students will discover how faithlessness and disobedience led to the destruction of Jerusalem and to the end of Israel and Judah. They will listen to the prophets call for repentance and then foretell of doom and destruction. And they will watch as God's people were led captive from their homeland into exile in the distant city of Babylon.

Some things ended, but others began. God's people began to see Him with powerful new understanding. God was *not* limited by the boundaries of Jerusalem or Judah. Worship of God was *not* restricted to the Temple of Jerusalem. God is everywhere—even in the distant land of Babylon. And God's people could worship Him no matter where they were. It was during their years of exile that some of God's people came to an exciting new awareness of God's presence in their lives.

The worship focus of these sessions is the benediction, the blessing which marks the end of church worship and sends us on our way to begin worshiping God by the way we live. As students study the benediction and its purpose and meaning, they will grow in the understanding that worship is an everyday, minute-by-minute experience of living in God's love and praising God with the whole of their lives. ■

Journey into Isaiah; Jeremiah 1, 20—36; II Kings 22—23: Isaiah and Jeremiah accept God's call to witness to the Jews (pp. 461-469).

Special Things You'll Need:
☐ Materials for "Make a Relief Map," page 50 in *THE Idea Book*
☐ "Divided Kingdom" map
☐ Copies of pictures 1 and 2 from the "Photo Album" activity piece 12A in the back of this book
☐ Materials for different types of benedictions, pages 82 and 83 in *THE Idea Book*
☐ Globe or world map (Optional)

GETTING STARTED

Today the children will read the sad story of the fall of Judah, and the scattering of God's people. They will see how the prophet Jeremiah continued to share God's message in spite of persecution. As students arrive, involve them in one or more of these activities.

☐ Introduce the "Make a Relief Map." Let students begin to create the map of the exile and captivity. Have them place the two figures for Session 48 near Jerusalem on the map. You can use this map in all sessions of the unit.

☐ Write the word "Benediction" on the chalkboard or a large sheet of paper. Ask students to define it.

☐ On the chalkboard, write "How I Hear God's Message" and have students list various means of hearing about God (Bible; TV; parents; pastor; Sunday school teachers; etc.).

● When you share God's message with your friends, what do you tell them? List student responses on the chalkboard.

● Suppose a good friend were stealing something from a grocery store. What message from God might he need to hear?

Explain that sometimes God's message is good news, and sometimes it is bad news. Today students will hear about some men who shared God's good and bad news with a whole nation.

EXPLORING THE BIBLE

Students have seen how God guided the people of both Judah and Israel. At the time of today's story, only Judah remained intact. But because of sin, soon the nation of Judah would also be destroyed.

Let a student point out the location of Israel on a map.

● We have learned how God sent two messengers, Elijah and Elisha, to warn the people of Israel that there was trouble ahead if they did not stop worshiping idols. What were these messengers called? If students need a clue, begin to spell "prophets" on the chalkboard.

Even though these prophets gave many warnings, the people wouldn't listen. Finally, Assyrian soldiers conquered the nation of Israel and took away its people as captives. Now only the small nation of Judah remained. If students have used the relief map in Getting Started, point to Assyria and Judah. As you discuss today's story, continue using this map as a visual aid.

Write "Isaiah" and "Jeremiah" on the board and pronounce them for the class. These men shared God's message with the people of Judah. In today's Bible story we will see how God called these prophets. We will also study the messages God gave them to share.

Have students silently read pages 461-469 in the *Picture Bible*, and look for both good and bad news that the prophets shared.

● **How did God call Isaiah to become a prophet?** Let kids describe Isaiah's vision and encounter with God in the Temple. Note Isaiah's willingness to serve God: "Here I am; send me."

● **What was Isaiah's message to his people? When the people refused to listen, Isaiah's message changed.**

● **What was Isaiah's final warning to the sinful nation?**

Isaiah also gave the people God's Good News. Have students read aloud Isaiah's message on the bottom of page 462. Help students understand that Isaiah was telling the people that God planned to send a special Person who would save the world from sin. This Person would be called the Messiah or Christ.

● **Why did Jeremiah object when God called him to be a prophet?**

● **What was Jeremiah's message to his people?**

Review the final picture frame on page 465 in the *Picture Bible*. Show how Jeremiah's prophecy of doom was beginning to come true—first by Egypt and then by Babylon who conquered Jerusalem, Judah's capital city.

● **How did the people react to Jeremiah's warnings of destruction?**

● **Why do you think Jeremiah kept on repeating the same warning in spite of all these difficulties?**

Ask students to recall a time when they were doing something dangerous and someone warned them to stop. Maybe they were hitting balls into a busy street, climbing too high in a tree, or experimenting with things not good for them (cigarettes, drugs, even junk food).

● **Did you believe the person who warned you? Why or why not?**

● **What might have happened if the person had not given you the warning?**

Help students understand that when someone gives us a warning, we should ask ourselves, "Would God give me this same warning?" If the answer is yes, we should change our actions.

Hand out the first two pictures from the "Photo Album." Let students summarize the stories of Isaiah's and Jeremiah's calls by completing the picture captions in their own words. Refer to pages 462 and 464 in the *Picture Bible*, if necessary. (. . . told the people of Judah that they should destroy their idols and worship God . . . most of the people refused to listen, kept on sinning . . . if the people didn't repent, they would be destroyed by enemies.) After completing the captions, they can color the "photos" and glue them onto a construction paper "album page."

EXPLORING WORSHIP

Since this is the final unit in our worship journey through the Bible, review the preceding units on Invocation, Creed, Hymns, Scripture Readings, Our Response, Offering, Prayer, Sermon, Worship Leaders, Our Role, and the Sanctuary. Explain that this final unit explores what happens after we worship.

When we sit through a church service, singing hymns, hearing God's Word, and praying to God, we are brought close to God.

● **What should happen when we go back to our families, neighborhoods, and schools?**

Refer to the word "benediction" which you printed on the board earlier (or print it on the board now). **At the end of most church services, as we get ready to go out and share God's message, the pastor speaks the words of benediction.** Explain that *benediction* means to speak well of, or to say good words or something good to someone. We also call the benediction a blessing.

If your pastor recites a regular benediction each week, make a copy of it for the kids to examine or let students turn to where it is printed in your church hymnal or worship book. Read this benediction aloud together, and discuss its meaning.

Two of the most frequently used benedictions come from passages in Scripture. Let the students look these up in Numbers 6:24-26 ("The Lord bless you and keep you . . .") and II Corinthians 13:14 ("May the grace of the Lord Jesus Christ . . ."). If these are used in your church services, you might want to let students memorize them in the weeks ahead.

Point out how most benedictions are wishes or reminders that God will be with us and surround us with His love, strength, and protection.

● **Why do you think the pastor says these words to us as we get ready to**

And this is my prayer: that your love may abound more and more in knowledge and depth of insight.
—Philippians 1:9

leave church and go out to tell others about God?

WORSHIPING TOGETHER

Review with students the place and purpose of the benediction. Encourage them to be listening for it during In Worship.

In keeping with this week's worship aim—to tell others God's message—try to select hymns that focus on sharing our faith with others. You might start with the hymn, "O for a Thousand Tongues to Sing." "I Can Join," page 31, and "I Need You and You Need Me," page 15, from *Worship Time Music Book*, would be appropriate songs to use.

aren't limited to the benedictions that are suggested in the projects. Encourage them to come up with blessings that might be more appropriate or personal to the people who will receive the gifts. ■

RESPONDING PERSONALLY

To conclude this session, give the children a chance to personalize what they have gained from the worship experience and their study of the benediction.

Remind students that the benediction—or blessing—sends us on our way with confidence that God loves us.

● **When might people need to hear a benediction during the week?**

Think of a person you know who might be encouraged by a reminder of God's love. If you were able to bring in apples, oranges, and donuts, let students choose from the "Benedictions to Eat" as well as the "Stand-up Benediction Card" idea.

Be ready to offer help if the kids have problems with any of the projects. It would be a good idea to make a sample stand-up card, explaining each step as the kids watch. Remind students that they

IN WORSHIP
WE TELL OTHERS ABOUT GOD

1. Call to Worship—Psalm 105:1, 2

2. Invocation—Dear Lord, we are together here today to worship You. Let our thoughts and our voices praise You. Help us to learn what You want us to. In Jesus' name. Amen.

3. Hymn

4. Our Statement of Faith—*Read this aloud together.*

5. Scripture Reading—Read Isaiah 6:1-8 and
   Jeremiah 1:4-8.

6. Prayer—*Complete the following prayer sentences.*
   Dear God, we praise You because You are _____.
   Give us strength to tell others about You. They may need to hear that _____. We know that You hear our prayers and will answer them in the best way. In Jesus' name. Amen.

7. Hymn

8. Student Worship Talk—*Complete the sentences below.*
   I. Read Jeremiah 1:4, 5.
      A. In these verses, God told Jeremiah to be a prophet who would speak for God. God wants me to speak for Him, too.
      B. There are people whom I know who need to hear that
         _____.
   II. Read Jeremiah 1:6.
      A. At first, Jeremiah was afraid to be God's prophet. He argued that he was _____.
      B. Sometimes I am like Jeremiah. I try to get out of speaking for God because I'm worried that _____.
   III. Read verses 7 and 8.
      A. God told Jeremiah not to worry about being too young. And God promised to _____.
      B. God also promises to be with me when I speak to others about Him. Knowing that God will be with me makes me feel _____.
      C. I know that, with God helping me, I can talk to others and tell them that _____.
   IV. Read Isaiah 6:8.
      A. When Isaiah heard God ask for someone to be His prophet, Isaiah answered _____.
      B. I can offer to speak for God whenever _____.

9. Benediction—Read II Corinthians 13:14.
   May God give us power to share that love and friendship as we tell others about Him in the weeks ahead. ■

203

SESSION 49
WORSHIP AIM:

PREPARING FOR PROBLEMS

Journey into II Kings 24; Jeremiah 27—43: Jeremiah urges the Jews to turn back to God as the Babylonians attack them (pp. 470-478).

Special Things You'll Need:
☐ Materials for "Make a Relief Map," page 50 in *THE Idea Book*
☐ Copies of pictures 3 and 4 from "Photo Album," activity piece 12B in the back of this book
☐ Materials for "Stand-up Benedictions," page 82, and "Benedictions to Eat," page 83, in *THE Idea Book*

GETTING STARTED

Choose one or more of the following activities to do with your group.

☐ Students who are working on the relief map can add glue and yarn to trace the captives' route from Jerusalem to Babylon and place the figure for Session 49 on the map. If you have a globe or world map, let children use it to locate some of the areas pictured on the map they're making. Talk about events taking place in these countries today.

☐ Ask children to recall a time when they saw a person being treated badly because of his or her religious beliefs. Maybe the child was teased for missing a sports practice on Sunday morning. Or maybe the child was laughed at because he or she wouldn't swear or tell a dirty story.

● How did the person seem to feel during this time?

● Did any other kid help the one who was being treated badly? If so, what did the person say or do?

● Most people who take their Christian faith seriously are treated badly at one time or another. What might help us prepare for such times?

The object of this discussion is to make students aware that standing up for one's religious faith is not easy. It helps to be prepared ahead of time.

EXPLORING THE BIBLE

To help students put today's Bible story in context, let them quickly summarize last week's story about the call and assignment given to Isaiah and Jeremiah. The kids can use their "photo album" pages to help them review.

If students are making the relief map, use it to show students how, because the people of Judah refused to listen to the prophets, Judah was conquered first by Egypt and later by Babylon. Let a volunteer come to the map and trace the long route taken by the first bunch of captives from Jerusalem to Babylon.

To set the stage for today's story, read the caption of the last frame on page 469 in the *Picture Bible* and have a student read Jeremiah's speech.

In today's story, we will see how God's prophet Jeremiah and the kings of Judah usually disagreed about how to rule the people.
Have students read pages 470-473.

● **What did the kings of Judah usually want to do about their Babylonian rulers?**

● **What did Jeremiah say they should do?**

● **If you were a king of Judah, what would you do? Why?**

Have students read pages 474-478.

● **Why did Jerusalem finally fall to the Babylonian army?** (The army surrounded the city for 30 months—two and one-half years! Jerusalem's people were probably weak from

hunger, disease, and casualties.)

Time and again, Jeremiah begged his king and his people to give in to the Babylonians. He told his people that God had sent the Babylonians as punishment and that Judah should accept that punishment.
● Why do you suppose the people refused to listen to Jeremiah's warnings?
● Why didn't Jeremiah give up when he saw how stubborn the people were?

Jeremiah had a really tough job to do. Almost everything God told him to say was bad news.
● How did the people of Judah bring the bad news on themselves? If students can't recall, refer to page 465. After Babylonian soldiers had surrounded the city of Jerusalem, Jeremiah had more bad news. He said the city would be destroyed if the king didn't surrender.

What made Jeremiah's job even harder was that his people refused to listen to him—even when his words started coming true. It took a lot of courage and strength for Jeremiah to keep up the job God had given him.

Distribute copies of pictures 3 and 4 from the "Photo Album." Let kids find these frames on pages 470-478 in the *Picture Bible* and use the captions and speech balloons on the frames to help them complete the captions on their album pictures. (. . . if Judah did revolt, the Babylonians would destroy the city; . . . took its people captive and burned the city to the ground.)

Then give kids time to color their pictures and glue or tape them onto a construction paper "album page." As the kids work at assembling their albums, offer suggestions for placement of the pictures, ideas on how to color the pictures (keeping a

character's clothes consistent, for example); and get the kids thinking about what they might do for their album covers (an appropriate design and title).

EXPLORING WORSHIP

Write the word "benediction" on the board.
● What is a benediction? (A blessing which asks for God's love and protection on us.)

The pastor speaks words of the benediction just before we leave church. The benediction helps us remember that God is going to be with us in the week ahead. It is especially good to hear the benediction when we face difficult times.

See if the kids can remember any of the benedictions mentioned in last week's session.
● What kind of benediction do you think Jeremiah would have needed to hear?
● What blessing or reminder would have helped him face all the problems he ran into? Help the kids put words of blessing and encouragement into a benediction for Jeremiah. Start them out by writing some beginning words on the board: "May God, who is stronger and more loving than we can imagine, be with you when . . ."

When we stand up for what's right and speak to others about God's will, we may need a blessing, too. Share an example of a time when you faced opposition for speaking out against wrong. Tell the kids how you felt and what you did to seek God's help in that experience. Did someone encourage you with a blessing from God?

It can seem easy to be a Christian when we're sitting in church listening to God's Word, surrounded by other Christians. But when we leave church, we often run into problems which make living like a Christian seem pretty hard. At those times, it can help to remember the blessing and promise of God's love in the benediction.

WORSHIPING TOGETHER

Today your students have learned that sometimes Christians must face difficult times because of their faith. Students have looked at the example of Jeremiah, who continued to give God's message to his people in spite of their unbelief and hostility. The benediction offered at the conclusion of the worship service is designed to encourage us when we must face hard times.

Pass out index cards or small slips of paper to the kids and let them create benedictions that would be especially good for kids who are facing problems. Have children name problems that young Christians like themselves might face. List these on the board. Then turn these problems into the beginnings of benedictions using the following format:

The teacher who is attempting to teach without inspiring the pupil with a desire to learn is hammering on cold iron.
—Horace Mann

When a classmate wants to cheat from you, may God . . .

When your friends laugh at you because you go to church, may God . . .

When you hear people using God's name in vain, may God . . .

When it doesn't seem like your prayers are being answered, may God . . .

Try to list a phrase for each student in class. Assign the phrases to the kids and let them create benedictions by completing the phrases on their index cards or slips of paper. Explain that volunteers will read these benedictions at the conclusion of the worship service.

Help students worship God by selecting songs that praise Him because He helps us prepare for problems. You could start the worship time by singing "O God, Our Help in Ages Past." From *Worship Time Music Book* you could sing "God's Way, the Best Way," page 20, and "You Know, Lord," page 19.

RESPONDING PERSONALLY

Conclude the session by giving children an opportunity to personalize what they have gained from the worship experience.

☐ Use one or more of the ideas suggested in "Stand-up Benedictions" and "Benedictions to Eat." Let students tackle the benediction projects during the sessions of this unit. If a student made the stand-up card last week, for example, he or she could make one of the "Benedictions to Eat" this week. Distribute sheets of construction paper for the cards and apples, oranges, or donuts for the other projects. Students can use the benedictions suggested on the project

sheets or choose some of the ones they made up for the worship in today's session.

☐ If you were able to bring refreshments today, suggest that kids use this time as they eat together as a chance to share when God helped them face problems as they stood up for what was right. You can help get these sharing experiences moving by telling kids about times when God helped you face such problems. Move around the group, talking about your own experiences and asking leading questions of the kids. ■

IN WORSHIP
WE PREPARE FOR PROBLEMS

1. Call to Worship—Psalm 105:1, 2

2. Invocation—Dear God, we have gathered to worship You. Be with us as we praise You for helping us with our problems. You are a great God, and we love You. In Jesus' name. Amen.

3. Hymn

4. Our Statement of Faith—*Repeat this together.*

5. Scripture Reading—Jeremiah 26:7, 8, 12-16

6. Prayer—*Complete the following sentences.*

Dear God, we praise You because You are _____.

We admit that we sometimes do wrong by _____.

We are sorry and ask You to forgive us. We're thankful that You still love us and that You sent Your Son, Jesus, to teach us Your ways. Help us, Lord, to do better in _____. Amen.

7. Hymn

8. Student Worship Talk—*Complete the sentences below.*

I. Read Jeremiah 26:7, 8.

  A. Jeremiah stood before his people and told them everything God had commanded him to say. Sometimes I need to stand up and talk for God, too. I need to tell my friends or family that _____.

  B. When the people refused to listen to Jeremiah or when they got angry about what he said, he must have felt _____.

  C. Sometimes I don't stand up for God because I'm afraid that if I do _____.

II. Read verses 12, 13.

  A. Even though the people were so angry that they wanted to kill Jeremiah, he repeated what God had told him to say. He must have really believed that _____.

  B. And Jeremiah must have trusted that God would _____.

  C. When I feel afraid to speak for God or have problems because I stand up for what's right, it helps me to remember that _____.

  D. Two ways God helps me with problems are by _____ and by_____.

9. Benediction—*(Read benedictions you wrote.)*

May the promise of God's love and protection keep you strong as you face problems because of your faith. ■

HAVING FAITH IN GOD

I f anyone would be a true Christian teacher, let him deny his own prejudices and take up Christ's methods, though they're not the easy ones, and follow the Master Teacher.

For whosoever would save himself shall lose the real thrill of teaching; and whosoever shall give himself wholly to teaching in the distinctive Christian way shall reap eternal results.

For what doth it profit a teacher to give out the whole truth if he loses his pupil?

But the Savior will reveal Himself by the Spirit when He is again allowed to teach in His own way through the teacher. (After Mark 8:43-36)
—Lois E. LeBar

Journey into Ezekiel: Ezekiel instructs the captive Jews to wait patiently for the Lord to restore their homeland (pp. 479-484).

Special Things You'll Need:
☐ Materials for "Make a Relief Map," page 50 in *THE Idea Book*
☐ Copies of pictures 5 and 6 from the "Photo Album," activity piece 12B in the back of this book
☐ Materials for "Stand-up Benedictions," page 85, and "Benedictions to Eat," page 86, in *THE Idea Book*

GETTING STARTED

Today your students will be encouraged to trust God to bring good from the difficulties in their lives. As students arrive and settle down, have them do one or more of the following activities.
☐ Let students work on the relief map. Kids could glue two more strips of different-colored yarn along the captives' route from Jerusalem to Babylon, to indicate the three times when Babylonians led captives from Judah. Have students place the two figures for Session 50 near Babylon on the map.
☐ If any children need to complete pages of their "Photo Album," let them use this time to do so.
☐ Share with the children a bad time in your life. Maybe a parent was seriously ill; you had to move to another town; your car was wrecked; etc. Then have children think of a bad time in their lives.
● **How did you feel when this happened to you?**
● **Did your family or the people in church pray for you or help in other ways?**

● **Did anything good come from this bad time?**
Help the children realize that everyone has bad times. God wants us to have hope that our Lord can bring good even from the hard times in our lives.

EXPLORING THE BIBLE

Today's Bible story is about a really hard time for the people of Judah. They had lost their homes, some of their relatives had probably been killed, and now they had to move far, far away to a foreign country.
To help students put today's story in context, briefly review the conclusion to last week's Bible story. **Jeremiah had begged the king of Judah to surrender to the Babylonian army. But the king refused.**
● **What happened to the king and the city of Jerusalem?** (Babylonian soldiers broke through the city wall, blinded the king, took the remaining people captive to Babylon, and burned Jerusalem to the ground.)
If students have made a relief map let a volunteer indicate the 900-mile route which the captives took from Jerusalem to Babylon.
● **How do you think the captives felt as they left behind their beloved city and headed toward an unknown future?**
Today's story moves us from Jerusalem to Babylon. **We'll look at some of the captives who had gone to Babylon before the city of Jerusalem was destroyed.** Read the opening caption on page 479 in the *Picture Bible:* "To understand the Book of Ezekiel . . ." Then assign parts for reading pages 479-484 aloud.

You take the lines of narration and assign students to read the speech balloons. Ezekiel has the largest role; characters with one speech balloon are Ezekiel's wife, a Babylonian soldier, and ten other captives.

Read through pages 479-481; then pause for a brief discussion. Help students understand that the city of Babylon was unlike anything which these captives had ever seen. The Babylonians had gathered riches from many lands they had conquered. Their capital city was filled with beautiful gates, palaces, temples, and houses. Point to the hanging gardens which kids added to the map they made. **The greatest king of Babylon was Nebuchadnezzar. To please one of his wives, Nebuchadnezzar had built a many-leveled palace which rose high into the sky. On each level of the palace, the king planted beautiful flowers, shrubs, and trees. These "hanging gardens," as they were called, were considered one of the seven wonders of the world.**

● **How do you suppose the poor, ragged, exhausted captives must have felt when their long journey was finally over and they looked around at Babylon?**

Use the student map to indicate the Euphrates River which flowed past the city. Explain that Babylon had built rich farmlands by digging canals which let the river flow into fields. The captives from Judah were allowed to build homes and farm the fields along these canals, so life wasn't really too bad for them. Note how Ezekiel farmed the land and built a house. He was sure that God wanted the captives to remain in Babylon for a long time.

Most of the captives were very unhappy in Babylon, even though life wasn't hard for them. They **believed that God had deserted them. The captives thought that God had stayed behind in the Temple of Jerusalem.**

● **What was wrong with the captives' attitude about Jerusalem?**

Study the vision which God sent to Ezekiel (shown on page 481 in the *Picture Bible*). In this vision, Ezekiel saw God's throne set on special wheels which turned in all directions. Help kids understand how the wheels illustrate that God moves everywhere; God is always with us.

Read the rest of the story on pages 482-484.

● **What terrible thing happened to the people of Judah?**

● **How did God bring something good out of this bad happening?**

Help children understand that the story has a hopeful ending, despite the news of Jerusalem's destruction. The captives had to give up their foolish ideas about Jerusalem and begin to worship God in this distant land. They had begun to learn that God's power extends beyond a building or country. Let a student reread Ezekiel's final words of challenge and promise on page 484.

Then distribute copies of pictures 5 and 6 from the "Photo Album." Let students complete the captions, color the pictures, and add them to their photo album page. (Picture 5: . . . because God can be everywhere; Picture 6: . . . some day they would return to Jerusalem)

After Jerusalem was destroyed, Ezekiel continued preaching words of hope to the unhappy captives. He helped them see that God had not deserted them and that God would one day bring His faithful people back to rebuild Jerusalem.

Help students understand that when Christians today worship God or think about God only in church on Sundays, they are acting like the unhappy captives in Babylon.

● **How do some Christians act like they've left God behind when they leave church?**

● **What are some good ways that we can worship God anytime and anyplace?**

Have students look again to the vision which God sent to Ezekiel on (page 481 of the *Picture Bible*). **This visual or picture of God helped to remind Ezekiel that God was always with him.**

● **How is the benediction at the end of our worship service a kind of reminder for us as we leave church?** (It reassures us that as we leave, God will go with us to guide and protect us.)

EXPLORING WORSHIP

Examine some visual symbols which we use to remind ourselves of God's presence.

● **Can you think of any pictures or visual symbols—other than the cross—that could remind us of God's love and protection?** List student responses on the board. (An outstretched hand—God's protection and care; a sunrise—the light and

Children respect parents who play that role—parents! . . . The same is true of you, the teacher. . . .

love of God, Jesus' resurrection; a butterfly—the new life Jesus gave us.) Symbols are a bit heavy for third and fourth graders, so don't push this activity too far. But do encourage the kids to suggest *pictures* that remind them of God's love.

Give the children sheets of paper and crayons or markers and let them work in pairs to draw simple picture reminders of God's love. They can choose from the list on the board or else make up their own visual symbols. Have each pair write one sentence telling how the picture reminds them of God.

WORSHIPING TOGETHER

This week's worship aim—to be encouraged to trust God to work things out for our best—try to select hymns that focus on trust and faith. From your hymnal you might sing "Holy, Holy, Holy" to begin In Worship with musical praise to our God. Other appropriate songs are "The Lord Is My Shepherd," page 28, and "Psalm 100," page 5, from *Worship Time Music Book.*

. . . *You are an adult, contributing to the lives of your pupils as an adult—a contribution that can never be made by peers.*
—Lawrence O. Richards and Marlene LeFever

RESPONDING PERSONALLY

Conclude the session by giving children an opportunity to personalize what they have gained from the worship experience.

☐ Let students make a big bulletin board or wall display of their picture reminders of God's presence. Encourage the class to make up a good title for the display: "Things That Remind Me of God"; "God Is Everywhere"; "Remember That God Is with You!"

☐ Have children work on the benediction projects. Students who make the Stand-up Benediction Card may want to replace the heart shapes with circles which they design to look like globes of the world. The inside benediction could reflect the assurance that God is with us no matter where we are.

As the kids work on their cards and gifts, talk with them about who they plan to give these benedictions to and how such reminders of God's love and protection might help those people. ■

IN WORSHIP
WE HAVE FAITH IN GOD

1. Call to Worship—Psalm 105:1, 2

2. Invocation—Dear Lord, we are together here today to worship You. Let our thoughts and our voices praise You. Help us to learn what You want us to. In Jesus' name. Amen.

3. Hymn

4. Our Statement of Faith—*Read this aloud together.*

5. Scripture Reading—Ezekiel 11:16-20

6. Prayer—*Complete the following prayer sentences.*

Dear God, we praise You because You are _____. We ask You to help those who are sick or in need of _____. In Jesus' name. Amen.

7. Hymn

8. Student Worship Talk—*Complete the sentences below.*

I. Read Ezekiel 11:16.
  A. This verse begins a message that Ezekiel heard from the Lord. At this time, the people of Judah were sad because _____.
  B. But Ezekiel told them that God had been guiding them. God had _____.
  C. Sometimes we forget that God is guiding us, and we are sad, too. I feel that way once in a while, too, when I _____.

II. Read Ezekiel 11:17, 18.
  A. Here, God tells Ezekiel that He will continue to watch over the people. He will _____.
  B. God wanted His sad, discouraged people to see that He had the power to _____.
  C. Whenever I feel sad or lonely, it helps me to remember that God is with me and that God can _____.

III. Read verses 19, 20.
  A. God would do more than take His people back to their home country. God would change His people's hearts. He would _____.
  B. God is also changing my heart. He helps me to stop _____. Times that God has helped me feel like a new person were _____.
  C. I know that, no matter how bad things seem, I will be all right, because _____.

9. Benediction—God is everywhere. God is with you wherever you go and whatever you do. May you always remember that God is nearby to love and guide you. ■

SESSION 51
WORSHIP AIM:

RESISTING TEMPTATION

Journey into Daniel 1—5: Daniel and his friends refuse to adopt the evil ways of Babylon (pp. 485-496).
Special Things You'll Need:
☐ Materials for "Make a Relief Map," page 50 in *THE Idea Book*
☐ Copies of pictures 7 and 8 from the "Photo Album" activity piece 12C in the back of this book
☐ Materials for "Stand-up Benedictions," page 82, and "Benedictions to Eat," page 83, in *THE Idea Book*

GETTING STARTED

☐ Let the students work on the "Photo Album" project. Anyone who hasn't completed pages for the pictures in Sessions 48-50 can do so now. Distribute sheets of construction paper so students can begin to make covers for their albums. Talk with the kids about ways to decorate the cover and possible titles for the picture albums. Help students use a sharp scissors or punch to put holes in the pages and covers of the books. They will finish and bind their albums during the next session.
☐ Several students can put the figure for Session 51 near the city of Babylon on the relief map and do any necessary work to complete the map.
☐ Begin planning for the "Old Testament Jamboree" review project suggested on page 218 in next week's Responding Personally section. Children can look through their *Picture Bibles* and list favorite Bible stories, which you can use as bases for charades. Look over suggested Bible-time refreshments and let students volunteer to bring some of these.
☐ The following activity should help students become aware of how

they decide whether to resist temptation. On a chalkboard, write "Reasons to Do It" "Reasons Not to Do It." Leave space under each for student responses.

Suppose you are tempted to eat a wonderful chocolate-covered, cream-filled cream puff. But your mom says, "Don't eat it!"
● **Why might you decide to eat it anyway?**
● **Why might you decide not to eat it?**
● **Would it be easy for you to resist this temptation?**

EXPLORING THE BIBLE

Temptation is something that every person must cope with. It can be especially hard to resist when we don't have our parents around to tell us how to act. Today's Bible story shows how some young men reacted to temptation when they were far from home.

The session's material in the *Picture Bible* breaks down nicely into four episodes or stories.

1. Daniel and his friends are given positions in the king's court: pages 485-486. Assign the roles of narrator, Shadrach, Daniel, the king's officer, and King Nebuchadnezzar. After reading these pages, explain that Daniel and his friends were rather special captives: they had been members of the royal family and nobility in Jerusalem.

Note the mental and physical abilities of Daniel and his friends. After three years of study with the wisest teachers in the land, these young captives would be candidates for posts in the king's court.
● **How did Daniel react when he learned they had passed the tests?**

God had given His people special rules about the kind of food which they could and could not eat. When Daniel and his friends refused the rich Babylonian food, they were obeying God's rules.

● Why might it have been hard for them to refuse the food?

● How did God bless them for their obedience?

2. Nebuchadnezzar's strange dream: pages 487-489. Assign roles of narrator, king, adviser, guard, Daniel, and Meshach; then read these pages with the class. Point out the courage which Daniel and his friend showed in what seemed like an impossible situation.

● How do these friends manage to find out about the king's dream—when none of the wisest men in the kingdom know the answer? Let a student again read Daniel's interpretation of the dream in the final frame on page 489. Daniel told mighty Nebuchadnezzar that his kingdom would one day crumble, but that God's Kingdom would last forever.

● Why did it take courage to tell the king what his dream meant? But God was with Daniel, and Nebuchadnezzar rewarded him by making Daniel and his friends important rulers in the Kingdom.

3. The fiery furnace: pages 490-494 (top frame). Assign the parts of narrator, Daniel, Shadrach, four evil advisers, Nebuchadnezzar, and a Babylonian soldier. Let students read this famous story of faith.

● Why were the king's wicked advisers out to get Daniel's friends?

● What bad thing might happen if the friends didn't worship the statue? Point out that the three friends knew that everybody else was going to bow down to the statue—

even though some people probably didn't believe that the statue was a real god.

● Wouldn't Daniel's friends have been smarter to go along with everyone else and pretend to worship the statue? Why or why not?

4. Nebuchadnezzar's second dream and the new kings of Babylon: pages 494 (bottom frame)-496. Assign roles of narrator, Nebuchadnezzar, Daniel, and Belshazzar and let students read these pages. Again point out the courage it took for Daniel to reveal the unpleasant meaning of the king's dream.

The final frame on page 496 leaves us with an exciting cliff-hanger. Let children guess what Belshazzar might have seen. Tell them that next week, in the final session, they will find out the answer.

Daniel and his friends were prisoners in a strange land nearly a thousand miles away from Jerusalem. But life for Daniel and his friends was far different than life for Ezekiel and the rest of the captives that we read about last week.

● How were these young men treated differently from the other captives? List the differences as students name them.

● Who do you think had an easier time remaining faithful to God: Daniel and his friends or the other captives who lived together on farms outside the city? Have students give reasons for their answers.

● How do you think Daniel and his friends were able to remain faithful to God in spite of temptations?

We're luckier than these young captives in our story, because we can get together every week to worship God with lots of friends and

family who are also Christians. But when we leave church and go back to our neighborhoods and schools, we sometimes face the same kinds of temptations that Daniel faced.

Let children describe some times when they've been tempted to follow the crowd, even though they knew they would be disobeying God. Tell about some temptations that you face in your life outside church.

Distribute copies of pictures 7 and 8 from the "Photo Album." Let students complete the captions, color the pictures, and add them to their photo album page. (Picture 7: . . . rulers of provinces; Picture 8: . . . saved them from death.)

EXPLORING WORSHIP

Your students have been been studying about all the wonderful things that go into church services. They have seen how each part of the service can help them grow closer to God and to other Christians. Now, as they look at the last part of the church service—the benediction—they also need to think about what will happen after they worship together.

Be sure the kids understand that, though taking part in the church

Children enter school as question marks and leave as periods. Why does that have to be?
—Neil Postman

service is a beautiful way to worship God, it is *not* only in church that we can or should worship God. In fact, one of the most important reasons for church worship is to "fuel up" to go out and worship and praise and pray to God in our everyday lives. The benediction sends us on our way prepared to worship with our lives.

Daniel and his friend were able to help one another avoid the temptation to follow the evil ways of Babylon.

● **What are some ways we could help each other overcome temptations to follow the crowd and disobey God?** Make a list of ideas on the board or a sheet of paper. Here are some ideas; let students suggest others:

1. Send notes of encouragement (or "benediction" cards like the kids have been making).

2. Pray for one another.

3. Call each other or visit one another to give encouragement.

4. Read the Bible and pray together.

Encourage students to try out some of these ideas in the weeks ahead.

WORSHIPING TOGETHER

In keeping with this week's worship aim—to be strengthened to resist the temptation to follow the crowd—choose hymns that focus on obedience and Christian living. You might want worshipers to sing the familiar song "Trust and Obey." An old song that fits very well with this lesson is "Dare to Be a Daniel." From *Worship Time Music Book* you might select "Be Very Careful," page 29, and "Psalm 119," and page 27.

RESPONDING PERSONALLY

Select one or more of the following activities.

☐ This will be the last session that students can work on the benediction cards and gifts. Let children try any suggestions they haven't used in previous sessions. If they have been making benediction gifts for other people, encourage the kids to make a stand-up card for themselves. Let them select their favorite benediction from the worship services or from the suggested Bible verses to print on the inside of the card. Or else suggest that they use the benediction from today's Worshiping Together and send their cards as messages of encouragement to one another during the coming week.

☐ Have a last-minute check on who will bring which Bible-time food for the refreshments portion of the jamboree. You may want to send reminder notes home with the kids. ■

IN WORSHIP
WE RESIST TEMPTATION

1. Call to Worship—Psalm 105:1, 2

2. Invocation—O Lord, be with us now and bless our worship so we will be stronger to face temptations as we live our lives from day to day. We ask this in Jesus' name. Amen.

3. Hymn

4. Our Statement of Faith—*Read this aloud together.*

5. Scripture Reading—Daniel 3:13-28

6. Prayer—*Complete the following sentences.*

Dear God, we praise You because You are _____.
We admit that we sometimes do wrong by _____.
We are sorry and ask You to forgive us. Help us, Lord, to resist temptations such as _____.
We know that You hear our prayers and will answer them in the best way. In Jesus' name we pray. Amen.

7. Hymn

8. Student Worship Talk—*Complete the sentences below with your own words and ideas.*

  I. Read Daniel 3:13-18.
    A. When Nebuchadnezzar gave Daniel's friends this second chance to worship the idol he had made, it would have been really easy for them to _____.
    B. When everyone else is doing something that I know is wrong, I'm sometimes tempted to do it, too, because _____.
    C. Shadrach, Meshach, and Abednego refused to obey the king because _____.

  II. Read Daniel 3:19-23.
    A. The king was so angry that he had the three men thrown into the furnace.
    B. One time when people got angry or made fun of me because I didn't follow the crowd was _____.

  III. Read Daniel 3: 24-28.
    A. Because Shadrach, Meshach, and Abednego refused to disobey God, King Nebuchadnezzar learned that _____.
    B. When I refuse to follow the crowd into wrongdoing, God can use me to show _____.

9. Benediction—May God give you the strength to be faithful to Him—even if no one else seems to be. (Read II Corinthians 13:14.) ■

SESSION 52
WORSHIP AIM:

STAYING CLOSE TO GOD

Journey into Daniel 5—6; Hosea—Malachi: Daniel goes into the lions' den rather than give up his daily prayers to God (pp. 497-509).

Special Things You'll Need:
☐ Materials for "Make a Relief Map," page 50 in *THE Idea Book*
☐ Copies of pictures 9 and 10 from the "Photo Album," activity piece 12C in the back of this book
☐ Yarn or string (Optional)
☐ Bible-time refreshments: butter and honey on wheat bread, raisins, almonds, cheese, grape juice, roasted sesame seeds, cucumbers, melons (Optional)

GETTING STARTED

Choose one or more of the following to do with your group:
☐ Let students put finishing touches on their "Photo Album" covers.
☐ Let students add the final two figures for Session 52 to the relief map.
☐ Hand out sheets of paper, and have students write the names of two friends.
● Put a check by the friend you spend more time with.
● Put a star by the friend who hears more of your thoughts and feelings.
● Put a dot by the friend you know better.
● Underline the friend who knows more of your faults.
● Which friend is closer to you?

Discuss with children what makes friends close. Help them understand that if we want to be close friends with God, we must do things that make us close to people.

EXPLORING THE BIBLE

Today's Bible story tells about many of God's messengers in the Old Testament. But one thing stands out: all of them were close to God.

Have five children prepare to read aloud Daniel's story on pages 499-503 of the *Picture Bible*. Also have teams of students read and prepare a brief report on several of minor prophets, "Twelve Men of God" (pages 504-506). Ask teams to discover what job God had for these men.

When children are ready, have them turn back to the final two frames on page 496 in the *Picture Bible*. Read these frames to the class and let a volunteer find the Persian Empire and its capital city of Persepolis on the relief map. Then read the first two pages of today's selection in the *Picture Bible* (pages 497 and 498)—which describe how the Persian army invaded Babylon and captured the palace.

Explain that when the Persians conquered a land, they sent leaders to rule over the cities of that land. Unlike the Babylonians, the Persians allowed the conquered people to remain in their homes. The Persian leader who was sent to rule the city of Babylon was a man called Darius.

Have the assigned students present the story of Daniel. Inform students that by the time this story took place, Daniel was probably nearly 80 years old. For over 60 years he had served as an adviser to many rulers—Babylonians and now Persians.
● Why do you think that ruler after ruler kept Daniel on as an adviser—even though he was a foreigner?
● What caused the problem for Daniel in this story?

Help students understand that if

Daniel had tried to hide his prayers, everyone would have thought Daniel's God didn't mean much to him. Also, after all the years of God's blessings and protection, Daniel was probably confident that God would be with him—even if he had to die in a den of lions.

Read the introductory paragraph to "Twelve Men of God" on top of page 504 in the *Picture Bible*. Then let students present brief reports on these twelve "minor prophets." They should see that God used the prophets to call God's people to repentance and new obedience.

Use pages 507 and 508 to briefly review the panorama of Old Testament history. If your class is small, hold up your *Picture Bible* so students can see the pictures. Cover captions in each frame with your fingers, and let students describe each scene. If your class is large, ask the kids to cover the copy on each picture. Use the picture captions to fill in details the students missed.

Read aloud page 509, which describes the return of the exiles and the words of warning and promise which close the Old Testament.

Distribute the final two pictures for the class photo album. Let children complete the captions with information from the story of Daniel. (. . . some wicked leaders saw Daniel and told the king; . . . he discovered that God had kept Daniel safe.)

After coloring pictures, students can glue or tape them into the last page of their photo albums. Give the class time to make up titles for them and put on finishing touches. Help the kids punch holes through the pages and covers, and use yarn or string to bind the albums.

EXPLORING WORSHIP

Print on the board the elements of the worship service which children have been studying during this past year: Invocation, Call to Worship; Creed; Hymns; Scripture Reading; Invitation to Salvation; Offering; Prayer; Worship Talk; Benediction.

Let students explain the part that each of those elements plays in the worship service. If necessary, ask, **Why do we do this?** or **How does this help us worship?** Also let students tell what they remember about the role of pastor and lay leaders, church holidays **(Why do we have these? What do we celebrate?)**, and the sanctuary or church building.
● **Which part of the church service is your favorite? Why?**

Then erase all the words on your list except "benediction." **We've said that the benediction ends the church service. The pastor sends us away from church with farewell words of blessing.**
● **How does this blessing help us feel close to God?**

Today we're going to look at several great ways to help us stay

close to God throughout the week.

Remind students that Daniel didn't have a church where he could worship God and grow stronger in his faith. So Daniel needed to come up with a way of worshiping God in his home.
● **How did Daniel give us an excellent example of daily worship?**
● **What are some ways that we can worship God in our homes or on our own during the week?** (Praying to God; singing hymns to God; reading the Bible; talking with other Christians about God; telling non-Christians about God.)

Have volunteers describe prayer and Bible-reading times in their homes, either with their families or by themselves. Explain that these activities help us to stay close to God. Encourage kids to build these habits into their lives.

WORSHIPING TOGETHER

Have students work in teams to compose benedictions for every day of the week—Monday through Saturday—on six separate slips of paper. Let the kids suggest special events that are coming up during the days of the next week and then build their blessings around these: "May

But grow in the grace and knowledge of our Lord and Savior Jesus Christ. To him be glory both now and forever! Amen.
—II Peter 3:18

God be with you on Monday and make you happy to go back to school"; "May God give you extra love on Thursday when you've got to miss your favorite TV programs to study for Friday's test"; etc.

Songs you might select for today's worship time are "I Was Glad" and "Psalm 119" from *Worship Time Music Book*. You also might repeat "Dare to Be a Daniel" from last week's session.

RESPONDING PERSONALLY

Help children to see that one way to be close to God is to learn as much as we can about God. That is why we study the Bible. Conclude this final session by giving the children a chance to review what they have learned from their study of the Old Testament.

Begin an "Old Testament Jamboree" by taping names of Bible characters on the children's backs. Let students tape a name on your back so you can join in the fun. After everyone has guessed the names—using only questions that can be answered with yes or no—have each person tell a favorite thing about his or her Bible character. Or, if the character is a villain, let the child tell what one thing he or she would change about the character.

Then divide the class into teams and play Bible story charades. Stay on the sidelines timing the teams and helping out. After teams have had a turn, check their times. The team which took the least amount of time is the winner.

Wind up the jamboree by serving Bible-time refreshments—bread and butter, raisins, almonds, cheese, grape juice, sesame seeds, cucumbers, melons. As the kids enjoy the

refreshments, talk with them about what they have learned about God through their study of the Old Testament. Also encourage the children to use what they've learned during children's church as they join the congregation in regular worship services during the weeks ahead.

Close by offering a special benediction asking God's blessings on your students. ■

IN WORSHIP
WE STAY CLOSE TO GOD

1. Call to Worship—Psalm 100:1-5

2. Invocation—O Lord, we ask that You would bless our final Old Testament worship service today. Help us to be strong and joyful so that we can worship You in days to come. Amen.

3. Hymn

4. Our Statement of Faith—*Recite our church's creed.*

5. Scripture Reading—Daniel 6:10-12, 16-23

6. Prayer—*Complete the following prayer sentences.*
Dear God, we praise You because You are _____.
We admit that we sometimes do wrong by _____.
We are sorry and ask You to forgive us.
Help us do what's right when _____. Amen.

7. Hymn

8. Student Worship Talk—*Complete the sentences below.*

I. Read Daniel 6:10, 11.
   A. We know Daniel stayed close to God. Two things he did were _____ and _____.
   B. Three things I can do to help me stay close to God are _____.

II. Read verse 12.
   A. The king's men reported Daniel for disobeying his decree. Daniel felt it was more important to _____.
   B. I must remember it is more important to stay close to God than do what my friends want. This is hard for me when _____.

III. Read verses 16-18.
   A. The king felt bad and could not sleep because _____.
   B. One time I felt bad when someone else was trying to do what was right. What happened was _____.

IV. Read verses 19-23.
   A. Daniel was safe in the lions' den because _____.
   B. If I stay close to God, a hard or scary time when I know God will be with me is _____.

9. Benediction—Our benediction for Sunday is—May you stay close to God and trust Him every day, in every situation. Monday's benediction is . . . Tuesday's benediction is . . . Wednesday's benediction is . . . Thursday's benediction is . . . Friday's benediction is . . . Saturday's benediction is . . . ■

219

ACTIVITY PIECES

*These activity pieces
may be reproduced
for each
of your students.*

WORSHIP QUESTIONNAIRE

Name _____

Telephone Number _____

During Junior Children's Church you could use your gifts to worship God.
In which of the ways listed below would you like to help:

_____ Hand out songbooks and bulletins.

_____ Read a Bible verse.

_____ Read a prayer.

_____ Lead the group in reading.

_____ Say a prayer.

_____ Give a short oral report.

_____ Give a short worship talk.

_____ Show something I have made and explain it.

_____ Sing in a small group.

_____ Sing a solo.

_____ Lead the group in singing.

_____ Play a musical instrument.

    _____ kazoo

    _____ harmonica

    _____ bells

    _____ piano

    _____ violin

    _____ guitar

    _____ drum

    _____ tambourine

    _____ other: _____

1A

CAN YOU DO THIS?

Read the whole page before following the rest of the instructions.

Work as quickly as possible.

1. What is the first book of the Bible? _____

2. What sign did God give Noah that there would never be another flood over the world? _____

3. What is your birthdate? _____

4. Who was the first murderer? _____

5. Stand beside your chair and clap three times.

6. Recite loudly the capitol of your country.

7. On what day did God rest? _____

8. Jump in place as high as you can.

9. The largest country in the world is _____ .

10. Do not follow any of the above instructions. If you did not do any of the items on this page, congratulations, you're a winner! This was a test to see if you would follow the first direction.

ABRAHAM'S FAMILY TREE

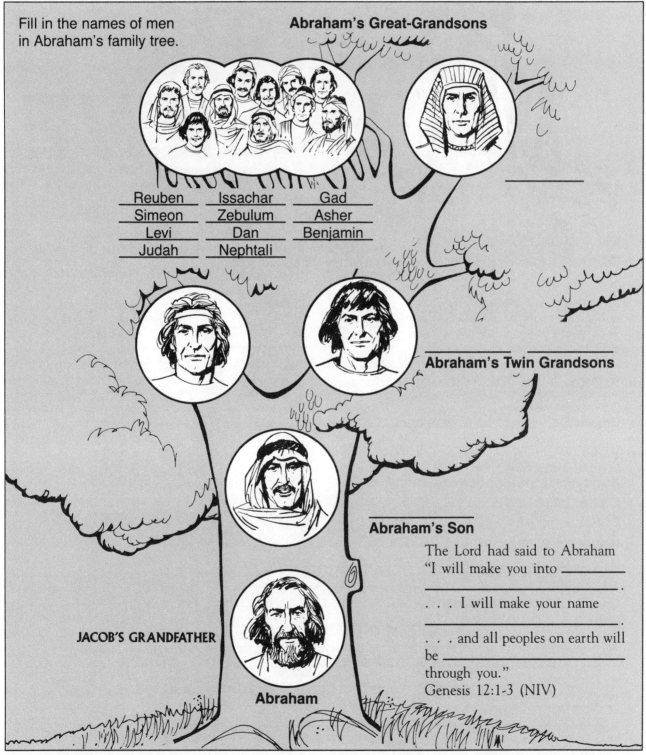

Fill in the names of men in Abraham's family tree.

Abraham's Great-Grandsons

Reuben	Issachar	Gad
Simeon	Zebulum	Asher
Levi	Dan	Benjamin
Judah	Nephtali	

Abraham's Twin Grandsons

Abraham's Son

The Lord had said to Abraham "I will make you into _____.

. . . I will make your name _____.

. . . and all peoples on earth will be _____

through you."
Genesis 12:1-3 (NIV)

JACOB'S GRANDFATHER

Abraham

Answers for this activity are on pages 255

WE BELIEVE IT!

Complete this conversation about your church's statement of faith.

Buddy: Hey! Listen to what I just learned. _____
_____
_____

Pal: People say that in church every Sunday. What does that mean, anyway?
Chum: Our church believes that _____
_____
_____

Buddy: How do we know that's true?
Chum: Because _____
Chum: I might forget if we don't practice some more. Let's say all we know so far. _____
_____
_____
_____
_____
_____
_____
_____
_____
_____
_____

PEACE SURVEY

Decide which of the following answers are true and circle the letter.

1. My friends and I get into fights . . .
   a. never.
   b. sometimes.
   c. often.
   d. always.
2. My friends get mad at me when . . .
   a. I try to be the best.
   b. I talk behind their backs.
   c. I won't do what they want to do.
   d. I cheat.
   e. other _____ .
3. My friends usually fight over . . .
   a. who wins a game.
   b. who gets to be first.
   c. who gets to tell the others what to do.
   d. other _____ .
4. The way I make peace with my friends is . . .
   a. to do things their way.
   b. to just forget the fight.
   c. to leave them alone for a while.
   d. to talk over the problem.
   e. to do something nice for them.
5. I wish I . . .
   a. could keep myself from getting into fights.
   b. knew how to keep my friends from fighting.
   c. were a better loser.
   d. other _____ .

PSALM 100

Leader: Shout for joy to the Lord, all the earth.

Group: Worship the Lord with gladness; come before him with joyful songs.

Leader: Know that the Lord is God. It is he who made us, and we are his; we are his people, the sheep of his pasture.

Group: Enter his gates with thanksgiving and his courts with praise;

Leader: Give thanks to him and praise his name.

Leader and Group: For the Lord is good and his love endures forever; his faithfulness continues through all generations.

Gripe Session
What did the Israelites complain about?

Below each picture, write the Israelites' complaint to God. Then draw an awful thing that happened because they didn't trust God.

Answers for this activity are on pages 255

POPCORN PROMISES GAME

By Kathy Lewis

Things You'll Need: ☐ popcorn box or bowl ☐ paper slips

Cut out the promise references below and place them in a popcorn box or large bowl.

To play the game, each student will need a Bible. Pass around the "popcorn" and have each student take two or three popcorn papers. Tell students not to look at their papers until you say "Go."

Explain that after the signal is given, students will become popcorn poppers. Popcorn usually pops slowly at first, but gradually it pops faster and faster.

When children find a promise in the Bible, they must pop up and read aloud the verse. If several of them pop at once, they should take turns reading their verses. Then they should sit down again and find the next verse.

Jeremiah 33:3	Proverbs 4:7, 8	Deuteronomy 28:15	Psalm 34:18
Jeremiah 29:13	Proverbs 4:23	Deuteronomy 29:9	Psalm 34:22
Isaiah 43:2	Proverbs 9:10	Deuteronomy 31:8	Psalm 37:3-5
Exodus 20:7	Proverbs 10:3	Psalm 103:11-13	Psalm 37:23
Malachi 3:10	Proverbs 10:16	Psalm 107:43	Psalm 40:4
Joel 2:32a	Proverbs 10:29	Psalm 116:5	Psalm 41:1, 2
Hosea 14:4	Proverbs 11:2	Psalm 1:1-3	Psalm 50:15
Deuteronomy 28:2	Proverbs 12:20	Lamentations 3:22-25	Isaiah 1:16-18
Genesis 9:13-15	Proverbs 12:28	Psalm 19:7	Jeremiah 3:15
Genesis 12:1-3	Proverbs 13:3	Psalm 25:12	Jeremiah 7:5-7
Deuteronomy 7:11-13	Proverbs 13:11	Psalm 27:14	Micah 7:19
Proverbs 3:5, 6	Proverbs 13:15	Psalm 27:10	Isaiah 53:6
Proverbs 3:9, 10	Proverbs 14:27	Psalm 34:16	Malachi 3:6a
Proverbs 3:13	Proverbs 15:1	Psalm 34:17, 19	Psalm 91:15

15 FIFTEEN EVENTS CARDS

The story events are printed below in correct order. Make copies of this sheet and cut out each card along the dotted line. Be sure to cut the numbers from the cards, but keep a copy of the sheet to help you check for proper order.

1 On the seventh day when the priests blow their trumpets and the marchers shout, the walls of Jericho (the mighty city) fall flat.

2 Two Israelite scouts search out the house of Rahab. They recognize it by the red rope in her window.

3 One Israelite scout tells Rahab that she will be safe at their camp.

4 Joshua says no one is to keep anything from the city for himself.

5 Achan decides to take some of the spoil (treasures) from the city.

6 Achan buries his stolen treasure.

7 Jericho is set on fire because its evil ways would have spread among the Israelites.

8 Joshua plans to attack Ai with his scouts. They volunteer to scout it out.

9 The scouts discover that the army of Ai is small.

10 The Israelites become frightened in battle and run away from Ai.

11 Joshua asks God why his men were afraid.

12 God replies that the people are being punished because someone disobeyed Him when they took Jericho.

13 God points out Achan as the guilty one, and Achan admits that he sinned against God and his people.

14 The same day thirty thousand men prepare to attack Ai.

15 When Joshua raises his spear, the Israelites set fire to the city and trap and defeat the soldiers of Ai.

5A

God Is Number One

Fill in the blanks with things from the list you just made in class.

God, You are more important to us than _____.

We love You more than _____.

We know You are more powerful than _____.

We want to give You more attention than we give _____.

We confess that sometimes we spend too much time with things like _____.

Help us make You most important in our lives. Amen.

STRENGTH BUSTERS

Put a check next to any item on the list below which sometimes makes you feel weak, frustrated, or helpless and weak.

_____ School
_____ Older brother
_____ Older sister
_____ Younger brother
_____ Younger sister
_____ Teacher
_____ Classmate
_____ Playmate
_____ Bully
_____ Sport
_____ Coach
_____ Neighbor
_____ Friend
_____ Homework
_____ Games

Look at what you checked on the list. Pick the thing or person that makes you feel most weak, frustrated, or helpless. In a sentence, tell why that person or thing makes you feel the way you do.

Chain of Kindness

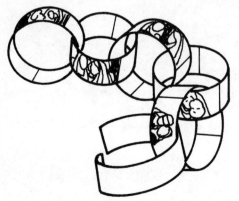

Color the pictures showing acts of kindness in the story of Ruth. Then draw an act of kindness you can do for someone in the empty box. Cut the strips apart, and staple or glue the ends together to make a chain. Have everyone in the class connect their chains and hang them in the classroom.

KINDNESS CONTRACT

I, _____ ,

am worshiping my Lord today, _____ ,

by doing the following acts of loving-kindness:

_____ , _____ , _____ .

Signed: _____   Witness: _____

Coupons

Giving in Faith

GOD ANSWERS HANNAH'S PRAYER—AND WHEN THE BOY IS OLD ENOUGH TO LEAVE HIS MOTHER, SHE BRINGS HIM TO ELI.

WHEN I ASKED GOD FOR A SON, I PROMISED THAT HE WOULD SERVE THE LORD ALL HIS LIFE. SO I HAVE BROUGHT HIM HERE TO BE TRAINED IN GOD'S HOUSE. HIS NAME IS SAMUEL.

GOD BLESS YOU, HANNAH. LEAVE THE BOY WITH ME, AND I WILL TEACH HIM TO BE A SERVANT OF THE LORD.

Who is giving a gift? _____
What is the gift? _____
What becomes of the gift? _____

Draw a picture of a gift you would like to give to God.

FORGIVE THY PEOPLE, LORD, AND HELP THEM. THEY HAVE TORN DOWN THE IDOLS, AND REPENTED FOR HAVING TURNED AWAY FROM THEE.

Who is giving a gift? _____
What is the gift? _____
What becomes of the gift? _____

Draw a picture of yourself giving the gift to God. Show the expression on your face.

Offering Attitudes Cards

1. Oh, do I have to give this quarter at children's church? If I keep it in my pocket, I can finally afford a new Barbie doll for myself.

5. I'm afraid God won't like me unless I give an offering.

2. Those children in Guatemala are suffering. I am going to give all the money that I earned dog-sitting to the special offering.

6. I've *got* to give an offering, because all my friends do.

3. Maybe if I give God a *big* offering, He will give me an A on my test.

7. I love the Lord so much. I wish I had more money to give Him.

4. I earned two dollars this week. I think I will tithe by giving God one tenth of it. One tenth is 20¢.

Adopt-a-Grandparent

This is to certify that

_____

has adopted

_____

to be his or her grandparent—to be
visited and loved as one way that
this above named Junior Children's
Church member can be an offering
to God.

_____
Date

BIBLE SPIES

Answer the five W questions and then fill out your spy report. Hint: You may need to read more than just your assigned page or pages to answer the questions.

Who are the people in this part of the story?

What are these people doing?

Where does this story happen?

When are these events taking place?

Why are the people doing the things that they are doing?

SPY REPORT

Using the information above, write a brief summary of what happened in your part of the story.

_____

_____

_____

_____

CROSSWORD PUZZLE

Across

2. When David heard that _____ and his father had been killed, he sang a song about them.
3. David was glad that his wife, _____, was safe.
5. David and his men discovered that _____ had been burned.
6. A messenger told David that _____ was dead.
7. The messenger hoped to receive a _____ from David.
8. The man had been lying beside the road for _____ days.
10. The man lying on the side of the road was a _____.
11. David sang the "Song of the _____."

Down

1. David said that Saul and Jonathan were "Swifter than _____."
3. The _____ captured the wives and children of David and his men.
4. The man was left behind because he was _____.
9. To prove his story was true, the messenger showed David a _____.

7B

Answers are on pages 255

Activity Piece 7B by Eric Potter. ©1987 David C. Cook Publishing Co. Permission granted to reproduce for ministry use only—not for resale.

Private Eye Clue Sheet

Can you find the secret message hidden in the words below? Unscramble the words on the left and write them in the blanks in the middle. (If you have trouble figuring out the words, the number tells you on which page they are found in the *Picture Bible*.) Then, write the circled letter in each word in one of the boxes on the right and read the message in the boxes.

NESTILIPHI (301)

AHIRU (306)

KAR (301)

SICSNAIMU (302)

MISEORP (303)

PLECRIP (304)

NETT (302)

USEOH (303)

GASEESM (306)

TPLEEM (303)

AOJB (305)

REUSN (305)

VIDDA

Figure out what the sentence below says.

EMAN SIH OTNU EUD
YROLG EHT DROL EHT
OTNU EVIG

_____

_____

_____ .

Answers are provided on pages 255

Some words from today's story are hidden in the box. The words can go up or down, forward or backward. See how many of the words listed below you can find.

Beauty
Servant
Worship
Ten Commandments
Jerusalem
Temple
Battle
Palace
Lame
Glory
Ark
Promise
Tent

```
P W A L J E I M O N Z K B A D
N Y S P O Q R X T B E A U T Y
A S E R V A N T K E J X M O R
L J O W O R S H I P F U Z V P
T E N C O M M A N D M E N T S
J T A E U Q N C U N G I J Y A
K L R P O M B F A Y O B E L V
G A E C A L A P D E K H R T K
J M L Q E O T H M L Z P U F U
P E O K R A T M D P N B S T C
S I C Q S M L Z N M R I A W P
J G L O R Y E B Z E P E L V I
R X M G H S D K V T V T E N T
O P R O M I S E G L H B M K X
W E C X V Y A E G P R O A M T
```

Tillie's Terrible Troubles

Tillie is excited. This is the day of the big art show at school, and Tillie's painting has been chosen to be in it.

When the last bell rings, Tillie hurries to the place in the gym where the paintings are hung, but she doesn't see hers. It is not where she hung it the night before. Out of the corner of her eye, Tillie sees Bart and Theodore giggling and watching her. Suddenly she realizes that Bart and Theodore have hidden her painting so that they will win the prize ribbons.

Tillie is angry. She wants to cry and scream at the same time. What should Tillie do?

Read Psalm 37:1-8 in a modern translation. Using these verses, write Tillie a letter that will help her know how to handle her problem. Verse 8 is especially important.

Dear Tillie,

Sample Shape Poetry

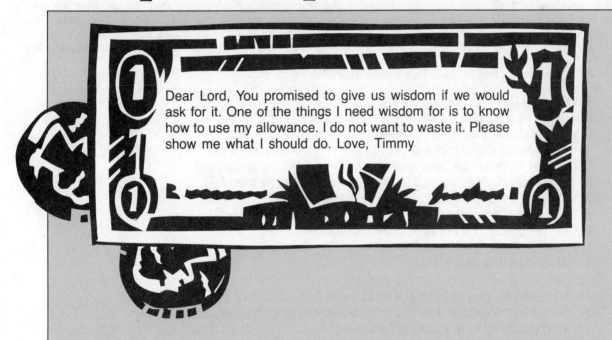

Dear Lord, You promised to give us wisdom if we would ask for it. One of the things I need wisdom for is to know how to use my allowance. I do not want to waste it. Please show me what I should do. Love, Timmy

In this space draw the shape of something with which you need God's help. Then write a poem, a letter, or a story to ask God for help with that thing.

Bible Tic-Tac-Toe

In order to play Bible Tic-Tac-Toe, choose two contestants. Then choose nine other students to sit in chairs arranged in three rows of three like a tic-tac-toe board. When the game begins have all of these students stand in front of their chairs. In "Bible Tic-Tac-Toe" (page 8C in the back of this book), you will find 25 questions. Give the X contestant a chance to choose a person from the nine. Then ask the question. If the person chosen can answer it correctly, he or she will sit down as an X. He or she should be given a card with an X so that there will be no confusion about who sat for whom. Then it is the Y contestant's turn. The first contestant to get three students sitting in a row wins. Children who are not participating may act as cheering sections for the two players. You should be able to play a couple of rounds with the questions provided.

1. Who was David's general? *Joab*
2. Amnon was killed by which brother? *Absalom*
3. Who did David send to bring Absalom to Jerusalem? *Joab*
4. What rule did David make about Absalom? *He could not live in the palace or see David.*
5. How did Absalom get Joab's attention? *By setting fire to his field.*
6. To what city did Absalom go to crown himself king? *Hebron*
7. Who did David tell to stay behind and give Absalom bad advice? *Hushai*
8. To whom did Absalom listen concerning the attack on David? *Hushai*
9. Who did Joab tell not to fight in the battle? *David*
10. How did David's army catch Absalom? *His hair was caught in a tree.*
11. Who killed Absalom? *Joab*
12. Why did Joab's soldier not kill Absalom? *David had told them to protect Absalom.*
13. Who was the prophet who talked to David about Solomon? *Nathan*
14. Who was the second son who tried to take the kingdom? *Adonijah*
15. Who did David crown as king? *Solomon*
16. Why was Adonijah's life spared? *He grabbed the horns on the altar of sacrifice.*
17. How long did David rule? *40 years*
18. What psalm is called the Shepherd's Psalm? *23*
19. What kind of trees were cut to make God's Temple? *cedar*
20. How long did it take to build the Temple? *seven years*
21. What other large building did Solomon build? *palace*
22. What queen visited Solomon? *Queen of Sheba*
23. Who was Solomon's chief labor foreman? *Jeroboam*
24. What caused Solomon's downfall? *idol worship*
25. Who was the prophet who foretold the tearing of the kingdom? *Ahijah*

Problems! Problems!

All kids face problems from time to time. Read the following problems and think about what you have learned from your church leaders and parents. Then offer some advice. If the problem is really tough, write the name of a person you might ask for advice.

1. My best friend, Suzy, is the most popular girl in my Sunday school class. She says we shouldn't talk to the new girl because she wears weird clothes. The new girl looks so sad. I'm afraid that if I talk to her, Suzy and the other girls won't talk to me anymore. What should I do?

2. I've been taking music lessons on my clarinet. My music teacher says I have to give a recital. I get shaky every time I think about it because I'm not ready to give a recital yet. I'm afraid to tell my teacher how I feel. What should I do?

3. My mom and dad are getting a divorce. I think it's all my fault! My insides hurt all the time. What should I do?

4. My parents read Bible stories at our house, so I know all the answers in Sunday school. My friend calls me Smarty Barty every time I get an answer right. Now all the kids are calling me that. What should I do?

5. I play on a really great soccer team. Last year I was one of the best players, and we won a trophy. Coach wants us to practice on Sunday mornings at 10:00. If I don't go to practice, I won't be able to play. But if I do go, I'll miss Sunday school. What should I do?

6. My friend Ted was hit by a car, and he died in the hospital. Ever since then, I've been scared of the dark. When I'm in bed at night, I think about Ted, and I cry. What should I do?

Faith-Sharing Letter

DEAR _____ ,

👁 M N ⛪. 👁 LIKE 2 COME

2 ⛪ B-CAUSE 👁 🥫 HEAR

GOD'S WORD. 2-DAY 👁 LEARNED

THAT ...

_____

_____

_____

U SHOULD COME 2 ⛪ WITH ME.

👁 COULD PICK U UP NEXT ☀ DAY

IF YOU WANT ME 2

YOUR FRIEND, _____

God's Team
Membership Requirements

This is the requirement I must meet to be a member of God's team:			
This is the equipment I need to be on God's team:			
Here are things I must do to stay in shape for God's team:			
Because I am on God's team, I will not do these things:			

This is where members of God's team meet regularly:

_____ (time),

_____ (place).

_____
Your signature

_____
Date

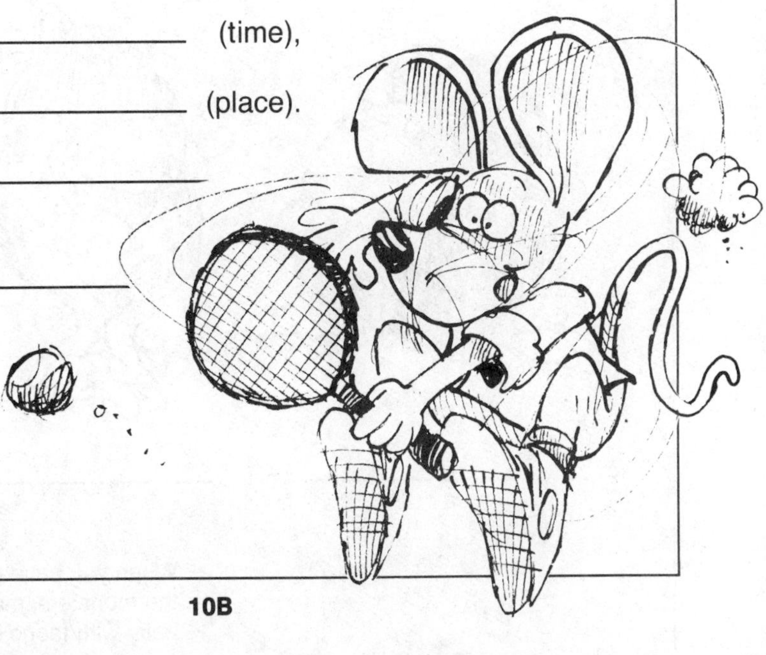

10B

Worship Monsters

Name the three monsters or enemies Jehu had to defeat to worship God.

Name three monsters (problems) you need to defeat so you can worship God.

When you have named the monsters, make them hairy with fabric or yarn.

Hezekiah Club Membership Kit

Cut out this "badge" and color it.
Fasten it on with a pin or tape.

Hezekiah Club

This is to certify that

_____

_____

has agreed to abide by the rules of
the Hezekiah Club and is a member
in good standing.

_____
Date

_____
Signed

10D

I Have Hidden

Look up the Bible verse and find the missing words.
Then draw pictures of those words in the boxes.

I have hidden

your ☐ in my

☐ that I

might not ☐

against you.

Ps. 119:11 (NIV)

I Was Glad

by Neta Jackson

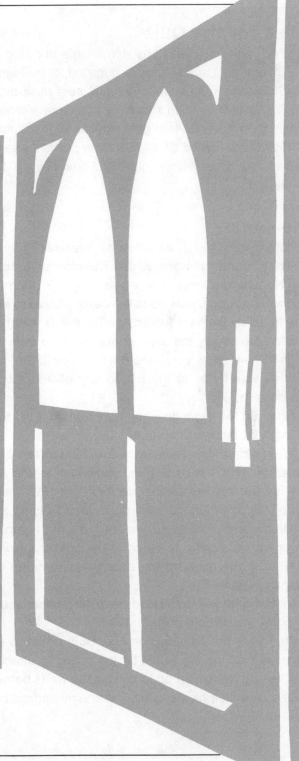

Reader 1: I was glad when they said to me,
Reader 2: "Let us go into the House of the Lord!"
Reader 3: What makes this God's House?
Reader 1: Simply that we are gathered . . .
Reader 2: the hands . . .
Reader 3: the feet . . .
Reader 2: the tongue . . .
Reader 3: the eyes . . .
Reader 2: the ears . . .
Reader 3: the knees . . .
Reader 2: of the Body of Christ, brought together into our wholeness.
Reader 1: ALONE we are each His children.
Reader 1, 2: TOGETHER we are His Body.
All: GATHERED there is a power for praise . . . encouragement . . . witness . . . hope.

©1983, Neta Jackson

Captivity Quiz Game

Rules for the Quiz

1. Each team will take turns answering a question (Team A first question, Team B second question, etc.). If Team A can't answer its question, then Team B gets a chance, and vice versa.

2. Students on the answering team must raise their hands to get called on.

3. The answering team should try to answer without looking in the *Picture Bible.* If neither team can answer, then the first team gets another try, this time looking at the story (pp. 438-446).

4. Points are earned as follows: three points if a team answers its own question; two points if a team answers the *other team's* question; one point if the team has to look up the answer. Select a scorekeeper.

The Quiz

Q: Where were the Jews taken as captives? (To Babylon, p. 438.)

Q: What country conquered the Babylonian Empire? (Persia, p. 438.)

Q: Who was the king of this new empire? (King Cyrus, p. 439.)

Q: What did King Cyrus do to the Jews who were still captives in Babylon? (He said they should go back to Jerusalem and rebuild the Temple, p. 439.)

Q: What did he say the Jews should do who didn't want to go back? (They should give money and goods to help those who were returning, p. 439.)

Q: What was living in the ruined city of Jerusalem when the Jews returned home? Wild dogs, p. 440.)

Q: What did the Jews do when they had built the foundation of the Temple? (They had a service of worship and thanksgiving, p. 441.)

Q: Why didn't the Jews want the Samaritans to help them build the Temple? (Because the Samaritans didn't worship in the same way as the Jews, p. 442.)

Q: What did the Samaritans do for revenge? (They wrote King Cyrus and said the Jews wanted to destroy his power, so he made them stop building the Temple, p. 442.)

Q: After many years the Jews started work again and finished the Temple. What is the name of the priest who came to teach the people the laws of God? (Ezra, p. 443.)

Q: What is the name of the stranger who came at night to examine the city walls? (Nehemiah, p. 444.)

Q: What did he say to the leaders of Jerusalem about the walls? (That the city was defenseless, and the walls should be rebuilt, p. 445.)

Q: Why were the neighboring countries upset to see the walls around Jerusalem getting built? (Because then the city would be too strong to attack, p. 445.)

Q: What did Nehemiah do to defend the walls before they were finished? (The workers worked with a weapon in their hands; when the enemy approached the workers, they became warriors, p. 446.)

Who's Who?

Find someone who fits the following description. Have them sign their name in the right-hand spaces.

Find someone who . . .

Has blue eyes _____

Likes spinach _____

Ties double knots in their shoelaces _____

Is wearing green _____

Has a pet dog _____

Hates black jelly beans _____

Plays soccer _____

Has an older brother _____

Has a younger brother _____

Has two sisters _____

Has brown eyes _____

Brought a Bible with them _____

Wears glasses _____

Likes to roller-skate _____

Is wearing a barrette _____

Went camping this past year _____

Plays the piano _____

Has a missing tooth _____

Can spell Mississippi _____

Has pet goldfish _____

Photo Album

Students can use these pictures to build a photo album which illustrates events leading up to Jerusalem's destruction and the captivity of Judah. Children will complete the picture captions in their own words, summarizing the central idea of each lesson, and then use crayons or felt-tip markers to turn the black and white pictures into colored "photos."

Make enough photocopies of the three work sheets so that each student has a copy of all three. (Two "photos" are used per session.) Each session, cut apart the two designated pictures with captions and distribute these to the kids. After they've completed the captions and colored the pictures, let the students glue or tape these onto pieces of black construction paper to make the pages of their albums. (Four pictures will fit on one 8½″ × 11″ sheet of construction paper.)

When all the pages are assembled, students can make covers out of different-colored sheets of construction paper, punch holes through the covers and pages, and bind their albums with yarn.

Session 48

1. Isaiah accepted God's call to tell the people of Judah that they should . . . But despite Isaiah's warnings, most of the people . . .

_____

_____

2. Jeremiah was another prophet who told the people of Judah to repent. In a vision, God showed Jeremiah that if the people didn't repent, they would . . .

_____

_____

3. Finally, Babylon captured Judah. When Judah's king decided to revolt, Jeremiah warned him that, if Judah did revolt, the Babylonians would . . .

_____

_____

4. The foolish king refused to listen. After a long siege, the army of Babylon defeated Jerusalem, took its people captive, and . . .

_____

_____

5. The captives in Babylon thought God had behind in Jerusalem.Ezekiel saw a vision of a throne on wheels moving in all directions. The vision meant that God hadn't stayed in Jerusalem, because God can . . .

_____

6. When the captives learned that Jerusalem had been destroyed, they felt hopeless. Ezekiel told them that if they repented and obeyed God, someday they . . .

_____

7. Daniel was a young captive in Babylon who remained true to God. When God helped him explain King Nebuchadnezzar's dream, the king made Daniel and his friends . . .

_____

_____

8. When Daniel's friends disobeyed Nebuchadnezzar's order to worship a statue, the king had them thrown into a fiery furnace. But because they were faithful to Him, God . . .

_____

_____

Session 52

9. A new king made a law forbidding people to pray to anyone but him. When Daniel continued to pray to God each day, some wicked leaders . . .

_____

_____

10. Daniel was thrown into a den of lions because he prayed to God. But when the king looked into the lions' den, he discovered that God . . .

_____

_____

Answers for Activity Piece 2A

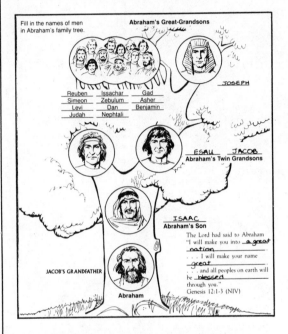

Answers for Activity Piece 7B

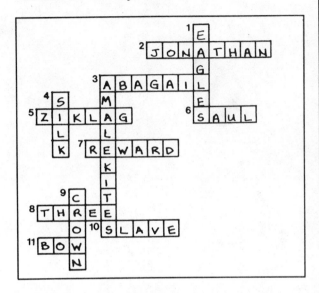

Answers for Activity Piece 4B
Gripe Session

Top picture shows Israelites complaining about their food.

Middle picture shows Israelites complaining about no meat.

Bottom picture shows Miriam and Aaron complaining about Moses' leadership.

Answers for Activity Piece 6C
Giving in Faith

Top picture—
Hannah is giving the gift. She is giving her son Samuel. The gift, her son Samuel, becomes a great prophet for God.

Bottom picture—
Samuel is giving the gift. The gift is an animal that is sacrificed to God. The gift is consumed by fire so the sins of the people will be forgiven.

Answers for Activity Piece 7C

NESTILIPHI (301)	PHILISTINE P
AHIRU (306)	URIAH R
KAR (301)	ARK A
SICSNAIMU (302)	MUSICIANS I
MISEORP (303)	PROMISES S
PLECRIP (304)	CRIPPLE E
NETT (302)	TENT T
USEOH (303)	HOUSE H
GASEESM (306)	MESSAGE E
TPLEEM (303)	TEMPLE L
AOJB (305)	JOAB O
REUSN (305)	NURSE R
VIDDA	DAVID D

```
P W A L J E I M O N Z K B A D
N Y S P O Q R X T BEAUTY R
A SERVANT K E J X M O R
L J WORSHIP F U Z V P
TENCOMMANDMENTS
J T A E U Q N C U N G I Y A
K R P O M F A Y O B L V
G A E C A L A D B K H T K
J M L Q E O T H M Z R F U
P E O KRA T M D N B S T C
S I C Q S M Z N M R I A W P
J GLORY B Z E P L V I
R X M G H S D K V V T E N T
O PROMISE G L H B M K X
W E C X V Y A E G P R O A M T
```

Figure out what the sentence below says.

EMAN SIH OTNU EUD
YROLG EHT DROL EHT
OTNU EVIG

Give unto the Lord
the glory due unto
His name.

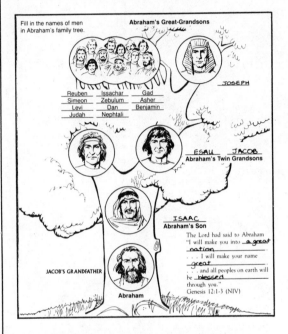 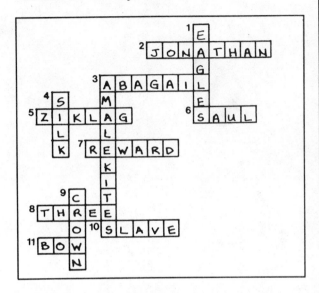